The Woman o...

THE LIFE AND...

BARBARA TAYLOR BRADFORD

Barbara Taylor Bradford was born in Leeds, and by the age of twenty was an editor and columnist on Fleet Street. Her first novel, *A Woman of Substance*, became an enduring bestseller and was followed by twenty others, most recently *Just Rewards*. Her books have sold more than seventy-five million copies worldwide in more than ninety countries and forty languages, and ten of her books have been made into mini-series and television movies. She lives in New York with her husband, producer Robert Bradford.

Piers Dudgeon is the author of fifteen works of non-fiction. He worked for ten years as a publisher before starting his own company and developing books with authors as diverse as John Fowles, Ted Hughes, Daphne Du Maurier, Catherine Cookson and Peter Ackroyd. In 1933 he moved to a village on the North Yorkshire Moors where he has written a number of books, including biographies of Sir John Tavener, Edward de Bono and Catherine Cookson, *The Girl from Leam Lane* becoming a no. 1 bestseller.

Visit www.AuthorTracker.co.uk for exclusive information on your favourite HarperCollins authors.

By the same author

The Woman of Substance

THE LIFE AND BOOKS OF
BARBARA TAYLOR BRADFORD

Piers Dudgeon

HarperCollins*Publishers*

HarperCollins*Publishers*
77–85 Fulham Palace Road,
Hammersmith, London W6 8JB

www.harpercollins.co.uk

This paperback edition 2006
1 3 5 7 9 8 6 4 2

First published in Great Britain by
HarperCollins*Publishers* 2005

A catalogue record for this book
is available from the British Library

ISBN-13 978–0–00–716569–8
ISBN-10 0–00–716569–2

Set in PostScript Linotype Sabon by
Rowland Phototypesetting Ltd, Bury St Edmunds, Suffolk
Printed and bound in Great Britain by
Clays Ltd, St Ives plc

CONTENTS

LIST OF ILLUSTRATIONS

for London to work as a Fashion Editor on *Woman's Own*. (Bradford Photo Archive)

40. Peter O'Toole with Omar Sharif in *Lawrence of Arabia*. (Columbia Pictures)

41. Barbara's husband, film producer Robert Bradford. (Bradford Photo Archive)

42. Barbara after her uprooting to New York. (Cris Alexander/Bradford Photo Archive)

43. Barbara's mother, Freda Taylor, a long way from home on Fifth Avenue, New York.

44. Barbara, the writer. (Bradford Photo Archive)

45. Barbara, multi-million-selling author of *A Woman of Substance*. (Cris Alexander/Bradford Photo Archive)

Section 4

46. Robert Bradford with the book that realised a dream. (Bradford Photo Archive).

47. Jenny Seagrove as Emma Harte, the woman of substance. (Bradford Photo Archive)

48. Deborah Kerr takes over as the older Emma, with Sir John Mills as Henry Rossiter, Emma's financial adviser. (Bradford Photo Archive)

49. Stars of *To Be the Best*, Lindsay Wagner and Sir Anthony Hopkins. (Bradford Photo Archive)

50. Barbara with the stars of *To Be the Best*, Fiona Fullerton, Lindsay Wagner, Christopher Cazenove and Sir Anthony Hopkins (Bradford Photo Archive)

51. Victoria Tenant as Audra Crowther and Kevin McNally as Vincent Crowther in *Act of Will*. (Odyssey Video from the DVD release *Act of Will*)

PREFACE

Exploring one of the world's most successful writers through the looking glass of her fiction is an idea particularly well suited in the case of Barbara Taylor Bradford, whose fictional heroines draw on their creator's character and chart the emotional contours of her own experience, and whose own history so often emerges from the shadowland between fact and fiction.

She turned out to be unstintingly generous with her time, advising me about real-life places, episodes and events in the novels, despite a hectic round of her own, which included the writing of two novels, the launch of her nineteenth novel, *Emma's Secret* (2003), a high-profile legal action in India against a TV film company suspected of purloining her books and films, a grand party celebrating a quarter of a century with publishers HarperCollins, and a schedule of charity events, which film producer, business manager and husband Robert Bradford arranged for her – oh, and a week or so's holiday.

Barbara's first novel, *A Woman of Substance*, is, according to *Publishers Weekly*, the eighth biggest-selling novel ever to be published. It has sold more than twenty-five million copies worldwide. In it, so reviewers will tell you, we have the classic Cinderella story. Emma Harte rises from maid to matriarch; the impoverished Edwardian kitchen maid comes, through her own efforts, to rule over a business empire that stretches from Yorkshire to America and Australia.

What it took to escape the constraints of the Edwardian and later twentieth-century English class system is at the heart of Barbara's family's own story too. Her rise to bestselling novelist and icon for emancipated womanhood, currently valued at some $170 million, from a two-up two-down in Leeds is by any standard extraordinary. Her elevation coincided with the post-war drift from an Edwardian upstairs/downstairs class system (into which Barbara's mother Freda was born), reconstructed by socialism in the period of Barbara's own childhood, to one ultimately sensible to merit, a transformation which finds symbolic incidence in the year 1979, in which *A Woman of Substance* was first published and that champion of meritocracy, Margaret Thatcher, who had risen from the lower middle classes to become Britain's first female Prime Minister, arrived at No. 10 Downing Street.

Barbara's novels, which encourage women to believe they can conquer the world, whatever their class or background and despite the fact that they are operating in a man's domain, tapped into the aspirational energy of this era and served to expedite social change. Indeed, it might be said that Barbara Taylor

Bradford would have invented Margaret Thatcher if she had not already existed. When they met, there was a memorable double take of where ambition had led them. 'I was invited to a reception at Number Ten,' Barbara recalls. 'I saw a picture of Churchill in the hall outside the reception room and slipped out to look at it. Mrs Thatcher followed me out and asked if I was all right. I just said: "I never thought a girl from Yorkshire like me would be standing here at the invitation of the Prime Minister looking at a portrait of Churchill inside ten Downing Street," and she whispered: "I know what you mean." '

More intriguingly, in the process of writing fiction, ideas arise which owe their genesis not to the culture of an era, but to the author's inner experience, and here, as any editor knows, lie the most compelling parts of a writer's work. Barbara is the first to agree: 'It's very hard when you've just finished a novel to define what you've really written about other than what seems to be the verity on paper. There's something else there underlying it subconsciously in the writer's mind, and that I might be able to give you later.' She promised this to journalist Billie Figg in the early 1980s, but never delivered, though the prospect is especially enticing, given that she can also say: 'My typewriter is my psychiatrist.'

There is no pearl without first there being grit in the oyster. The grit may lie in childhood experience, possibly only partly understood or deliberately blanked out, buried and unresolved by the defence mechanisms of the conscious mind. Unawares, the subconscious generates the ideas that claw at a writer's inner self and drive his or her best fiction.

Barbara shies away from such talk, denouncing inspiration – it is, she says, something that she has never 'had'. She admits that on occasion she finds herself strangely moved by a place and gets feelings of *déjà vu*, even of having been part of something that happened before she was born, but mostly she sees herself as a storyteller, a creator of stories, happy to draw on her own life, all of it perfectly conscious and practical. Later we will see how she works up a novel out of her characters, which is indeed a conscious process. But subconscious influences are by their very nature not known to the conscious mind, and we will also see that echoes of a past unknown do indeed inhabit her writing.

Barbara will tell you that it was her mother, Freda, who made her who she is today. Mother and daughter were so close, and Freda so determined an influence, that their relationship reads almost like a conspiracy in Barbara's future success. Freda was on a mission, 'a crusade', but it wasn't quite the selfless mission that Barbara supposed, for Freda had an agenda: she was driven to realise ambition in her daughter by a need to resolve the disastrous experiences of her own childhood, about which Barbara, and possibly even Freda's husband, knew nothing.

In fact, Barbara's story turns out to be an inextricable part of the story of not two but three women – herself, her mother Freda, and Freda's mother, Edith, whose own dream of rising in the world turned horribly sour when the man she loved failed her and reduced her family to penury. It left her eldest daughter Freda with enormous problems to resolve, and a sense of loss which, on account of her extraordinarily close relationship with Barbara, found its way into the novels. One might even say that in resolving it in the lives of her characters Barbara appeased Freda and, in her material success, actually realised Edith's dream.

Barbara told me very little about her mother and grandmother before I began writing this book, and as my own research progressed I had to assume that she did not know their incredible story. If she had known, surely she would have told me. If she had not wanted me to know, why set me loose on research geared to finding out? At the end, when I showed her the manuscript, her shock confirmed that she had not known, and she found it very difficult to accept that she had written about these things of which she had no conscious knowledge.

That the novels own something of which their creator is not master, to my mind adds to their magic, the subconscious process signifying Freda's power over Barbara, which Barbara would not deny. She may not have been aware of all that happened to Freda, but she was 'joined at the hip', as she put it, to one who was aware.

No one was closer to Barbara at the most impressionable moments of her life than Freda. They were inseparable, and the child's subconscious could not have failed to imbibe a sense of what assailed her mother. Even if Freda withheld the detail, or Barbara blanked it out, the adult Barbara allows an impression of 'a great sense of loss' in Freda, which is indeed the very feeling that so many of her fictional characters must overcome.

Freda's legacy of deprivation – her loss – became the grit around which the pearls of Barbara's success were layered. So closely woven were the threads of these three women's lives that Barbara's part in the plot – the end game, the novels – seems in a real sense predestined. In reality, everything in Freda's history, and that of Edith's, required Barbara to happen. In the garden of her fiction, they are one seed. None is strictly one character or another, although Barbara regards Freda as most closely Audra Kenton in *Act of Will*. Nevertheless, their preoccupations are what the novels are about.

Of secrets, she writes in *Everything to Gain*, 'there were so many in our family . . . I never wanted to face those secrets from my childhood. Better to forget them; better still to pretend they did not exist. But they did. My childhood was constructed on secrets layered one on top of the other.' In *Her Own Rules*, Meredith Stratton quantifies the challenge of the project: 'For years she had lived with half-truths, had hidden so much, that it was difficult to unearth it all now.'

Secrets produce rumour, which challenges the literary detective to run down the truth at the heart of the most fantastic storylines. Known facts act like an adhesive for the calcium layers of fictional storyline which make up the 'pearl' that is the author's work.

These secrets empower Barbara's best fiction. They find expression in the desire for revenge, which Edith will have felt and which drives Emma Harte's rise in *A Woman of Substance*. They find expression in the unnatural force of Audra Kenton's determination in *Act of Will* that her daughter Christina will live a better life than she, and in the driving ambition of dispossessed Maximilian West in *The Women in His Life*.

My project is not, therefore, as simple as matching Barbara's character with the woman of substance she created in the novels, but I believe it takes us a lot closer to explaining why *A Woman of Substance* is the eighth biggest-selling novel in the history of the world than merely observing such a match or studying the marketing plan. That is not to belittle the marketing of this novel, which set new records in the industry; nor is it to underestimate the significance of the timing of the venture; nor to underrate the talents of the author in helping fashion Eighties' *Zeitgeist*.

It is just that these 'secrets', which come to us across a gulf of one hundred years, have exerted an impressive power in the lives of these women, and although we live in a time when the market rules, deep down we still reserve our highest regard for works not planned for the market but which come from just such an elemental drive of the author, especially when, as in the case of *A Woman of Substance*, that drive finds so universal a significance among its readers in the most pressing business of our times – that of rising in the world.

PART ONE

CHAPTER ONE

The Party

'The ambience in the dining room was decidedly romantic, had an almost fairytale quality . . . The flickering candlelight, the women beautiful in their elegant gowns and glittering jewels, the men handsome in their dinner jackets, the conversation brisk, sparkling, entertaining . . .'

Voice of the Heart

The Bradfords' elegant fourteen-room apartment occupies the sixth floor of a 1930s landmark building overlooking Manhattan's East River. The approach is via a grand ground-floor lobby, classical in style, replete with red-silk chaise longues, massive wall-recessed urns, and busy uniformed porters skating around black marbled floors.

A mahogany-lined lift delivers visitors to the front door, which, on the evening of the party, lay open, leaving arrivals naked to the all-at-once gaze of the already gathered. Fortunately I had been warned about the possibility of this and had balanced the rather outré effect of my gift – a jar of Yorkshire moorland honey (my bees, Barbara's moor) – by cutting what I hoped would be a rather sophisticated, shadowy, Jack-the-Ripper dash with a high-collared leather coat. If I was successful, no one was impolite enough to mention it.

One is met at the door by Mohammed, aptly named spiriter away of material effects – coats, hats, even, to my chagrin, gifts. Barbara arrives and we move swiftly from reception area, which I would later see spills into a bar, to the drawing room, positioned centrally between dining room and library, and occupying the riverside frontage of an apartment which must measure all of five thousand square feet.

The immediate impression is of classical splendour – spacious rooms, picture windows, high ceilings and crystal chandeliers. These three main rooms, an enfilade and open-doored to one another that night, arise from oak-wood floors bestrewn with antique carpets, elegant ground for silk-upholstered walls hung with Venetian mirrors, and, as readers of her novels would expect, a European mix of Biedermeier and Art Deco furniture, Impressionist paintings and silk-upholstered chairs.

This is not, as it happens, the apartment that she draws on in her fiction. The Bradfords have been here for ten years only. Between 1983 and 1995 they lived a few blocks away, many storeys higher up, with views of the East River and exclusive Sutton Place from almost every room. But it was here that Allison Pearson came to interview Barbara in 1999, and, swept up in the glamour, took the tack that from this

similarly privileged vantage point it is 'easy to forget that there is a world down there, a world full of
pain and ugliness', while at the same time wanting
some of it: 'Any journalist going to see Barbara Taylor
Bradford in New York,' she wrote, 'will find herself
asking the question I asked myself as I stood in exclusive Sutton Place, craning my neck and staring up
at the north face of the author's mighty apartment
building. What has this one-time cub reporter on the
Yorkshire Evening Post got that I haven't?' It was a
good starting point, but Allison's answer: 'Well, about
$600 million,' kept the burden of her question at bay.

Before long the river draws my gaze, a pleasure
boat all lit up, a full moon and the clear night sky, and
even if Queens is not exactly the Houses of Parliament
there is great breadth that the Thames cannot match,
and a touch of mystery from an illuminated ruin, a
hospital or sometime asylum marooned on an island
directly opposite. It is indeed a privileged view.

Champagne and cocktails are available. I opt for
the former and remember my daughter's advice to
drink no more than the top quarter of a glass. She, an
American resident whose childhood slumbers were
disturbed by rather more louche, deep-into-the-
night London dinner parties, had been so afeared that
I would disgrace myself that she had earlier sent me
a copy of Toby Young's *How To Lose Friends &
Alienate People*.

I find no need for it here. People know one another
and are immediately, but not at all overbearingly,
welcoming. In among it all, Barbara doesn't just

Europeanise the scene, she colloquialises it. For me that night she had the timbre of home and the enduring excitement of the little girl barely out of her teens who had not only the guts but the *joie de vivre* to get up and discover the world when that was rarely done. She is fun. I would have thought so then, and do so now, and at once see that no one has any reason for being here except to enjoy this in her too.

It is a fluid scene. People swim in and out of view, and finding myself close to the library I slip away and find a woman alone on the far side of the room looking out across the street through a side window. Hers is the first name I will remember, though by then half a dozen have been put past me. I ask the lady what can possibly be absorbing her. I see only another apartment block, more severe, brick built, stark even. 'I used to live there,' she says. 'My neighbour was Greta Garbo . . . until she died.' This, then, was where the greatest of all screen goddesses found it possible finally to be alone, or might have done had it not been for my interlocutor.

'Where do you live now?' I venture.

She looks at me quizzically, as if I should know. 'In Switzerland and the South of France. New York only for the winter months.'

Then I make the faux pas of the evening, thankful that only she and I will have heard it: 'What on earth do you *do*?'

Barbara swoops to rescue me (or the lady) with an introduction. Garbo's friend is Rex Harrison's widow, Mercia. She does not *do*. Suddenly it seems that I have opened up the library; people are following Barbara in. I find myself being introduced to comedienne Joan Rivers and fashion designer Arnold Scaasi, whose history Barbara peppers with names such as Liz Taylor, Natalie Wood, Joan Crawford, Candice Bergen, Barbra Streisand, Joan Rivers of course, and, as of now, all the President's women. Barbara and movie-producer husband Bob are regular visitors to the White House.

It is November 2002 and talk turns naturally to Bob Woodward's *Bush at War*, which I am told will help establish GB as the greatest president of all time. I am asked my opinion and once again my daughter's voice comes like a distant echo – her second rule: no politics (she knows me too well). Barbara has already told me that she and Bob know the Bush family and I just caught sight of a photograph of them with the President on the campaign trail. They are Republicans. When I limit myself to saying that I can empathise with the shock and hurt of September 11, that I had a friend who died in the disaster, but war seems old-fashioned, so primitive a solution, Barbara takes my daughter's line and confesses that she herself makes it a rule not to talk politics with close friend Diahn McGrath, a lawyer and staunch Democrat, to whom she at once directs me.

Barbara is the perfect hostess, this pre-dinner hour the complete introduction that will allow me to relax at table, even to contribute a little. There's a former publishing executive, one Parker Ladd, with the demeanour of a Somerset Maugham, or possibly a

Noel Coward (Barbara's champagne is good), who tells me he is a friend of Ralph Fields, the first person to give me rein in publishing, and who turns out – to my amazement – still to be alive.

So, even in the midst of this Manhattan scene I find myself comfortable anchorage not only in contact through Barbara with my home county of Yorkshire, but in fond memories of the publishing scene. It was not at all what I had expected to find. I am led in to dinner by a woman introduced to me as Edwina Kaplan, a sculptor and painter whose husband is an architect, but who talks heatedly (and at the time quite inexplicably) about tapes she has discovered of Winston Churchill's war-time speeches. Would people be interested? she wonders. Later I would see a couple of her works on Barbara's walls, but for some reason nobody thought it pertinent until the following day to explain that Edwina was Sir Winston's granddaughter, Edwina Sandys. Churchill, of course, is one of Barbara's heroes; in her childhood she contributed to his wife Clementine's Aid to Russia fund and still has one of her letters, now framed in the library.

The table, set for fourteen, is exquisite, its furniture dancing to the light of a generously decked antique crystal chandelier. The theme is red, from the walls to the central floral display through floral napkin rings to what seems to be a china zoo occupying the few spaces left by the flower-bowls, crystal tableware and place settings. Beautifully crafted porcelain elephants and giraffes peek out from between silver water goblets and crystal glasses of every conceivable size and design.

There are named place-cards and I begin the hunt for my seat. I am last to find mine, and as soon as I sit, Barbara erupts with annoyance. She had specially chosen a white rose for my napkin ring – the White Rose of Yorkshire – which is lying on the plate of my neighbour to the right. Someone has switched my placement card! Immediately I wonder whether the culprit has made the switch to be near me or to get away, but as I settle, and the white rose is restored, my neighbour to the left leaves me in no doubt that I am particularly welcome. She tells me that she is a divorce lawyer, a role of no small importance in the marital chess games of the Manhattan wealthy. How many around this table might she have served? Was switching my place-card the first step in a strategy aimed at my own marriage?

I reach for the neat vodka in the smallest stem of my glass cluster and steady my nerves, turning our conversation to Bob and Barbara and soon realising that here, around this table, among their friends, are the answers to so many questions I have for my subject's Manhattan years. I set to work, both on my left and to my right, where I find Nancy Evans, Barbara's former publisher at the mighty Doubleday in the mid-1980s.

By this time we have progressed from the caviar and smoked salmon on to the couscous and lamb, and Barbara deems it time to widen our perspectives. It would be the first of two calls to order, on this occasion to introduce everyone to everyone, a party game rather than a necessity, I think, except in my case. Thumbnail sketches of each participant, edged devilishly with in-group barb, courted ripostes and laughter, but it was only when she came around the table and settled on me, mentioning the words 'guest of honour' that I realised for the first time that I was to be the star turn. I needn't have worried; there was at least one other special guest in Joan Rivers and she more than made up for my sadly unimaginative response.

Barbara tells me that Joan is very 'in' with Prince Charles: 'She greeted me with, "I've just come back from a painting trip . . . with Prince Charles." A friend of hers, Robert Higdon, runs the Prince's Trust. Joan is very involved with that, giving them money. So she was there with Charles and Camilla and the Forbses at some château somewhere. She always says, "Prince Charles likes me a lot; he always laughs at my jokes." But Joan is actually a very ladylike creature when she is off the stage, where she can be a bit edgy sometimes. In real life she is very sweet and she loves me and Bob.'

Joan is deftly egging Arnold Scaasi on as he heaps compliments on Barbara from the far end of the table. At the very height of his paean of praise, the comedienne rejoins that Arnold's regard for his hostess is clearly so great that he will no doubt wish to make one of his new creations a *gift* to her. The designer's face is a picture as he realises he has walked straight into a game at his expense, in which the very ethos of celebrity Manhattan is at stake. The table applauds his generosity, while Arnold begins an interminable descent into get-out: Alas, he does not have the multifarious talents of Joan to allow such generosity, he cannot *eat* publicity, etc., etc.

I felt I was being drawn in to Bob and Barbara's private world. When we first met I had said to Barbara that I would need to be so, and she had begun the process that night. After cheese and dessert, coffee and liqueurs were served in the drawing room and one after another of her guests offered themselves for interview.

The evening reminded me of the glittering birthday party in the Bavarian ski resort of Konigsee in *Voice of the Heart*. The table setting was remarkably similar – the candlelight and bowls of flowers that 'march down the centre of the table', interspersed with 'Meissen porcelain birds in the most radiant of colours', the table itself 'set with the finest china, crystal and silver ... The flickering candlelight, the women beautiful in their elegant gowns and glittering jewels, the men handsome in their dinner jackets ...', and the conversation 'brisk, sparkling, entertaining ...'

In *Act of Will* the Manhattan apartment is added to the mix. As guests of Christina Newman and her husband Alex in their Sutton Place apartment, we, like Christina's mother, Audra Crowther (née Kenton, and the fictional counterpart of Barbara's mother, Freda Taylor), are stung by the beauty of 'the priceless art on the walls, two Cézannes, a Gauguin ... the

11

English antiques with their dark glossy woods ... bronze sculpture by Arp ... the profusion of flowers in tall crystal vases ... all illuminated by silk-shaded lamps of rare and ancient Chinese porcelains'.

Barbara's passion for antique furniture and modern Impressionist paintings was born of her own upbringing in Upper Armley, Leeds. 'My mother used to take me to stately homes because she loved furniture, she loved the patinas of wood. She often took me to Temple Newsam, just outside Leeds [where the gardens also found a way into the fiction – Emma Harte's rhododendron walk in *A Woman of Substance* is Temple Newsam's], and also to Harewood House, home of the Lascelles family ... to Ripley Castle [Langley Castle in *Voice of the Heart*], and to Fountains Abbey and Fountains Hall at Studley Royal.' These were Barbara's childhood haunts, and it was Freda Taylor who first tuned her in to beautiful artefacts and styles of design, as if preparing her for the day when such things might be her daughter's: 'I always remember she used to say to me, "Barbara, keep your eyes open and then you will see all the beautiful things in the world."'

In *A Woman of Substance* the optimum architecture is Georgian, and Emma Harte's soul mate Blackie O'Neill's dream is to have a house with Robert Adam fireplaces, Sheraton and Hepplewhite furniture, 'and maybe a little Chippendale'.

In *Angel*, Johnny dwells on the paintings and antiques in his living room – a Sisley landscape, a Rouault, a Cézanne, a couple of early Van Goghs, 'an antique Chinese coffee table of carved mahogany, French bergères from the Louis XV period, upholstered in striped cream silk ... antique occasional tables ... a long sofa table holding a small sculpture by Brancusi and a black basalt urn ...' Costume designer Rose Madigan's attention is caught by a pair of dessert stands, 'each one composed of two puttis standing on a raised base on either side of a leopard, their plump young arms upstretched to support a silver bowl with a crystal liner', the silver made by master silversmith Paul Storr. There are George III candlesticks also by Storr dated 1815.

In *Everything to Gain*, Mallory Keswick feasts her eyes on a pair of elegant eighteenth-century French, bronze doré candlesticks, and her mother-in-law Diana buys antiques from the great houses of Europe, specialising in eighteenth- and nineteenth-century French furniture, decorative objects, porcelain and paintings.

For a dozen or so years leading up to publication of her first novel, Barbara wrote a nationwide syndicated column in America three times a week, about design and interior decor. She also wrote a number of books on interior design, furniture and art for American publishers Doubleday, Simon & Schuster and Meredith, long before the first commissioned *A Woman of Substance*. So, this design thing is, if not bred in the bone, part and parcel of her being.

But these mother and daughter trips out into the countryside had a more fundamental effect: they introduced Barbara to the landscape and spirit of

Yorkshire, in which her fiction is rooted. In *A Woman of Substance*, Barbara sets Fairley village, where teen-ager Emma Harte lives with her parents and brother, Frank, in the lee of the moors which rise above the River Aire as it finds its way down into Leeds. 'It was an isolated spot,' she wrote, 'desolate and uninviting, and only the pale lights that gleamed in some of the cottage windows gave credence to the idea that it was inhabited.'

Today she will say: 'Fairley village is Haworth, but not exactly; it is the Haworth of my imagination.' It could be anywhere in the area of the Brontës' Haworth, Keighley or Rombalds moors. Barbara knows the area well. It lies within the regular expeditionary curtilage of her childhood home in Leeds.

The hills that rise up in an undulating sweep to dominate Fairley village and the stretch of the Aire Valley below it are always dark and brooding in the most clement of weather. But when the winter sets in for its long and deadly siege the landscape is brushstroked in grisaille beneath ashen clouds and the moors take on a savage desolateness, the stark fells and bare hillsides drained of all colour and bereft of life. The rain and snow drive down endlessly and the wind that blows in from the North Sea is fierce and raw. These gritstone hills, infinitely more sombre than the green moors of the nearby limestone dale country, sweep through vast silences broken only by the mournful wailing of the wind, for even the numerous little becks, those tumbling, dappled streams that relieve the monotony in spring and summer, are frozen and stilled.

This great plateau of moorland stretches across countless untenanted miles towards Shipley and the vigorous industrial city of Leeds beyond. It is amazingly featureless, except for the occasional soaring crags, a few blackened trees, shrivelled thorns, and abandoned ruined cottages that barely punctuate its cold and empty spaces. Perpetual mists, pervasive and thick, float over the rugged landscape, obscuring the highest peaks and demolishing the foothills, so that land and sky merge in an endless mass of grey that is dank and enveloping, and everything is diffused, without motion, wrapped in unearthly solitude. There is little evidence here of humanity, little to invite man into this inhospitable land at this time of year, and few venture out into its stark and lonely reaches.

Near here, at Ramsden Ghyll (Brimham Rocks in the film), 'a dell between two hills ... an eerie place, filled with grotesque rock formations and blasted tree stumps', Lord of the Manor Adam Fairley seduces Emma's mother, Elizabeth. There, years later, Adam's son Edwin Fairley makes love to teenage virgin Emma Harte, the Fairley Hall kitchen maid who conceives their illegitimate child, Edwina, this episode the impetus behind a succession of events that will realise Emma's destiny.

The heather and bracken brushed against her feet, the wind caught at her long skirts so that they billowed out like puffy clouds, and her hair was a stream of russet-brown silk ribbons flying behind her as she ran. The sky was as blue as speedwells and the larks wheeled and turned against the face of the sun. She could see Edwin quite clearly now, standing by the huge rocks just under the shadow of the Crags above Ramsden Ghyll. When he saw her he waved, and began to climb upwards towards the ledge where they always sat protected from the wind, surveying the world far below. He did not look back, but went on climbing.

'Edwin! Edwin! Wait for me,' she called, but her voice was blown away by the wind and he did not hear. When she reached Ramsden Crags she was out of breath and her usually pale face was flushed from exertion.

'I ran so hard I thought I would die,' she gasped as he helped her up on the ledge.

He smiled at her. 'You will never die, Emma. We are both going to live for ever and ever at the Top of the World.'

When Edwin abandons Emma she wreaks vengeance on the Fairleys, at length razing Fairley Hall to the ground. Meanwhile, the geography moves some miles to the north. Emma's centre in Yorkshire becomes Penniston Royal, with its 'Renaissance and Jacobean architecture . . . crenellated towers . . . mullioned leaded windows' and 'clipped green lawns that rolled down to the lily pond far below the long flagged terrace'. The model is Fountains Hall on the Studley Royal Estate, Ripon, gateway to the Yorkshire Dales and another of Barbara's childhood haunts, while Pennistone Royal village is neighbouring Studley Roger.

Why should an author who left North Yorkshire as soon as she could, found success and glamour in London as a journalist on Fleet Street, married a Hollywood film producer and moved lock, stock and barrel to a swish apartment in New York City, return to her homeland for the setting of her first novel, a novel that featured a character whose spirit seems at first sight more closely in tune with the go-getting ethos of Manhattan than the dour North Yorkshire moors? The answer to that is, broadly, the text of this book.

Barbara's novels are novels principally of character. The dominant traits are the emotional light and shade of the landscape of her birth. When she came to write the novels, she had no hesitation in anchoring them there, even though she was, by then, cast miles away in her Manhattan eyrie.

The county is blessed with large tracts of wide-open spaces – breathtaking views of varied character – so that even if you are brought up in one of the great industrial cities of the county, as Barbara was, you are but a walk away from natural beauty. There is a longing in her for the Yorkshire Dales which living in Manhattan keeps constantly on the boil. Like Mallory

Keswick in *Everything to Gain*, 'I had grown to love this beautiful, sprawling county, the largest in England, with its bucolic green dales, vast empty moors, soaring fells, ancient cathedrals and dramatic ruins of mediaeval abbeys . . . Wensleydale and the Valley of the Ure was the area I knew best.'

The author's sense that landscape is more than topography may first have been awakened when Freda introduced Barbara to the wild workshop out of which Emily Brontë's Heathcliff was hewn. 'My mother took me to the Brontë parsonage at Haworth, and over the moors to Top Withens, the old ruined farm that was supposed to be the setting for *Wuthering Heights*. I loved the fact that this great work of literature was set right there. I loved the landscape: those endless, empty, windswept moors where the trees all bend one way. I loved Heathcliff.'

There are many allusions to *Wuthering Heights* in Barbara's novels. For example, *Voice of the Heart* tells of the making of a film of it. Shot in the late 1950s, the film stars heart-throb Terence Ogden as Heathcliff and dark-haired, volatile, manipulative Katharine Tempest as Catherine Earnshaw. *The Triumph of Katie Byrne* is about an actress whose first big break is to play Emily Brontë in a play-within-the-novel about life in Haworth parsonage. In *A Woman of Substance* the principal love story between Emma and Edwin Fairley, though Edwin is no Heathcliff, draws on Brontë's idea of Cathy's sublimation of her self in Heathcliff and in the spirit of the moor: 'My love for Heathcliff resembles the eternal rocks beneath . . .'

Brontë wrote. 'Nelly, I AM Heathcliff.' When Emma makes love with Edwin literally within 'the eternal rocks beneath' the moor – in a cave at Ramsden Ghyll – 'Emma thought she was slowly dissolving under Edwin, becoming part of him. Becoming him. They were one person now. She *was* Edwin.'

There is scarcely any landscape description as such in *Wuthering Heights*, but Emily Brontë (1818–48) was the greatest of all geniuses when it comes to evocation of place. Charlotte, her sister, worried what primitive forces Emily had released from the bleak moorland around Haworth, 'Whether it be right or advisable to create things like Heathcliff, I do not know,' she wrote, 'I scarcely think it is.' She compared her sister's genius to a genius for statuary, Heathcliff hewn out of 'a granite block on a solitary moor', his head, 'savage, swart, sinister', elicited from the crag, 'a form moulded with at least one element of grandeur . . . power'. The mark of genius was the writer working an involuntary act – 'The writer who possesses the creative gift owns something of which he is not always master – something that at times strangely wills and works for itself . . . With time and labour, the crag took human shape; and there it stands colossal, dark, and frowning . . . terrible and goblin-like . . .'

Readers of *A Woman of Substance* will know just how central this 'element of grandeur . . . power' is to the character of the woman of substance. Are we to understand that it is hewn from the same granite crag whence *Wuthering Heights* came? The natural assumption is that Barbara takes from the imagery of that 'nursling of the moors' and transports it to the boardrooms and salons of Manhattan, London and Paris. Certainly, wherever the settings of Barbara's novels take us, her values are Yorkshire based, but hers is a moral focus on the *history* of place, and the spirit of Yorkshire speaks to her through its history as much as through Nature's demeanour.

She owes to her mother Freda's expeditions the sense of drama she shares with mediaeval historian Paul Murray Kendall from 'this region of wild spaces and fierce loyalties and baronial "menies" of fighting men, with craggy castles and great abbeys scattered over the lonely moors . . . a breeding ground of violence and civil strife'. Freda saw to that; she took her to castles – Middleham and Ripley – and to ruined abbeys – Kirkstall Abbey in Leeds and Fountains Abbey on the Studley Royal Estate in Ripon.

Centuries before Emily trod the Brontë 'heath, with its blooming bells and balmy fragrance', and created Heathcliff out of its darker aspects, a real-life personification of power came forth in Wensleydale, the most pastoral, gentle and green of all the Yorkshire Dales, and appealed to Barbara's imaginative sense that the spirit of place is the spirit of the past. For her, Yorkshire is a living ideological and architectural archive of the past, a palimpsest or manuscript on which each successive culture has written its own indelible, enduring text.

Wensleydale lies less than a half-hour's drive from Ripon, the tiny city north of Leeds where Freda was brought up. The dale has two centres of power,

Middleham and Bolton castles, and it is the former that commanded her attentions. Middleham was the fifteenth-century stronghold of the Earl of Warwick, one of the most dynamic figures in English history. 'The castle at Middleham is all blown-out walls and windows that no longer exist,' Barbara told me, 'but Richard Neville, Earl of Warwick, who was raised there and lived there, was devastating as a young man, devastating in the sense that he was very driven and ambitious ... and a great warrior.' Within 'the roofless halls and ghostly chambers' of Middleham Castle, Freda introduced her daughter to the story of the Earl of Warwick, the 'reach' of his ambitions and many of the traits that would define her woman of substance. 'She told me all about Richard Neville, the Kingmaker ... He put Edward IV on the throne of England, and he was one of the last great magnates. He held a fascination for my mother.'

Warwick's tireless constitution was rooted in the hard-bitten culture of the North. When Richard was a boy he lined up next to his father to repel attempts to wrest their lands away from them. At eighteen he won his spurs and was hardened further by action in skirmishes to avenge rustling and looting of villages within family territories. He was instinctively the Yorkshire man, but he was also someone who, like the woman of substance herself, was not bound to his home culture. The vitality of his character awakened him to recognise and seize his moment in the wider world when it occurred.

It was in the Wars of the Roses (1455–85), the

struggle between the houses of York and Lancaster for the throne of England, that he really came to the fore. His role in changing the English monarchy in the fifteenth century affected England for two centuries afterwards, but his relevance is for all times, as his biographer Paul Murray Kendall records: 'The pilgrimage of mankind is, at bottom, a story of human energy, how it has been used and the ends it has sought to encompass . . . Warwick's prime meaning is the *reach* of human nature he exemplifies and – type of all human struggle – the combat he waged with the shape of things in his time.'

For Barbara the spirit is all, and in Warwick, as in Middleham Castle itself, it is powerfully northern. Born on 28th November 1428 to Richard, Earl of Salisbury, and his wife Alice, 'on his father's side he was sprung from a hardy northern tribe who had been rooted in their land for centuries . . . The North was in Richard's blood, and it nourished his first experiences with the turbulent society of his day,' Kendall writes in *Warwick the Kingmaker*. And yet Richard would hold sway over lands so far distant – more than fifty estates from South Wales across some twenty counties of England – that he, like Barbara, could never be said to have been anchored down by the northern culture in which he was raised.

Neither Kendall nor Barbara go along with the Warwick that Shakespeare gives us in the three parts of *Henry VI* – a 'bellicose baron of a turbulent time'. Kendall's Warwick is 'an amalgam of legend and deeds', a figure whose character and actions attracted heroic levels of adulation and gave him mythic status throughout the land, as he rode in triumph through his vast estates; a figure who, like Barbara herself and her charismatic heroines, seems to have been marked with a strong sense of destiny from the start. Warwick, writes Kendall, never doubted for one moment that he could achieve what he set out to do: 'He refused to admit there were disadvantages he could not over-come and defeats from which he could not recover, and he had the courage, and vanity, to press his game to the end. In other words, he is a Western European man, and in him lies concentrated the reason why that small corner of the earth, in the four centuries after his death, came to dominate all the rest.'

From an early age he gave the impression of a man awaiting his moment, of a 'depth of will' as yet untapped but equal to any challenge that truly merited his time. And when the moment came, when the dream promised to become the man, he recognised it, gave up his subordinate role without second thought, seized it and won it, not with sleight of hand, subter-fuge or trickery, but with valour, the occasion the defeat of the King's troops in the city of St Albans in 1455.

His role had been as back-up to the dukes of York and Salisbury against forces raised by Somerset from a full quarter of the nobility of England. They had approached the city making clear their intention to rescue the King from the clutches of Margaret of Anjou, beautiful and feisty niece of Charles VII of France and now wife of King Henry and *the* divisive force in the land. When battle commenced in the narrow lanes that led up to Holywell, York and Salisbury found themselves in serious difficulties and it was then that Warwick took it upon himself to lead his men forward on the run, dashing across domestic gardens and through private houses to attack Somerset's men from the rear. From the moment his archers burst into St Peter's Street shouting 'A Warwick! A Warwick!' his reputation flew. With 'Somerset's host broken,' as Kendall describes, 'Warwick, York and Salisbury approached the peaked King, standing alone and bewildered in the doorway of a house, his neck bleeding from an arrow graze. Down on their knees they went, beseeching Henry the Sixth for his grace and swearing they never meant to harm him. Helplessly, he nodded his head. The battle was over.'

There is in Kendall's Warwick the same unifying robustness to which the nation rises when the England rugby team presses its game to the end, seizing the Webb Ellis trophy against a background of fans clad in the livery of St George. What Kendall is identifying is what attracts Barbara to Winston Churchill and Maggie Thatcher: the character that won us an Empire and coloured what is understood to be our very Englishness.

It is a spirit often given to excess, bigotry, even fanaticism, so that Barbara can say defensively and with evident contradiction: 'There was no bigotry in our family. The only thing my father said was, "Nobody listens to Enoch Powell."' But there is no hint of fanaticism in Barbara's ideals. It is not in her character to support it, and through husband Bob, a German Jew, dispossessed by the Nazis as a boy, Barbara is alert to the danger more than most. She would probably avoid politics altogether if she could, and draws any political sting in the novels by introducing a crucial element of compassion in her heroic notion of power.

In the young Warwick, Barbara found the epitome of the person of substance for whom integrity is all. In her novels, power is 'the most potent of weapons', and it only corrupts 'when those with power will do anything to hold on to that power. Sometimes,' she tells us in full agreement with the Warwick legend, 'it can even be ennobling.'

The character of Warwick that got through to Barbara encompassed more than soldier values. The fierce loyalties of those times were, in young Warwick's case, not forged in greed, nor were they all about holding on to, or wresting, power from an opponent for its own sake. Long before he fell out with his protégé Edward and, embittered, took sides against him; long before he 'sold what he was for what he thought he ought to be', as Kendall put it, his purpose really was to defend the values which true Englishmen held as good.

Freda made sure that Barbara picked up on this heroic aspect. As a child, her mother 'instilled in her a sense of honour, duty and purpose', the need for 'integrity in the face of incredible pressure and opposition' and 'not only an honesty with those people who occupied her life, but with herself'. These noble values arise in *Act of Will* and *A Woman of Substance*, but they first found impetus in Freda's expeditions into Wensleydale; they are what Barbara always understood to be the values of the landscape of her birth. The seed took root when Freda led her by the hand up the hill through Middleham into the old castle keep, even if she was unable to articulate and bring it to flower until she sat down many years later to write *A Woman of Substance*.

In the novel, Paul McGill recognises the woman of substance in Emma with reference to Henry VI – 'O tiger's heart wrapp'd in a woman's hide'. The heroic values Barbara garnered in her childhood as a result of Freda's influence – the sense of honour, duty and purpose – ensures a strong moral code. 'Emma has such a lot of inner strength,' as Barbara says, 'physical and mental strength, but also an understanding heart. She is tough, but tough is not hard,' an allusion that brings us from Shakespeare to Ernest Hemingway, who once said, 'I love tough broads but I can't stand hard dames.'

Emma is tireless, obsessive, ruthlessly determined and dispassionate. She has a 'contained and regal' posture, there is an imperiousness about her, but she is also 'fastidious, honest, and quietly reserved'. She wears a characteristically inscrutable expression and cannot abide timidity where it indicates fear of failing, which she says has 'stopped more people achieving their goals than I care to think about.' She is physically strong and has a large capacity for hard work. 'Moderation is a vastly overrated virtue,' she believes,

26

'particularly when applied to work.' Emma is 'tough and resilient, an indomitable woman', with 'strength of will' and 'nerves of steel'. To her PA, Gaye Sloane, she is 'as indestructible as the coldest steel'.

To Blackie's wife, sweet Laura Spencer, with whom Emma lodges, 'there was something frightening about her', the feeling that 'she might turn out to be ruthless and expedient, if that was necessary. And yet, in spite of their intrinsic difference, they shared several common traits – integrity, courage, and compassion.' While 'understanding of problems on a personal level, [she] was hard-headed and without sentiment when it came to business. Joe [Lowther, her husband] had once accused her of having ice water in her veins.' But granddaughter Paula admires Emma's 'integrity in the face of incredible pressure and opposition', and while she can be 'austere and somewhat stern of eye' and there is a 'canny Yorkshire wariness' about her, when her guard is down it is 'a vulnerable face, open and fine and full of wisdom.'

References to Middleham are legion in the novels. In *Angel*, research for a film takes us there. In *Where You Belong* Barbara chooses it as the site for the restaurant, Pig on the Roof, and there's a lovely Yorkshire Christmas there. In *Voice of the Heart*, Francesca Cunningham guides Jerry Massingham and his assistant Ginny to the castle in search of film locations. Key scenes in the film of *A Woman of Substance* were shot in the village, and when you climb up the main street towards the castle you will see to your right the iron-work canopied shop, which, though placed elsewhere in Barbara's imagination, became the film location for Harte's Emporium (Emma's first shop in her empire).

When I visited Middleham with Barbara, an army of horses clattered down the road from the castle to meet us, descending from the gallops and tipping me straightaway into the pages of *Emma's Secret* and *Hold the Dream*, where Allington Hall is one of the greatest riding stables in all England. Barbara, however, was back in her childhood with Freda: 'We'd get the bus to Ripon and then my mother had various cousins who drove us from Ripon to Middleham . . .'

In *Hold the Dream*, past and present find a kind of poetic resolution in this place. Shane O'Neill believes that he is linked to its history through an ancestor on his mother's side. It is 'the one spot on earth where he felt he truly belonged', and at the end he and Emma's granddaughter Paula come together there. This sense of belonging plays an important role in the author's own imaginative life: 'I have very strange feelings there. I must have been about eight or nine when we first went. I thought, I know this place, as if I had lived there. I want to come back'

No matter whether it is Middleham Castle, Studley Royal or Temple Newsam, Barbara readily enters into an empathic relationship with Freda's favourite places, feeling herself into their history, and it is a strangely intense and markedly subjective relationship. Talking to me about Temple Newsam in Leeds, she said, 'I can't really explain this to you – how attracted I was to the place, my mother and I used to go a lot. It was a tram ride, you'd go on the tram to town and then take another tram . . . or was it a bus? I loved it there, I always loved to go and I felt very much *at home*, like I'd been there before. Yes, déjà vu. Completely.'

'Can you think why that was?' I asked her.

'No. I have no idea.'

'Did you say anything about it to your mother at the time?'

'No, she just knew I loved to go.'

When I drove Barbara to Middleham Castle, we had a similar conversation while exploring what remains of the massive two-storey twelfth-century Keep with Great Chamber and Great Hall above, 'the chief public space in the castle', I read from a sign. 'The Nevilles held court here. Walls were colourful with hangings and perhaps paintings. Clothes were colourful and included heraldic designs . . .'

Barbara interrupted me: 'I have always been attracted to Middleham and I have always had an eerie feeling that I was here in another life, hundreds of years ago. I know it; why do I know it all? *How* do I know it all? Was I here? I know this *place*, and it is not known because I came in my childhood.'

From outside came the sound of children playing. We made our way gingerly up steps nearly one thousand years old, the blue sky our roof now, held in place by tall, howling, windowless walls that supported scattered clumps of epiphytic lichen and wild flowers. Barbara stood still in the Great Hall, taking it all in with almost religious reverence. Then, inevitably, the larking children burst in. She turned, her look silencing them before even she opened her mouth: 'Now look, you've got to stop making a lot of noise. You're disturbing other people. This is not a place for you to play!' It was as if they had desecrated a church. We descended to areas which were once kitchens and inspected huge fireplaces at one time used as roasting hearths, and discovered two wells and a couple of circular stone pits, which a signpost guide suggested may have been fish tanks.

'It was much taller than this, it has lost a lot,' she sighed, and then asked, 'Would it have been crenellated?'

I said I thought that likely, adding, 'It is gothic, dark,' before my eyes returned to the wild flowers in search of a lighter tone. 'Look at the harebells,' I said, but Barbara was not to be deterred. She had come from New York to be there, she wanted me to grasp a point.

'I don't understand why I have this feeling. I don't understand why it is so meaningful to me.'

'There *is* a very strong sense of place here,' I agreed.

'For *me* there is.'

I felt a compulsion to test the subjectivity of Barbara's vision. 'I think *anyone* would find that there is a strong sense of place here,' I said.

She leapt back at me immediately: 'No, no, I *know* this, I have been here, not in this life.' Then, as suddenly, the spell was broken: 'And then you see, you can go down here . . . I had the feeling as a child, I thought I knew it. I had this really strong pull, and

I don't know why. I feel I was here in that time, in the Wars of the Roses. I feel that I lived here in the time of Warwick.'

An ability to empathise with the spirit of place is a characteristic of all writers grouped together in the nineteenth-century Romantic movement, not least William Wordsworth, whose poem, 'I wandered lonely as a cloud . . .' was one of Freda's favourites and crops up time and again in Barbara's novels. The verses tell of an empathic moment in the woods beyond Gowbarrow Park, near Ullswater in the Lake District, where the poet and his sister, Dorothy, come upon the most beautiful daffodils they have ever seen: 'Some rested their heads upon these stones as on a pillow for weariness and the rest tossed and peeled and danced and seemed as if they verily laughed with the wind that blew them over the lake . . . ever glancing, ever changing,' Dorothy recorded in her diary. But Barbara's déjà vu experiences are different in an important respect from those of the Romantics. For her, sympathetic identification with Middleham Castle or Temple Newsam or Studley Royal always carries with it a conviction not only that the past is contained in the present, but of *herself* as part of it. The Romantic notion of empathy is absolutely the opposite of this: it is the disappearance of self. Empathy between Keats and the nightingale was contingent on the poet *becoming* the immortal spirit of the bird. Barbara's feeling that she has been to a place before, in another life perhaps, comes from somewhere else. The 'experience' carries a sense of *belonging*. She seems on the verge of finding out more about herself by being there. It has something to do with identity.

Also inherent in what she terms déjà vu (literally 'already seen') is a feeling of *disassociation* with what is felt to have been experienced before; a sense of loss, a sense that there is a past which was hers and has been lost to her. Such a sense of loss can be a powerful inspiration for an author. For instance, Thomas Hardy's novels were inspired by the loss he felt deeply of the land-based, deep-truth culture into which he had been born at Bockhampton in Dorset in the nineteenth century, and we will see that only after Barbara made her return in imagination to the landscape of her birth, and drew on the values that she associated with it, could she write the novels that made her famous.

But unlike Hardy, Barbara was *not* born into the culture or spirit of the times that inspired these values, and there was nothing that she could give me about her past to suggest that something in her identity had been lost to the passing of the times of which Middleham, Temple Newsam or Studley Royal belonged. I was, however, strongly aware that these experiences occurred and had been repeated on many occasions in the company of her mother. The image came to mind of Freda standing hand-in-hand with her daughter in the Keep at Middleham. Everything seemed to lead back to Freda. Why had Freda thought it so important to take Barbara to these places? Was it a committed mother's desire to share their history, or can we see in the intensity of feeling that the trips engendered something more?

Interestingly, Wordsworth's 'Daffodils' poem is used in Barbara's novel *Her Own Rules* to demonstrate that Meredith Stratton has a problem of identity – a terrible feeling of loss, of being robbed, of being incomplete, which is resolved in the novel when she discovers who her mother is. Meredith hears the poem and thinks she has heard it before – but not here, not in this life. It is the first of many so-called déjà vu experiences linked to Meri's true identity, her secret past. '*Her Own Rules* is about a woman who doesn't know who she really is,' as Barbara confirmed.

Was this how it was for Freda? Was she, like Meredith Stratton, drawing something from the spirit of the place that answered questions about her own identity? Was she sublimating the sense of loss, which her daughter noticed in her but could never explain, in the noble spirit of places like Middleham, Temple Newsam, Fountains Abbey and Studley Royal? And did the intensity of the experience encourage her daughter Barbara, with whom she was 'joined at the hip', to identify with their history and experience this déjà vu?

Freda's very being was redolent of the sense of loss which permeates not only the narrative but also some of the best imagery of Barbara's novels, as when the winter sets in 'for its long and deadly siege' and the landscape is 'brush-stroked in grisaille' – a technique to which Barbara alludes not only in *A Woman of Substance* but also in *The Women in His Life* and *Act of Will* invariably to describe a beauty pained by loss.

Barbara, who knew no more about Freda's problems than I did at the time of our trip to Middleham, allowed only that her mother did definitely want her to have a fascination for the history of the places they visited. But she herself had connected these déjà vu experiences with Meredith Stratton's search for her roots of existence, and, as I mulled over our trip to Middleham, I remembered her appraisal that the fundamental theme of all her novels – including *A Woman of Substance* – is one of identity: 'to know who you are and what you are'.

It would be some time, however, before the burden of the theme could be laid at Freda's door.

CHAPTER TWO

Beginnings

'I was the kind of little girl who always looked ironed from top to toe, in ankle socks, patent leather shoes and starched dresses. My parents were well dressed, too.'

Barbara was born on 10th May 1933 to Freda and Winston Taylor of 38 Tower Lane, Upper Armley, on the west side of Leeds. 'Tower Lane was my first home,' Barbara agreed, 'but I was born in St Mary's Hospital in the area called Hill Top. My mother, being a nurse, probably thought it was safer.'

Hill Top crests the main road a short walk from Tower Lane. St Mary's Hospital is set back from the road and today more or less hidden behind trees within its own large site. A map dated the year of Barbara's birth still carries the hospital's original name, 'Bramley Union Workhouse' (Bramley is the next 'village' to the west of Armley). The Local Government Act of 1929 had empowered all local authorities to convert workhouse infirmaries to general hospitals, and by the time Barbara was born, it was probably already admitting patients from all social classes.

As the crow flies, Armley is little more than a mile and a half west of the centre of Leeds, which is the capital of the North of England, second only to London in finance, the law, and for theatre – the Yorkshire Playhouse being known as the National Theatre of the North. More than 50,000 students of its two universities and arts colleges also ensure that it is today one of the great nights out in the British Isles. Straddling the River Aire, which, with the Aire & Calder Navigation (the Leeds canal), helped sustain its once great manufacturing past, Leeds is positioned at the north end of the M1, Britain's first motorway, almost equidistant between London and Edinburgh.

Armley, now a western suburb of the city, sits between the A647 Stanningley Road, which connects Leeds to Bradford, and Tong Road a mile to the south, where the father of playwright Alan Bennett, a contemporary of Barbara's at school, had his butcher's shop.

Armley's name holds the secret of its beginnings, its second syllable meaning 'open place in a wood' and indicating that once it was but a clearing in forest land. Barbara will appreciate this. Oft heard celebrating the 'bucolic' nature of the Armley of old (it is one of her favourite adjectives both in the novels and in life), she recalls: 'In the 1930s this was the edge of Leeds. There were a lot of open spaces . . . little moors – so called – fields, playing fields for football, as well as parks, such as Gott's Park and Armley Park.' There is still a fair today on Armley Moor, close to where Barbara first went to school: 'Every September the fair or "feast" came, with carousels, stalls, candy floss, etc. We all went there when we were children.'

The Manor of Armley and, on the south side of Tong Road, that of Wortley, appear in the *Domesday Book* of 1086 as Ermelai and Ristone respectively. Together they were valued at ten shillings, which was half what they had been worth before the Normans had devastated the North in 1069. In King William's great survey of England, Armley is described as comprising six carucates of taxable land for ploughing, six acres of meadow and a wood roughly one mile by three-quarters of a mile in area.

Not until the eighteenth century did the village come into its own, thanks to one Benjamin Gott, who was *the* outstanding figure among the Leeds woollen manufacturers of the industrial revolution. He was born in Woodall, near Calverley, a few miles west of the town, in 1762. At eighteen, he was apprenticed to the leading Leeds cloth merchant, Wormald and Fountaine. By 1800 the Fountaines had bowed out and in 1816 the Wormald family sold up too. Just how far all this was down to manoeuvring on the part of the acquisitive Gott does not come down to us. What is clear is that long before the firm was renamed Benjamin Gott and Sons it was his energy that made it the most successful woollen firm in England.

Gott's mills – Bean Ing on the bank of the Aire, and a second one in Armley – brought railway terminals, factories and rows of terraced houses for workers, so that Armley was already part of Leeds by the mid-nineteenth century and the whole area was covered in a pall of smoke. So bad was the pollution that as early as 1823 Gott was taken to court. At his trial, the judge concluded that 'in such a place as Leeds, which flourishes in consequence of these nuisances, some inconveniences are to be expected.'

Such attitudes made Gott a rich man. He bought Armley lock, stock and smoky barrel, built himself a big house there and hung it with his European art collection. Like many Victorian entrepreneurs, he was a philanthropist – he built a school and almshouses, organised worker pensions and gave to the Church's pastoral work in the area. After he died in 1840, two sons carried on the business, made some improvements to the mill, but refused to compromise the quality of their high-grade cloths and take advantage of the ready-made clothing industry, which burgeoned after 1850, preferring to exercise their main interest as art and rare-book collectors. Inevitably their markets shrank. When one of the next generation went into the Church, parts of Bean Ing were let out, and by 1897 one tenant had a lease on the entire building.

William Ewart Gott, the third-generation son who stayed in Armley, is lambasted by David Kallinski in *A Woman of Substance* for having built statues and fountains rather than helping the poor, although in fact he provided the land for the foundation – in 1872 – of Christ Church, Armley, where Barbara was christened, received her first Communion and attended service every Sunday, going to Sunday

School there as well. He gave towards the building of it and appointed its first vicar, the Reverend J. Thompson, who served a longer term (thirteen years) than any vicar since.

Barbara likes to say that she was 'born in 1933 to ordinary parents in an ordinary part of Leeds and had a similarly ordinary childhood,' but there was nothing unexceptional in the times into which she was born. The industrial revolution had finally ground to a halt. Two years before she was born, in the General Election of 1931, the Conservatives had romped home with some twelve million votes, the party having been elected to stem the economic crisis. It was the last year they would enjoy anything like that tally for some time to come.

The steps leading up to economic crisis and the Tory majority in 1931 led also to Adolf Hitler becoming German Chancellor two years later, and, seemingly inexorably, to war six years after that. Those who lived through it will tell you that the slump started in 1928 in the North of England, but it became world news in October 1929 with the Wall Street crash. Between 1930 and 1933, following President Hoover's decision to raise tariff barriers, world trade fell by two-thirds. Unemployment in America rose to twelve million (it had been but two million in 1920); in 1931 nearly six million were out of work in Germany. In Britain, in the January of the year of Barbara's birth – 1933 – the same year that Walter Greenwood's classic novel of life in a northern town during the slump, *Love on the Dole*, was published – it reached an all-time peak of 2,979,000. The Depression was on. Barbara was born at the height of it.

There is no doubt that there was great suffering in areas of the northwest and northeast of England. Figures of the unemployed seeking 'relief' in the work-houses in these regions confirm it, but for some there was a less drastic and emotive story. Barbara's family seem not to have suffered too badly, even though her father was unemployed 'for most of my childhood', and was once reduced to shovelling snow, getting paid sixpence for his work and later telling his daughter: 'At that time, Barbara, there was a blight on the land.' The memory went into *Act of Will*, the 'blight on the land' line causing Barbara some grief when her American editor cut it out.

So how did the Taylors make ends meet? 'My mother worked. She worked at nursing and she did all sorts of things. She was a housekeeper for a woman for a while. Do you remember that part of *Act of Will* when Christina gives her mother Audra a party? I remember that party, and I remember having those strawberries. My editor in England, Patricia Parkin, said nothing in the book summed up the Depression better than the strawberries. I cried when I wrote it because I remembered it so clearly – when I say, "their eyes shone and they smiled at each other . . ." I mean, I still choke up now!'

'It's time for the strawberries, Mam, I'll serve,' Christina cried, jumping down off her chair. 'And you get to get the most, 'cos it's your birthday.'

40

'Don't be so silly,' Audra demurred, 'we'll all have exactly the same amount, it's share and share alike in this family.'

'No, you have to have the most,' Christina insisted as she carefully spooned the fruit into the small glass dishes she had brought from the sideboard. They had not had strawberries for a long time because they were so expensive and such a special treat. And so none of them spoke as they ate them slowly, savouring every bite, but their eyes shone and they smiled at each other with their eyes. And when they had finished they all three agreed that these were the best strawberries they had ever eaten . . .

The dole, or unemployment benefit, was £1 a week in 1930, thirty shillings for man, woman and child. Barbara's father may also have received some sort of disability allowance, for he had lost a leg. A day's work might bring Freda in five shillings, say eighteen shillings a week, cash in hand. That's only 90p in the British decimalised economy, an old shilling being the current 5p piece, but its value was many times greater. In 1930, best butter cost a shilling a pound, bacon threepence for flank, fourpence-halfpenny for side, fivepence or sixpence for ham, two dozen eggs (small) were a shilling, margarine was fourpence a pound, and one pound of steak and rabbit was a shilling. It was quite possible to live on the Taylor income.

Indeed, there was money over to maintain Barbara's 'ironed look from top to toe, in ankle socks, patent leather shoes and starched dresses'. Her parents, she tells us, were well dressed, too. Of course, it was easier to be well dressed in those days. Men wore suits to work whether they were working class or middle class, and few changes of clothing were actually required; women for their part were adept at making do. There is no doubt also that there was the usual Yorkshire care with money in the Taylor household, which Barbara will tell you she has to this day. Certainly, when she was a child there was money left over for her father's beer, a flutter on the horses and even for summer holidays, taken at the east coast resort of Bridlington, the seaside holiday being a pastime whose popularity was on the increase, while foreign travel remained an elite pursuit for the very rich.

Another apparent anachronism of the depressed 1930s is that it was also the decade of the mass communication and leisure revolution, which facilitated industries that would be Barbara's playground as an adult. British cinema began as a working-class pastime, films offering escapism, excitement and a new focus for hero worship more palatable than the aristocracy, as well as a warm, dark haven for courting couples. The first talkie arrived in Britain in 1929. By 1934 there was an average weekly cinema attendance of 18.5 million (more than a third of the population), and more than 20 million people had a radio in the home.

Sales of newspapers also burgeoned, with door-to-door salesmen offering free gifts for those who registered as readers – it was rumoured that a family could be clothed from head to foot for the price of reading the *Daily Express* for eight weeks. In 1937 the typical popular daily employed five times as many canvassers as editorial staff. It is interesting that Barbara is wont to say in interview, 'I'd read the whole of Dickens by the time I was twelve,' because complete sets of Dickens were a typical 'attraction' offered to prospective readers – perhaps to *Daily Mirror* readers in particular, for 'When I was a child,' Barbara once said, 'we had the *Mirror* in our house and I have always been fond of it.'

Literacy increased throughout the country at this time, partly due to the expansion of the popular press, the sterling work of libraries and the coming of the paperback book. Allen Lane founded the Penguin Press in 1936 and Victor Gollancz set up the Left Book Club in the same year. Literature, as well as books not classifiable as such, was now available to the masses: 85.7 million books were loaned by libraries in 1924, but in 1939 the figure had risen to 247.3 million.

Freda took full advantage. 'She was a great reader and force-fed books to me. I went to the library as a child. My mother used to take me and plonk me down somewhere while she got her books.'

Armley Library in Town Street was purpose-built in 1902 at a cost of £5,121.14s. It is five minutes' walk from the family's first house in Tower Lane and even less from Greenock Terrace, to which the Taylors repaired during the war. Libraries in the North of

England are often supreme examples of Victorian architecture, like other corporation buildings an excuse to shout about the industrial wealth of a city. Though Armley's is relatively small, there is something celebratory about its trim, and the steps leading up to the original entrance give, in miniature, the feeling of grandeur you find in Leeds or Manchester libraries, for example. What's more, the architect, one Percy F. Robinson, incorporated a patented water-cooled air-conditioning system in the design. 'It was a beautiful building,' Barbara agreed when I told her that I was having difficulty getting access to local archives because it was now closed. 'Don't tell me they are destroying it!' she exclaimed in alarm. It was closed in fact for renovation, and today there is a pricey-looking plaque commemorating Barbara's reopening of it in November 2003.

'My mother exposed me to a lot of things,' Barbara continued. 'She once said, "I want you to have a better life than I've had." She showed me – she *taught* me to look, she taught me to read when I was very young. She felt education was very important. She would take me to the Theatre Royal in Leeds to see, yes, the pantomime, but also anything she thought might be suitable. For instance, I remember her taking me to see Sadlers Wells when it came to the Grand Theatre in Leeds. I remember it very well because Svetlana Beriosova was the dancer and I was a young girl, fifteen maybe. I loved the theatre and I would have probably been an actress if not a writer. I remember all the plays I was in, the Sunday School plays: I was a fairy – I have a photograph of myself! – and a witch! And then I was in the Leeds Amateur Dramatics Society, but only ever as a walk-on maid. We did a lot of open-air plays at Temple Newsam, mostly Shakespeare. I have a picture somewhere of me in an Elizabethan gown as one of the maids of honour.' The involvement of Barbara and some of her school-friends in these plays was organised by Arthur Cox, a head teacher in the Leeds education system, whose wife was a teacher at Northcote School, which Barbara attended from 1945. A friend at the time, June Exelby, remembers: 'We used to go and be extras in things like *Midsummer Night's Dream* – as fairies and things like that. Barbara used to particularly enjoy it. I can't remember whether she was any good at it.'

Affluence in Armley seemed to rise and fall with the topography of the place. Going west from Town Street at Wingate Junction, which was where the Leeds tram turned around in Barbara's day, up Hill Top Road and over the other side to St Mary's Hospital and St Bede's Church, where Barbara went to dances as a girl, the houses were bigger and owner-occupied by the wealthier professional classes: 'It was considered to be the posh end of Armley,' she recalled.

Tower Lane, where Barbara lived with Freda and Winston, is a pretty, leafy little enclave of modest but characterful, indigenous-stone cottages. It is set below Hill Top but hidden away from the redbrick industrial terraces off Town Street to the east, in which most of the working-class community lived. It must have seemed a magical resort to Barbara in the first ten years of her life, and certainly she remembered Armley with a fairytale glow when she came to write about it in *A Woman of Substance* and *Act of Will*, Emma Harte and Audra Kenton both coming upon it first in the snow.

> *Audra saw at once that the village of Upper Armley was picturesque and that it had a quaint Victorian charm. And despite the darkly-mottled sky, sombre and presaging snow, and a landscape bereft of greenery, it was easy to see how pretty it must be in the summer weather.*

In *A Woman of Substance*, it is 'especially pretty in summer when the trees and flowers are blooming,' and in winter the snow-laden houses remind Emma explicitly of a scene from a fairytale:

> *Magically, the snow and ice had turned the mundane little dwellings into quaint gingerbread houses. The fences and the gates and the bare black trees were also encrusted with frozen snowflakes that, to Emma, resembled the silvery decorations on top of a magnificent Christmas cake. Paraffin lamps and firelight glowed through the windows and eddying whiffs of smoke drifted out of the chimneys, but these were the only signs of life on Town Street.*

It is a little girl's dream. Although the description is unrecognisable of Armley today, and its 'mundanity' is again deliberately discarded when Barbara selects Town Street as the spot where Emma Harte leases a shop and learns the art of retail, setting herself on the road to making millions, we accept it because it was plausible to the imaginative little girl who lived and grew up there: 'There are a number of good shops in Town Street catering to the Quality trade,' Blackie tells Emma when she first arrives:

> *They passed the fishmonger's, the haberdasher's, the chemist's, and the grand ladies' dress establishment, and Emma recognised that this was indeed a fine shopping area. She was enormously intrigued and an idea was germinating. It will be easier to get a shop here. Rents will be cheaper than in Leeds, she reasoned logically. Maybe I can open my first shop in Armley, after the baby comes. And it would be a start. She was so enthusiastic about this idea that by the time they reached the street where Laura Spencer lived she already had the shop and was envisioning its diverse merchandise.*

Today, beyond Town Street's maze of subsidiary terraces, where Barbara's father Winston's family once lived, stand Sixties tower blocks and back-to-back housing with more transient tenants not featured in Barbara's fiction. And at the end of the line stands Armley Prison, its architectural purpose clearly to strike terror into the would-be inmates. This does register in *A Woman of Substance* – future architect

Blackie O'Neill calls it a 'horrible dungeon of a place'. Nearly a century later, multiple murderer Peter Sutcliffe – 'the Yorkshire Ripper' – added to its reputation.

Now, twenty-five per cent of Armley's inhabitants are from ethnic minorities where English is a second language. The great change began as Barbara left for London in the 1950s. As a result, the culture of Armley village today is unlike anything she remembers, even though, according to local headmistress Judy Blanchland, inhabitants still feel part of a tradition with sturdy roots in the past, and have pride in the place. Certainly there is continuity in generations of the same families attending Christ Church School. The school, and the church opposite, remain very much the heart of the local community, with around 100 attending church on Sunday, seventy adults and some thirty children. There always has been a lot of to-ing and fro-ing between the two, even if changing the name of Armley National School, as it was in Barbara's day, to Christ Church School did cause something of a stir.

Barbara enrolled there on 31st August 1937, along with eleven other infants. Her school number was 364 until she was elevated to Junior status in 1941, when it became 891. Alan Bennett, born on 9th May 1934, one year after Barbara, joined on 5th September 1938, from his home at 12 Halliday Place. The families didn't know one another. 'My mother used to send me miles to a butcher that she decided she liked better [than Bennett's shop on Tong Road]. It was all the way down the hill, almost on Stanningley Road.' After leaving the school, the two forgot they had known one another until the day, fifty years later, when they were both honoured by Leeds University with a Doctor of Letters *Honoris Causa* degree.

Bennett became a household name in England from the moment in 1960 that he starred in and co-authored the satirical review *Beyond the Fringe* with Dudley Moore, Peter Cooke and Jonathan Miller at the world-famous Edinburgh Arts Festival. Later the show played to packed audiences in London's West End and New York. He was on a fast-track even at Christ Church School, passing out a year early, bound for West Leeds High School, according to the school log. From there the butcher's son won a place at Oxford University.

Barbara and I walked the area together in the summer of 2003, mourning the fact that generally little seems to have been done to retain the nineteenth-century stone buildings of her birthplace. Even many of the brick-built worker terraces, which have their own period-appeal, have been daubed with red masonry paint in a makeshift attempt to maintain them. There was, however, enough left to remind Barbara of her childhood there.

We drove up Town Street towards Tower Lane, where she lived until she was about ten. At Town Street's west end, you can filter right into Tower Lane or left into Whingate, site of the old tram terminal and the West Leeds High School, now an apartment block. (See 1933 map in the first picture section.) The small triangular green between Town Street and Whingate which appears at this point must have been a talking point for Barbara and her mother from earliest times, if only on account of its name – Charley Cake Park – mentioned in both *A Woman of Substance* and *Act of Will*. 'Laura told me that years ago a man called Charley hawked cakes there,' says Blackie. Emma believes him, but only because no-one could invent such a name for an otherwise totally insignificant strip of grass.

As we wind our way towards Barbara's first home, she has a mental picture of 'me at the age of three, sitting under a parasol outside 38 Tower Lane, near a rose bush. It *is* a lane, you know,' she emphasises, 'and it was a tiny little cottage where we lived. Do you think it is still there? We got off the tram here . . . Whingate Junction . . . then we walked across the road and up Tower Lane, and there was a very tall wall, and behind that wall were . . . sort of mansions; they were called The Towers.'

At the mouth of the lane she points to a cluster of streets called the Moorfields: 'That used to be where the doctor I went to practised – Doctor Stalker was his name. One of those streets went down to the shop where I got the vinegar. Did I tell you about the vinegar? Boyes, a corner shop, that's where I used to get it. I wonder if that's still there?'

The vinegar turns my mind to Barbara's penchant for fish and chips. I had heard that when she comes to Yorkshire she likes nothing better than to go for a slap-up meal of fish and chips, mushy peas, and lashings of vinegar. That very night I would find myself eating fish and chips with her in Harrogate. Nothing odd, you might say, about a Yorkshire woman eating a traditional Yorkshire meal, only Barbara has her posh cosmopolitan heroes and heroines do it in the novels too, and has herself been known to request, and get, a bottle of Sarson's served at table in the Dorchester Grill.

What is Emma Harte, the woman of substance's favourite dish? Fish and chips, preceded by a bowl of vegetable soup, served in Royal Worcester china of course, the only concession to Emma's transformation. Again there is this feeling of fairytale about it all, except that one knows that the writer has herself made the same journey as Emma Harte, and that she does in fact order fish and chips too. The desire seems to pass down the generations, so that Emma's grandson, the immensely wealthy Philip McGill Amory, insists on eating fish and chips with his wife Madelena – what matter if she is wearing a Pauline Trigère evening gown?

'My mother used to send me to get the household vinegar from Mr Boyes,' Barbara continues, 'and she sent me with a bottle because it was distilled from a keg, and when I returned with it she'd always look at the bottle and say, "Look at this, he's cheating me!" Until one day she went in herself with the bottle and she said to Mr Boyes, "You're cheating me. I *never* get a full bottle," and apparently Mr Boyes replied, "Eeh, ah knows. Tha' Barbara's drinking it." He was very broad Yorkshire, and it's true, I did drink a bit of it on the way home. Even today I like vinegar on many things, but especially on cabbage . . .

'There's Gisburne's Garage!' I slow down as we pass the garage on our right at the mouth of the lane, and she points out an old house, pebble-dashed since she was a girl. 'This was where Mrs Gisburne lived and it had a beautiful garden in the back. But where this is green there used to be a pavement, surely . . . but maybe it wasn't, perhaps I am seeing . . .'

This is the first time that Barbara has set foot in the place for fifty years. What will turn out to be real of her childhood memories? What part of imagination? Childhood memories play tricks on us. She looks for the 'tall wall' that she remembers should be on our left, containing the mansions known as The Towers. There is a wall, but it is not tall, nor have the original blackened stones been touched since the four- or five-foot construction was built all those years ago.

'That wall used to seem so *high* when I was a child,' she says in amazement. 'Anyway, these are called The Towers and this is where Emma had a house and they were considered to be very posh. It was all trees here.'

The Towers stretched many floors above us and must have seemed to a child's eye to reach into the sky. Their castellated construction of blackened West Riding stone gives them a powerful, gothic feel, and it was the majesty of the site that captured Barbara's wonder when she was growing up here. Her eyes must have fallen upon the building virtually every day during her most impressionable years, whenever she emerged from the garden of her house opposite:

The Towers stood in a private and secluded little park in Upper Armley that was surrounded by high walls and fronted by great iron gates. A circular driveway led up to the eight fine mansions situated within the park's precincts, each one self-contained, encircled by low walls and boasting a lavish garden. The moment Emma had walked into the house on that cold December day she had wanted it, marvelling at its grandness and delighted with its charming outlook over the garden and the park itself.

A Woman of Substance

But where was No. 38 Tower Lane, supposedly opposite the tall wall of The Towers? There is No. 42 and 44 . . . but no label indicating No. 38. 'We *were* thirty-eight,' Barbara insists as she alights from the car to get a better look. We move through a gate into a front garden, and, set back from the lane, we see what might have once been a row of three tiny, terraced stone cottages, all that was left of the courtyard where they lived, 'the small cul-de-sac of cottages,' as she wrote in *A Woman of Substance*, describing the neighbourhood of Emma's childhood home.

'This seems very narrow,' she says as we make our way gingerly down the flagged path like trespassers in time. 'They've knocked it all down, I think, and turned it into this. All right, well, I'll find it! There was a house across the bottom,' she muses for her own benefit. 'This, the first of the line [of cottages] was number thirty-eight. You went down some steps. Here it was a sort of garden bit, and where the trees are . . . There were three cottages along here and then a house at the bottom, which has gone. Wait a minute, are there three cottages or only two? Have they torn our house down? Well, this is the site of it anyway.' Her voice breaks as she says this. 'There *were* three houses there. There was our cottage, the people in the corner and the lady at the bottom. There *were* three houses.' She then shows me the site of their air-raid shelter, where she and Freda would sit when the sirens sounded during the early years of the war. In the whole of the war only a handful of bombs actually fell on Leeds, but the preparations were thorough, the windows of trams and shops covered with netting to prevent glass shattering all over the place from bomb blast, entrances to precincts and markets sandbagged against explosions.

'I went to school with a gas mask, I remember,' said Barbara. 'We all had them in a canvas bag on our shoulders and there used to be a funny picture of me with these thin little legs – I've got thin legs even today – thin little legs with the stockings twisted and a coat and the gas mask and a fringe. My mother was cutting her rose bushes and I was playing with my dolls' pram that day in 1940 when a doodlebug, a flying bomb, came over, and she just dropped everything and dragged me into the air-raid shelter. I vaguely remember her saying to my father later – he was out somewhere – "Oh, I never thought I'd see that happen over England."'

No. 38 Tower Lane had two rooms downstairs and

two bedrooms on the upper floor. That is all: a sweet, flat-fronted cottage; a tiny, humble abode. The house at the bottom of the garden is long gone. Its absence offers by way of recompense a spectacular view across the top of Leeds, although Barbara's interest, as we walk the area, is only in how things were, and how they are no more.

Being an only child had various repercussions. Her parents will have been able to feed and clothe Barbara to a better standard than most working-class children, which we know to have been the case. But it would have set Barbara apart for other reasons, too – single-child families were unusual in those days before family planning, and in the single-child home the emphasis was on child-parent relationships rather than sibling friendships and rivalries, which can affect a child's ability to relate to other boys and girls at school; although when things are going well between child and parents it can make the relationship extra-special. 'There were plenty of times,' she says, 'when I just knew that we were special, the three of us. I always thought that we were special and they were special. I think when you are an only child you are a unit more. I always adored them. Yes, rather like Christina does in *Act of Will*.'

The closeness and reliance of Barbara on the family unit was never more clearly shown than in the only time she spent away from home during her early childhood, as an evacuee. The school log reads: '*1st September 1939, the school was evacuated to Lincoln this morning. Time of assembly 8.30, departure from school, 9, to Wortley Station, departure of train, 9.43.'*

The school stayed closed until 15th January 1940: *'Reopened this morning, three temporary teachers have been appointed to replace my staff, which are still scattered in the evacuation areas. Miss Laithwaite is at Sawbey, Miss Maitland at Ripon, Miss Musgrave at Lincoln and Miss Bolton is assisting at Meanwood Road. The cellars have been converted into air-raid shelters for the Infants. Accommodation in the shelters, 100. Only children over 6 can be admitted for the present.'*

'I went to Lincoln,' remembers Barbara, 'but I only stayed three weeks. It was so stupid to send us to Lincolnshire. I remember having a label on me, a luggage label, and my mother weeping as the school put us on a train. I was little. I wasn't very happy, that I know, I missed my parents terribly. I was very spoiled, I was a very adored child. My mother sent me some Wellington boots, so it must have been in winter. She'd managed to get some oranges and she'd put them in a boot with some other things, but the woman had never looked inside. So, when my father came to get me the oranges were still there and had gone bad. My mother was furious about that.

'Daddy came to get me. He'd gone to the house and they said, "She'll be coming home from school any moment." He said, "Which way is it? I'll go to meet her." And I saw him coming down the road and I was with the little girl who was at the house also. I remember it very well because I started to run – he was there on the road with his stick, walking towards me . . . and I'm screaming, "Daddy, Daddy, Daddy!" He said, "Come on, our Barbara, we're going home." We stood all the way on the train to Leeds. I was so happy because I missed my parents so much it was terrible. I was crying all the time – not all the time, but I cried a lot, I didn't like it. I didn't like being away from them. I loved them so much.'

I lead us back out of the gate and we return to the present with more sadness than joy. Walking further up the lane, which has a dogleg that leads eventually out onto Hill Top Road, we explore a steep track down the hill to the right, which Barbara calls 'the ginnel'. Later I discover from Doreen Armitage, who also grew up in the area and let us into the church, that this is an ancient weaver's track: 'They would bring up the wool to the looms from the barges on the canal there.' And, sure enough, I see on today's map that it is marked as a quarter-mile cut-through to the canal across Stanningley Road. Barbara was lost once more in her own memories – the fun she had as a little girl skipping down the ginnel – before again being arrested by the intrusive present: the gardens behind Gisburne's Garage, once so lovely, have been built upon and obscured.

Despondently we make our way back up the ginnel towards the moor where she would often play after school. Past the main gate of The Towers we emerge from a tunnel of trees into a wide-open space, flanked on our left by an estate of modern houses, which has replaced the 'lovely old stone houses' of her youth. Off to the right, we come to what was always referred

to as 'the moor', but is no more than half an acre of
open ground, where now a few strongly built cart-
horses are feeding. On the far side of it is a wall and
some trees. Barbara at once exclaims: 'That's the wall!
When you climbed over *that* wall, you were in something called the Baptist Field – I don't know why it
was called that, but . . . we used to play in that field,
some other children and I, we used to make little
villages, little fairylands in the roots of the trees, which
were all gnarled, with bits of moss and stones and bits
of broken glass, garnered from that field, and flowers.'

Memories of the Baptist Field had been magical
enough to earn it, too, a place in *A Woman of Substance* all of forty years later. In the novel, the field
promises entry to Ramsden Crags and the Top of the
World, symbol of the spirit of Yorkshire.

Barbara's fictional recipe may involve real places,
but it is the feelings recalled from her youth that are
especially true in the novels, and overlooking the Baptist's Field I felt in at the very source of a little girl's
teeming imagination. As with Emma Harte, the years
peeled away on her feelings as a child and 'she had a
sudden longing to go up to the moors, to climb that
familiar path through the Baptist Field that led to
Ramsden Crags and the Top of the World, where the
air was cool and bracing and filled with pale lavender
tints and misty pinks and greys . . . Innumerable memories assailed her, dragging her back into the past.' (*A
Woman of Substance*)

'My father used to walk up here sometimes and
go for a drink at the Traveller's Rest,' Barbara says,

breaking the silence. I had already noted the pub on Hill Top Road. Walking as far as we could up Tower Lane would bring us round to it. Later, Doreen Armitage would recall sitting up there 'with me father and me Uncle Fred; we used to sit there on a Sunday morning.' Barbara said she used to sit there with Winston: 'We were probably waiting for the pub to open, I should think! I used to come here with my father, and we would sit outside and my mother would have a shandy. He liked to go out for his pint, you know, and have his bet ... Ripon, York, Doncaster races. He bred in me a love of horses and racing.'

Barbara's father, Winston Taylor, was born on 13th June 1900 at 6 Wilton Place, Armley, the first child of Alfred and Esther Taylor. 'Daddy was called after Winston Churchill, who had just escaped from the Boer War.' On Barbara's admission, Winston is Vincent Crowther in *Act of Will*, the firstborn of Alfred and Eliza Crowther. He is also Emma Harte's brother, Winston, in *A Woman of Substance*. 'The fictional Winston Harte looked like him, thought like him, and had many of his characteristics,' Barbara told me.

I also learn that she based Emma Harte's father, 'Big Jack Harte', who, as a Seaforth Highlander, fought the Boers in 1900 and 'could kill a man with one blow from his massive fist', on Winston's father, big Alfred Taylor, 'because a certain ingredient of physical strength was required in the character of Emma', the woman of substance she was concocting.

'I loved my grandfather. He was in my mind when I created Jack Harte. He had a moustache, all lovely and furry white, and white hair. Big man, big moustache. He used to hold me on his knee, give me peppermints and tell me stories about when he was a Sergeant Major in the Seaforth Highlanders. He loved me and I loved him.'

Grandpa Alfred Crowther in *Act of Will* also serves as a Sergeant Major in the Seaforth Highlanders, and in *A Woman of Substance* Emma's first husband, Joe Lowther, and Blackie O'Neill join the regiment in the First World War.

The real-life Alfred Taylor, who occasioned these many references in Barbara's fiction, is described as a forgeman on his son Winston's birth certificate and as a cartman on Winston and Freda's marriage certificate. Barbara remembers him as the latter, as the Co-op drayman – the man who looked after the horses and drove the cart carrying stores for the Armley link in Britain's first supermarket chain.

The senior Taylors lived five minutes away from Tower Lane in Edinburgh Grove, off Town Street. 'The house was a Victorian terraced house with a series of front steps, but also a set of side steps leading down to the cellar kitchen. It was a through-house, not a back-to-back, but I can't remember if there were doors on both sides. They then moved to 5 St Ives Mount, two streets closer. This was also a Victorian terraced house with front steps down to the cellar kitchen, where you'd always see my grandmother baking. Both were tall houses as I recall.

'I also liked my grandmother, Esther Taylor. Her maiden name was Spence. She was very sweet and not quite Alfred Crowther's wife in *Act of Will*. Eliza Crowther is always the voice of doom, saying, "Happiness, that's for them that can afford it." My real grandmother was full of other sayings like, "A stitch in time saves nine", "You'd better watch your p's and q's", though I do remember her baking like Mrs Crowther – bacon-and-egg pies (we'd call them quiche Lorraine today), also apple pie, and sheep's-head broth and lamb stews. On Saturday morning I used to go for her to the Co-op, but we didn't call it the Co-op, it was called the *Cworp* – Armley dialect, I suppose. You could buy everything at the Cworp. It had a meat department, vegetables, groceries, cleaning products . . . She loved me. I think I was her favourite.'

All was as Barbara remembered of her grand-parents' houses, and she went on to tell me about the rest of the Taylor brood. 'Winston had a sister called Laura, who lived in Farsley, was married and had a child. She was my favourite aunt. She died of lung cancer during the war, when I was about seven; she died at home and it was a horrible death. I remember going to see her. She was a very heavy smoker. After Laura died, her husband went to live with his family with their little boy, but died not long after. Laura Spencer in *A Woman of Substance* was based on my Aunt Laura, except our family were not Catholic. She was sweet and gentle and so good.

'Then there was Olive, married to Harry Ogle. He had a motorbike and sidecar. He was in the RAF during the war. They never had children. And Aunt Margery, always called Madge . . . she was beautiful.'

Aunt Margery, I was to learn, had the 'uncommon widow's peak above the proud brow' that was Emma Harte's and granddaughter Paula's in *A Woman of Substance,* and Vincent's in *Act of Will.* It did not belong to Barbara, as I had imagined.

'Madge lived in Lower Wortley. She was married, but didn't have children either. I remember I was her bridesmaid when I was six. Olive was another favourite aunt. Everybody loved Olive. She managed a confectioner's shop, Jowett's at Hyde Park Corner – in Leeds, not London! – and I used to go and see her there. She used to let me serve a customer now and then. She lived in this house at twenty-one Cecil Grove, just the other side of the Stanningley Road, by Armley Park.

'We would go on picnics together. She always took her knitting. On one occasion, so the story goes, I nearly drowned. Olive suddenly looked up and said to Uncle Harry, "Where's Barbara?" They couldn't see me. Then, far out in the river, they saw my dress caught on a dead branch, they saw me actually bob up and go under the water again and I was flailing around because I couldn't swim. But the branch had hooked into my dress and was holding me up. Today I have a terrible fear of the sea where I can't put my feet on the bottom. I panic, which I think must go back to that. They got me out in the end, soaked and crying, and dried the dress in the sun, but you know the English sun! They took me home to their house and Auntie Olive ironed the dress and got me back home looking like the starched child that I was.

'So, Daddy had three sisters, and they spoiled me to death, of course, because two of them didn't have children. Their brothers were Winston – my father – Jack, Bill, and Don, the youngest, who sadly died just recently. He and his wife, Jean, my one surviving aunt, had a daughter, Vivienne, my only cousin.

'Jack and Bill Taylor lived at home with my grand-mother and never married. I didn't know them very well. Jack was in the army during the war, I think, and Bill was in minesweepers off the coast of Russia and places like that. Afterwards they came home and lived with my grandma, and then when she died they continued to live in that house – two bachelors, very straight, but very *dour*. I used to go and see my grand-mother, and they would be sitting in their chairs and nobody spoke. I hated it. I wasn't scared of them, I paid not a blind bit of notice because my focus was somewhere else.

Barbara says she owes her good looks to her father, and that 'he was very good-looking, dark-haired, green-eyed. My father in particular was always very well dressed and very well groomed, and even today I can't stand ungroomed men. Any man that I ever went out with before I knew my husband was always good-looking, always well dressed and well groomed. I loved my father. He would have charmed you.' In *Act of Will*, Vincent, Winston's fictional persona, boasts an almost feminine beauty, though 'there never was any question about his virility'. Barbara describes him in fact and fiction as a natural star, charismatic, one who drew others (especially women) to him by force of personality, dashing looks and more than his fair share of beguiling charm . . . plus he had 'the gift of the gab'.

Family legend boosted his reputation further with the adventurous story that at fourteen he ran away to sea and signed up in the Royal Navy, forging his father's signature on the application form. Barbara gives the story to Emma Harte's brother Winston in *A Woman of Substance*. It is not too far from the truth. The real Winston did join the Navy, but not until shortly before his sixteenth birthday. His naval record shows that he signed on as Boy (Class II) on 20th May 1916 in Leeds, that he had previously worked as a factory lad, and that he was at this stage quite small – height 5 ft 1 in, chest 31.5 ins. His first attachment was to *HMS Ganges*, a second-rate, 2284 ton, 84-gun ship with a ship's company of 800, built of teak in 1816 at the Bombay Dockyard under master shipbuilder Jamsetjee Bomanjee Wadia. By the time Winston joined it, *Ganges* was a shore-bound training establishment for boys at Shotley Gate. He remained in the Navy until 16th July 1924, when he was invalided out with a serious condition, which could have led to septicaemia and may have been the reason why he subsequently had one leg amputated.

They took him to what was then a naval hospital, Chapel Allerton in Leeds. Today there is still a specialist limb unit there. Barbara recalls that when he was lying in hospital, 'He said to his mother, "I don't want to have it off because I won't be able to dance." His mother said, "Winston, forget dancing. If you don't have the leg off, you won't live." Gangrene was travelling so rapidly that it had got to the knee. That was why it was taken off very high up. And so he couldn't dance, but he did go swimming. You can swim with one leg and two arms. He went swimming in Armley Baths.'

One can only speculate on the impact the loss would have had on one so sociable, though Barbara marks him out as pragmatic: 'I think I take after my father in that way. He didn't really give a damn what people thought, it was take it or leave me.' Yet, however brave Winston was, losing a leg would have been a huge thing; it would have taken tremendous determination to lead a normal life. Barbara agreed: 'He had to prove himself constantly, I think. I didn't know that when I was growing up.'

The artificial leg he was given was the best available and made of holed aluminium, which according to the specialist at Chapel Allerton would have been light and possibly easy enough to manoeuvre to allow Winston to engage in his favourite pastime, though perhaps not the jitterbug, which was sweeping the country in the years leading up to the war. Some years before rock 'n' roll, the jitterbug involved the disgraceful practice of leaving hold of your partner and improvising fairly frantic steps on your own. In *Act of Will*, when Audra meets Vincent at a dance, it is the less demanding waltz that brings them together:

Audra had almost given up hope that he would make an appearance again when he came barrelling through the door, looking slightly flushed and out of breath, and stood at the far side of the hall, glancing about. At the exact moment that the band leader announced the last waltz he spotted her. His eyes lit up, and he walked directly across the floor to her and, with a faint smile, he asked her if she would care to dance.

Gripped by a sudden internal shaking, unable to speak, Audra nodded and rose.

He was taller than she had realised, at least five feet nine, perhaps six feet, with long legs; lean and slenderly built though he was, he had broad shoulders. There was an easy, natural way about him that communicated itself to her instantly, and he moved with great confidence and panache. He led her on to the floor, took her in his arms masterfully, and swept her away as the band struck up 'The Blue Danube'.

During the course of the dance he made several casual remarks, but Audra, tongue-tied, remained mute, knowing she was unable to respond coherently. He said, at one moment, 'What's up then, cat got your tongue?'

She managed to whisper, 'No.'

Barbara's parents married on 14th August 1929. Winston was living at 26 Webster Row, Wortley, at the time, and described himself on their marriage certificate as a general labourer, while Freda, of 1 Winker Green, Armley, described herself as a domestic servant even though she had been working as a nurse. 'I don't actually know where they met,' admitted Barbara. 'Probably at a dance. If my father couldn't really dance any more because of the leg, perhaps he went just to listen to the music. I actually do think he met her at a dance; they used to have church dances and church-hall dances.'

Although Barbara adored her father, when she was a child there was little openly expressed of the love they shared. 'He didn't verbalise it perhaps in the way that Mummy did,' but the depth of it was expressed in a touching scene one day, which had to do with his artificial leg, symbol of the man's vulnerability.

It had been snowing and Barbara was walking with her father in Tower Lane when he fell and couldn't get up because of the slippery snow. 'He was down on his back, and there was nobody around, and he told me what to do. He said, "Go and find some stones and pile them up in the snow, near my foot." He was able to wedge his artificial leg against the stones in order to lever himself up. I got him sitting up, I couldn't lift him. I was six or seven years old. But he managed to heave himself to his feet eventually.'

But at least she had helped him, as she had always longed to do, and now he realised what a practical, efficient *doer* of a little girl he had fathered. The leg brought him close to her again when he died in 1981. 'My mother said, "Your father wanted his leg taken back to the hospital." So my Uncle Don drove me there with it, and three spare legs, and when I handed them over I just broke down in floods of tears. It was like giving away part of him and myself. I was very close to Mummy, but I was close to my father in a different way.'

After Barbara was born in 1933, however, relations between Winston and Freda were not all they might be. I knew that Barbara's mother Freda didn't always see eye to eye with Grandma Taylor. In *Act of Will* tension between wife and mother-in-law is created by Vincent being the favourite son – Grandma Crowther is forever undermining her daughter-in-law's position. In reality as in the fiction, Winston, I learned, was Esther Taylor's favourite, and Barbara recalls her father going 'maybe every day to see his mother. Why do I think my mother always used to say, "I know where you've been, you've been to . . ."?'

'Did it used to annoy Freda, his going to see his mother every day?' I asked.

'Probably. I should imagine it would. Don't you think it would?'

I thought it would be perfectly natural, particularly given the proximity of the houses. Extended families were supposed to be the great boon of working-class life, and Freda with her small child would surely have warmed to such support. Wortley, Farsley and Armley – Freda was surrounded by the entire Taylor family and she had been otherwise alone, having been brought up in Ripon.

Barbara's mother was not by nature big on company however, so perhaps she didn't find it easy to 'fit in' to this extended family scene, which at first must have seemed quite overpowering. She was 'a very sweet, rather retiring, quiet woman' in Barbara's words, 'rather reserved, shy, but with an iron will'. Freda told Barbara little about her past, only that her parents had brought her up in Ripon and that her father had died. 'Her mother Edith then married a man called Simpson. There were three daughters, Freda, Edith and Mary, and two sons, Frederick and Norman. I don't know, to tell you the honest truth, but as far as I remember there was only one Simpson, Norman Simpson.'

I would discover that Freda always had a particularly strong desire to return to the tiny city where she was brought up: 'My mother *always* wanted to be in Ripon,' Barbara recalled. 'All the time.'

'You mean, some time after you were born, when you were eight, nine or ten?' I asked.

'No, much younger, I went back as a baby.' Freda took Barbara back to Ripon from when she was a baby and constantly throughout her childhood. Was this a kind of escape? I wondered. Was marriage into the Taylor family so difficult an adjustment? It seemed unlikely, given that Barbara made Winston out to be such a catch and Freda as a woman who, in spite of her reserve, could fight her own corner with Esther.

In the novels we are given a number of reasons for a marriage hitting hard times. In *Act of Will* Audra is criticised by her mother-in-law for failing to see that her desire to go out to work is flouting the working man's code, which says that if a wife works, her husband loses his dignity. This is odd, as the mills of Armley and Leeds were filled with working wives, and pretty soon we discover that the real problem is that Audra comes from a better class background. She has fallen on hard times, but – she the lady, he the working man – it can never work, the mother-in-law says.

There may have been similar strife for Freda and Winston. There is speculation that Freda had come, or may have had the impression that she had come, from better stock than Winston. We know that mother-in-law Esther Taylor sounded warnings to Freda that giving Barbara ideas above her station would lead only to trouble. Her counterpart in *Act of Will* does the same. In the North of England there was a nasty word for girls with big ideas – 'upstart'. Barbara notes in the novel, 'the lower classes are just as bad as the aristocracy when it comes to that sort of thing. Snobs, too, in their own way.'

In *Everything to Gain*, on the other hand, the cause of strife is laid firmly at the husband's door. Mallory Keswick's father is 'very much a woman's man, not a man's man . . . He adores women, admires them, respects them . . . he has that knack, that ability to make a woman feel her best – attractive, feminine and desirable. [He] can make a woman believe she's special, *wanted*, when he's around her, even if he's not particularly interested in her for himself.'

In *Act of Will* we sense the same about Vincent. There are arguments not only about Audra's highfalutin ideas, but about Vincent's drinking and a 'fancy woman', and fears that he will leave home and never come back. ' "Go back to your fancy woman," I heard that,' said Barbara. 'That happened when I was little, I remembered it and I did ask Grandma, "What's a fancy woman?" And I know that my mother rejected Winston constantly. No, she didn't talk about it, but I knew about it somehow when I was in my teens. How do children know things?'

Recently, as guest on BBC Radio Four's *Desert Island Discs*, Barbara admitted that she hadn't been able to write *Act of Will* until after her parents had died, 'because I really wrote in a sense about this very tumultuous marriage that they had. They were either in each other's arms or at each other's throats. He was very good-looking and he had an eye for the girls at times.' Later, she said to me, 'But that's life. I think Winston had a bit of an eye for the ladies, but that doesn't mean that he did much about it. Listen, the more I write, the more I read of other people's lives, the more I realise how terribly flawed we all are.'

In the novels this is the message about fathers in general. In *Everything to Gain*, Mallory Keswick says: 'He was a human being after all, not a God, even if he had seemed like one to me when I was growing up. He had been all golden and shining and beautiful, the most handsome, the most dashing, the most brilliant man in the world. And the most perfect ... Yes, he had been all those things to me as a child.'

In *Act of Will*, although Vincent's family all dote on him, Grandpa Alfred has 'no illusions about him'. Vincent has 'temperament, stubbornness and a good measure of vanity', and is easily sidetracked from his purpose. His daughter gets her strength of purpose from elsewhere, from her mother's 'iron will', like Barbara.

Despite what Barbara said, that 'when you are an only child you are a unit more', one can imagine that this difference in character between mother and father was fertile ground for disagreement, and it is not uncommon for Barbara's fictional heroines to recall a childhood trauma of expecting the father to up and leave the family home. In *Everything to Gain*, Mallory is suddenly shaken one day 'not only by the memory but by the sudden knowledge that all the years I was growing up I had been terrified my father would leave us for ever, my mother and I, terrified that one day he would never come back.'

Mal and her mother discuss Edward, her archaeologist father, in this vein. Mal cannot understand 'why Dad was always away when I was a child growing up. Or why we didn't go with him.' Her mother talks about his not wanting either of them along 'on his digs'. Mallory is no fool, however. She remembers 'that fourth of July weekend so long ago, when I had been a little girl of five . . . that awful scene in the kitchen . . . their terrible quarrel [which] had stayed with me all these years.'

In the electoral records of Upper Armley, there is a period when Winston is not included as an inhabitant of the family home. Freda is the sole occupant of electoral age when they are living at Greenock Terrace in 1945, the first record available after the war years (when none were kept), and Barbara considers that 'the trauma [of expecting the father to leave] must spring from the war years. [In Tower Lane] we had an air-raid shelter at the end of the garden. My mother and I would go in with a torch and I'd worry about where my father was.'

'Your father was very often not there?'

'No, he was out having a drink. That was Daddy.'

Besides the Traveller's Rest on a Sunday, his favourite watering holes were 'the White Horse, and the other was the Commercial in Town Street. He'd have to walk home, and during the war I thought he was going to be killed,' said Barbara.

'So the picture I have is of you and your mother sitting in the shelter. Were you there alone or were the neighbours in there too?'

'No, it was ours. There were three in a row, but they were awful. There were seats to sit on, but no radio because you couldn't plug it in, could you? Yes, you put bottles of water and some things in there and a Thermos flask Mummy would fill. A woman wrote a very chastising letter about six months ago saying, "I don't know who did your research for the Anderson shelters, but they weren't like you made it out in *The Women in His Life*. I belong to the Society of Anderson Shelters People," or whatever . . . she will have been all of eighty!'

'It must have been strange to be in the dark with nothing to look at or do, in a makeshift shelter and in the knowledge that bombs could rain down on you at any time.'

'Well,' Barbara remembered, 'we had candles and

my mother always took a book, because she was a reader. She didn't knit like my Auntie Olive.'

'Did you take a book as well?'

'I can't remember, but I know that I listened for that unique, very particular step. It was like a missed step – because of the artificial leg, his was not an even step. There was a *lot* of worry about my father. I used to worry about my father, it's funny, isn't it?'

'Children do worry about their parents,' I say.

'Why? A fear of losing them?'

'Sometimes.'

'I used to worry about him being out when the sirens began to shrill. He always went out, not every night, but some nights a week he'd go down to the local for a pint. Usually he was down at the pub, locked in during the raid, and then later we'd hear his step down the garden. And I'd be so relieved I thought I would cry.'

What we have here is the classic 'only child' situation, touching in the extreme. You want to reach back in time and wipe the worry from the busy mind of this girl who took the responsibility for family relations upon herself. In reality, as in *Act of Will*, the only child was doing a balancing act between mother and father, which can't have been easy. Barbara would have had to stand alone under the burden of any unhappiness in her parents' marriage, and it was not done to complain about this. She would have had nobody to understand her worries and grief, and, clearly, the situation between Freda and Winston did become sadly polarised.

One day Barbara said to me about Freda, 'She neglected my father,' and, later, that Freda 'shut the bedroom door' on Winston. In *Everything to Gain*, Mal's parents, like Vincent and Audra in *Act of Will*, sleep in separate bedrooms, and this is deemed by Mal 'with a sinking feeling' to have been the reason why eventually her father must have romanced other women. And it comes out that, yes, her father was having affairs. The hindsight conclusion reached is that the Keswicks were 'a dysfunctional family', and the uncertainty of her parents' marriage made Mal want 'to have the perfect family when I got married. I wanted to be the perfect wife to Andrew, the perfect mother to Jamie and Lissa. I wanted it all to be . . . to be . . . *right* . . .'

We see this in Barbara also, when, after her marriage to Robert Bradford in 1963, she wrote a trio of manuals for the American publisher Simon & Schuster about being the perfect wife – *How to be the Perfect Wife: Etiquette to Please Him, Entertaining to Please Him* and *Fashions that Please Him*. When a journalist discovered these in the 1980s, the cry went up: Can this be the same woman who created Emma Harte? No journalist had an inkling of the fear out of which Barbara's desire for an even-keel marriage came.

However, it is also clear in both *Act of Will* and in reality that Winston, even if he was a bit flighty, was not the crucial factor. What led to separate bedrooms was the mother switching her attention away from the husband to the child – to Barbara – and that happened for reasons that went deeper than sex. One event that conspired to sharpen Freda's focus on Barbara at the expense of Winston was the tragic death of their firstborn, a boy called Vivian. 'He died from meningitis six months after he was born and some time before I was born,' Barbara told me. In a confusing and quite extraordinary and upsetting coincidence, Alfred and Esther Taylor also had a late son called Vivian, who died. 'She [Esther] would never lock the door at night and her youngest son, Don, who was probably still living at home in those days, said, "Mam, you've got to lock your door at night; it's not safe." And she'd say, "No, I can't in case Vivian wants to get in." He was her last child, I think, and he died as a baby, as a little boy. Then my parents had a son before me, who is Alfie in *Act of Will*, which is why I had Alfie also die of meningitis. Our Vivian Taylor was six or eight months old when he died, not even a year. It certainly affected my mother's relationship to me, because she focused every bit of love and attention on me. If there was a purpose in my mother's life it was *me*. That's rather sad actually.'

But there was more to it than Vivian. 'My mother didn't want any more children because she wasn't going to let anything stop her from giving me a better life than she had had,' Barbara told me. In *Act of Will*, Audra is fired by her need to *redeem her own lost opportunity*. No sacrifice is too great to enable her daughter, Christina, to realise the opportunities that were denied her in childhood. There is an obsessive quality about it from the moment Christina is born

Barbara's mother, Freda Walker, aged about 18 when working at Ripon Fever Hospital.

Winston Taylor, Barbara's father, in the Royal Navy, aged about 16.

Freda in her early twenties with baby Tony Ellwood.

Winston's sister, Laura, Barbara's favourite aunt who died of lung cancer during the Second World War. She was the model for Laura Spencer in *A Woman Of Substance*.

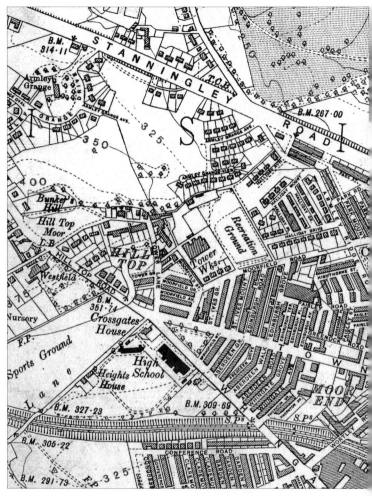

The map, dated 1933 (the year Barbara was born) shows Town Street, Armley, leading north-west past Charley Cake Park (the triangular green that figures in *A Woman Of Substance* and *Act Of Will*) into Tower Lane – Barbara's birthplace. Thence, past The Towers (Emma Harte's residence in the first novel) onto Hill Top Moor and the Baptist Field (another childhood haunt present in the fiction, shown here as Bunker's Hill). Opposite the moor, on Hill Top Road, still stands The Traveller's Rest, which Winston frequented, the road leading off the map to Bramley Union Workhouse (later St Mary's Hospital, where Barbara was born). To the north of Town Street can be seen St Ives Mount, where Winston's parents lived; and eastwards lie the Greenocks, to which Barbara's family moved during the war. Greenock Terrace, not named, is the second street at right angles to Greenock Road; Barbara lived at No. 5. The church and school she attended are off the map, a few streets further north.

Barbara's parents, Winston and Freda Taylor in 1929, the year they were married.

Barbara, a chubby two-year-old, walking in Gott's Park, Armley.

Left: Tower Lane, a surprise piece of rural bliss on the edge of dense industrial terraces. Barbara's first home was off to the right, The Towers are beyond the 'tall wall' on the left.

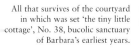

All that survives of the courtyard in which was set 'the tiny little cottage', No. 38, bucolic sanctuary of Barbara's earliest years.

Above: The Towers, the gothic, castellated construction of blackened West Riding stone which so commanded Barbara's attention as a child, reaching high above her home, that she included the house in her first novel.

Below: Armley National School (now Christ Church School), which Barbara attended from 31st August, 1937. Alan Bennett, son of a butcher on Tong Road, joined her a year later.

Freda in fur jacket and cloche hat, Barbara in her Whitsuntide clothes – leghorn straw bonnet, pale green coat and cream gloves – 'the kind of little girl who always looked ironed from top to toe'.

Barbara aged three. She remembers always wearing gloves.

Christ Church Armley, were Barbara was baptised and received her first Communion.

As a fairy in a Sunday School pantomime. Freda made the costume.

Barbara with bucket and spade, aged five – on holiday at Bridlington in Yorkshire.

Above: Leeds Market. 'Mummy and I used to go on Saturday mornings,' Barbara recalls. 'The first Mr Marks [of Marks & Spencer] had a stall there, which had the sign: "Don't ask the price it's a penny". So, I had Emma go into that market.' The food halls in Emma Harte's flag-ship store in *A Woman of Substance* owe much to the weekly trips. *Below:* 'Game Row' as it was then.

Barbara's mother took her over the moors to Top Withens, the setting for *Wuthering Heights*: 'I loved the fact that this great work of literature was set right there. I loved the landscape: those endless empty, windswept moors where the trees all bend one way.' Yorkshire awakened in her the notion that landscape can hold the the spirit of the past.

Within 'the roofless halls and ghostly chambers' of Middleham Castle, north of her own birthplace, Ripon, Freda introduced her to the story of Richard Neville, Earl of Warwick, and many of the traits that would define the character of her woman of substance.

and her mother announces, 'I am going to give her the world.'

Barbara remembers well how this was expressed for real in her relationship with Freda: 'We were very close. I was very close to Mummy. She totally and completely believed in me. There wasn't a day of her life that if she spoke to me, even after I'd gone to live in London and then America, when she didn't say, "I love you." There wasn't a time when she didn't tell me that I was the most beautiful and the cleverest and the most talented and the most charming and the most wonderful person and of course that's not true, we all know that we have faults. But what it did . . . it gave me tremendous self-confidence and a self-assurance that I had even when I was fifteen and sixteen. And she instilled in me a desire to excel. Her message was: "There's nothing you can't have if you try hard enough, work hard enough and strive towards a goal. And never, never limit yourself."'

Barbara took away from their relationship an absolute conviction that she was capable of anything to which she set her mind. Inadequacy was not a concept ever entertained. Her friend Billie Figg noted this as her defining characteristic in her early twenties: 'What she had was enormously high expectations of herself and a lot of assurance.'

In *Act of Will*, Vincent fears that Audra's motivation to do the same for Christina is tinged with obsession. He notes a possessiveness about his wife's relationship with their daughter, which seems to exclude him, and comes to frighten him. 'There was a cold implacability in the set of the mouth and the thrust of the jaw, a terrible relentlessness in those extraordinary cornflower-blue eyes . . .' And Vincent fears, 'She's going to make it a crusade.'

Audra announces her intention to give her daughter the world in the hospital, shortly after she is born. Both Audra's husband, Vincent, and his doctor friend, Mike Lesley, bridle at her naked aggression, not seen before.

When it is all over in the novel, and Audra's daughter, Christina, is the success she has made her, the girl says: 'I'll never be able to thank you enough, or repay you for everything you've done for me, Mummy. You've been the best, the most wonderful mother in the world.' But, as Emma's brother Winston says of his sister towards the end of *A Woman of Substance*, her success is attributable to '*Abnormal* ambition. *Abnormal* drive.'

In *Act of Will*, Vincent, convinced that his wife is victim to irrational forces, shows his mettle in his response to her. He is tender and loving. He masterminds a surprise birthday party for her. There is no hint of violence towards his wife, even when she brings him to his wits' end with her obsession. Moreover, he gives his wife one hundred per cent support over her sense of loss of status. He could have gained the whip hand in the class turmoil of their relationship – that she always believed she came from a better class than he – but nowhere does he use it as a weapon against her.

Knowing now what happened to Freda in her childhood, and the loss she suffered, knowing what it was that made her so determined that Barbara should have the opportunities that were denied herself, it is safe to say that Winston's response to Freda (if it is reflected in Vincent's) was the very best that could have been made. There was in Freda something running deeper even than the loss of her first child, something which possibly no project of success – not even Barbara – could ever quite resolve. Maybe Freda's mother-in-law, Esther, sensed it was never going to be resolved by her son Winston either – however good he was to her. Reason enough for her unsettled relationship with Freda.

The novels first tipped my research in Freda's direction, and it was the novels that gave me a sense of the deepest roots of dysfunction I would find. Turning again to *Everything to Gain*, Mal searches for the reason for her mother's unhappiness: 'Perhaps [she] had experienced humiliation and despair and more heartache than I ever realised. But I would never get the real truth from her. She never talked about the past, never confided in me. It was as if she wanted to bury those years, forget them, perhaps even pretend they never happened.'

In *Act of Will*, Audra's in-laws are all around her. She loves Vincent, but there is something getting in the way, a feeling of apartness certainly. Is it class, as in the novel? Is the belligerent 'outsider' in her really being outed by her better birth? Or is it, as in *Everything to Gain*, something in her childhood, some loss she suffered?

We never get to the heart of the matter in the fiction (because Barbara didn't know), but, like Mallory Keswick, we cannot but suspect there is something we are not being told; indeed we only accept Audra's strangely aggressive love for her daughter in *Act of Will* because we entertain such a suspicion.

In reality, I was to discover, there was every reason for Freda to behave so. Her story provides the crucial dysfunctional and motivational forces that led to her unique relationship with her daughter and Barbara's extraordinary will to succeed. Much of it remained hidden during Freda's lifetime, for Barbara's childhood 'was constructed on secrets layered one on top of the other,' as she wrote in *Everything to Gain*.

These secrets provided Barbara with many of the narrative possibilities of her best novels, and one reason why they have been so successful is that Barbara is not simply writing good ideas, but ideas that are her inheritance. The novels are the means by which she shares in the experience of her past, her mother's past, and that of her mother's own mother. More strangely still, she does so without knowing anything about Freda's history or that of her maternal grandmother, the extraordinary and beguiling Edith Walker.

CHAPTER THREE

Edith

*'I think we ought to go to Ripon. We've quite a
lot of things to review, and to discuss . . .'*
Meredith Stratton in *Her Own Rules*

Edith Walker, Freda's mother, was the daughter of
John and Mary Walker (née Scaife). John Walker was
a slater's apprentice when Edith was born on 4th
September 1880, the youngest of six children. The
occupation seems odd in that John was thirty-seven
at the time, which is late to consider being an apprentice in anything. The family lived at Primrose Hill,
Skipton Road (the Ripon side of Harrogate), close to
what is now a roundabout by a pub called The Little
Wonder.

It seems that Edith never knew her mother, for
John Walker was registered in the 1881 census as a
widower. Perhaps Mary Walker died in childbirth.
Living in the Primrose Hill house with John and Edith
in that year were his other children: Thomas (sixteen),
Elizabeth Ann (twelve), John William (ten), Minnie
(five), and Joseph (three).

One cannot help but wonder how her arrival on the scene was received by the rest of the family. Was she regarded as the final drain on the meagre resources available to a family of eight, in which the bread-winner was on apprenticeship wages? Was she rejected for being the cause of their mother's death? Or was her advent greeted with great love and pity for the poor little mite, and was she spoiled and fussed over by her elder sister, Elizabeth Ann, and, indeed, doted on by her father, John, who may even have caught glimpses of his lost wife in her?

Being motherless, even with the care of others in the family, Edith may have suffered from maternal deprivation, a condition believed to be as harmful as poor nourishment. It can have a child yearning throughout its life for the kind of unconditional love that only a mother can give, and which no substitute can hope to assuage. Edith may also have suffered physically, for feeding infants was mainly by mother's breast in those days.

The family does seem to have been a close one. It was largely still intact ten years later, and some members of it remained close for a considerable time into the future. It is indeed tempting to surmise that Edith was the apple of her father's eye. If so, it is all the more tragic that he was unable or, for some reason beyond resolution, unwilling to save Edith from the abyss into which she was to fall.

Typically for a working man of the period, John Walker stayed in one area for his entire lifetime. He was born in 1844 in Burton Leonard, a tiny village midway between Harrogate and Ripon, his parents having moved there from Pateley Bridge, ten miles to the west, where his elder sister Mary was born in 1839. After marrying, he went with his wife to live in Scotton, a village three miles to the south of Burton Leonard. Their first son, Thomas, was born there in 1865. The family then moved to Ripon in or around 1869, where siblings Elizabeth Ann, John William and Minnie were born. Then, around 1877, came the move to the outskirts of Harrogate, where first Joseph and then Edith (Barbara's grandmother) were born. By 1891 the family had moved back to Ripon.

The city, twenty miles or so north of Leeds, lies just west of the Vale of York, which runs north–south between the North York Moors to the east and the softer Dales to the west. To anyone who doesn't know Yorkshire, the names of these two great land masses may be misleading, because there are plenty of dales in the North York Moors and plenty of moors in the Dales. Dales are valleys; moors are high, largely unsettled tracts of wilderness, naturally enough separated by dales. Indeed, as we have seen, perhaps the most famous moor in all England – Haworth Moor – is not in the North York Moors at all, but way to the southwest, near Leeds.

In the immediate vicinity of Ripon there is some of the most beautiful countryside in all England. It was built at the confluence of three rivers. From Middleham to the north, a sense of Warwick's struggles washes down east of the city through Wensleydale on the Ure, the river's Celtic name – Isura – meaning physical and spiritual power. There it is met by the Skell, which is itself met southwest of the city by the River Laver.

In *Act of Will*, Audra refers to Ripon as 'a sleepy old backwater' compared to 'a great big metropolis like Leeds', but the description belies the tiny city's unique and many-faceted appeal. Its population was a mere 7500 at the time of the Walker family's incursion. Today it is little more than double that size, and retains the feel of a small, busy, rural community with tremendous reserves of history at its fingertips. There is a twelfth-century cathedral or minster, a seventeenth-century House of Correction, a nineteenth-century workhouse and debtor's prison, old inns bent and worn by time, and, nearby, twelfth-century monastic ruins – Fountains Abbey at Studley Royal.

Bronze-age earthworks and henges to the northeast suggest human habitation thousands of years BC, but Ripon itself can be said to have first drawn breath in AD 634 with the birth of the city's patron saint, Wilfrid, in Allhallowgate, Ripon's oldest street, just north of what was then a newly established Celtic Christian monastery.

The monks sent Wilfrid, an unusually able boy, to be educated in Lindisfarne (Holy Island) off the Northumberland coast, where St Aidan had founded a monastery in 635. Later, Wilfrid championed Catholicism over Celtic Christianity as the faith of the Church in England, and was appointed Abbot of the Ripon monastery, then Archbishop of York. The church he built in Ripon became a 'matrix' church of the See of York, and his work inspired the building of Ripon Minster in 1175 and the foundation of various hospital chapels, which established the city's definitive role in providing food and shelter for the poor and sick.

St Mary Magdalen's hospital and chapel were built in the twelfth century on the approach to the city from the north, and had a special brief to care for lepers and blind priests. St John the Baptist's chapel, mission room and almshouses lie at the southeast Bondgate and New Bridge approach to the city over the River Skell, which also offers a view of seventeenth-century Thorpe Prebend House, situated off High St Agnesgate in a peaceful precinct with another hospital chapel, St Anne's, already a ruin in Edith's time, but founded by the Nevilles of Middleham Castle. Thorpe Prebend was one of seven houses used by the prebendaries (canons) of the minster, and a house with a special place in Barbara's memory.

When Freda brought Barbara to Ripon as baby and child, they would invariably stay at Thorpe Prebend with a family by name of Wray, who were caretakers of the house. Joe Wray was married to Freda's cousin, Lillie, and Barbara became firm friends with Joe's niece, Margery Clarke (née Knowles). 'I spent a lot of weekends with Margery when I was a young girl,' Barbara recalls, and later as teenagers they would go to dances together at the Lawrence Café in the Market Place. The Lawrence had a first-floor ballroom famous because the dance floor was sprung: 'We used to go, she and I, to the Saturday night dance there at fifteen, sixteen . . . When I reminded her and I recalled that we stood waiting to be asked to dance, her swift retort was, "But not for long!" Apparently we were very popular.'

Margery still lives in Ripon today and took me to the spot beside Thorpe Prebend House where Freda and Margery's father, who went to school together, used to play on stepping-stones across the Skell. Later I learned from Barbara of the celebrated occasion when, according to Freda, he pushed her in. 'She was wearing a dress her mother Edith had dyed duck-egg blue and she dripped duck-egg blue all the way home on her white pinafore!'

Jim Gott, no obvious relation of the acquisitive Gott of Armley, but a working-class lad born seven years before Freda at 43 Allhallowgate, recalled in his memoir that playing on these stones was a popular pastime. What comes across in Jim Gott's book, *Bits & Blots of T'Owd Spot*, is the fun he had as a child and the empathy he and his contemporaries enjoyed with the spirit of Ripon – past and present fusing in its ancient architecture and traditions, and the daily round. These were the riches of a life that in other ways was hard, and Freda, despite the particular difficulties attached to her childhood, would have shared in them too, and, as an adult, looked back with similar wonder.

The spirit of the place, matured over time, was celebrated on a weekly basis at the twelfth-century Market Place, with its covered stalls, self-styled entertainers and livestock pens. It features in Barbara's novel, *Voice of the Heart*. Every Thursday, long before the market bell sounded at 11 a.m. to declare trade open, folk poured in from the surrounding moors and dales, and Ripon awoke to the clatter of vehicles laden with fresh produce and squawking hens, and the drovers' fretting sheep and lowing cattle as flocks and herds made their way through the city's narrow lanes to the colourful square on the final leg of what was often a two- or three-day journey. All came to an end at 9 p.m., as Gott recorded, when the Wakeman Hornblower announced the night watch, a tradition that survives in Ripon to this day.

Home for Edith and her family in 1891 was a small stone cottage just two minutes' walk south of the Market Place at No. 8 Water Skellgate, a whisper from where Barbara and Margery would dance the night away half a century later. (The 1909 map in the second picture section charts the area clearly.)

By this time Edith's father, John, was forty-seven and had married again, his second wife, Elizabeth, being four years his junior. Edith herself was ten, going on eleven, and very likely a pupil at the nearby Minster Girls Primary School. The only other alternative would have been the Industrial School, reserved for the very poor and substitute for the Workhouse School, which had closed its doors for the last time a few years earlier.

Siblings Elizabeth Ann, John William and Joseph (twenty-two, twenty and thirteen respectively) were still at home, but there is no sign of eldest brother

Thomas or of Minnie, who, if she was alive, would have been fifteen, old enough to be living out as a maid. Also sharing the house is a lodger, John Judson, and a 'grandson' (possibly Elizabeth's or even Minnie's child) by name of Gabriel Barker. It must have been a tight squeeze.

John had quite possibly made the move back to Ripon to avail himself of the wealth of job opportunities. The city's position on the western fringe of the Vale of York – good sheep-rearing country – had made it the centre of the mediaeval wool trade, its three rivers diverted into a millrace or water course, which flowed from High Cleugh, southwest of the city, through Water Skellgate, to Bondgate Green in the southeast, serving three mills in the process. Ripon's pre-eminence in this had continued into the late fifteenth century, but then steadily declined and various other industries had come to the fore. In the seventeenth century, Ripon rowels (spurs) had gained a worldwide reputation, so that Ben Jonson could write in his play *The Staple of News* (1626):

> *Why, there's an angel, if my spurs*
> *Be not right Rippon.*

The city was also renowned for its saddletrees, frames of saddles worked from local ash, elm and beech – horse racing has been part of Ripon's life since 1664, and fourteen days of flat racing are still staged between April and August at Yorkshire's Garden Racecourse. Button-making made another important economic contribution and, a century later, out of the French Revolution came a gift of an industry from a band of Ripon-bound French refugees, who were befriended by a French-speaking Yorkshireman called Daniel Williamson. In return for his welcome the immigrants handed Williamson the secret details of a varnish-making process, and the lucky man set up the first varnish-making business in England, becoming so successful that today Ripon manufacturers are still doing business in every major country of the world.

Besides these, an iron foundry made a significant contribution from the nineteenth century, and the city also supported a hive of little industries, such as bone- and rope-millers, tanners, fell-mongers, coachbuilders and chandlers. Finally, as many as nineteen per cent of those in employment in the city at this time were able to find work as unskilled labourers.

Upon arrival, Edith's brother, Joseph, found work as 'a rope twister', while his father, John, took up as a lamplighter. 'One of my earliest memories is of kneeling on a chair by a window waiting for the lamp-lighter,' wrote one J. Hilsdon, a Ripon citizen of those days. 'He was a tall figure, who carried a pole with a light on the end. The street lamps were gaslights and he tipped the arm to release the gas and lit the mantle. Presumably he made a second round to extinguish them.'

When one soaks up the history of Ripon in late Victorian and Edwardian times, the chief impression is of the huge divergence of lifestyle between rich and poor, who nevertheless lived on top of one another in so small a place as this. When Beryl Thompson arrived in 1956 she was spellbound by the accessibility of the city's history, and has spent her life looking into the plight of the poorest citizens ever since. 'I have done this over a period of about thirty or forty years,' she told me, 'and some of the places that children lived in Ripon at this time – if you read the medical inspectors' reports – were not fit to be in. They were no better than pigsties down St Marygate or Priest Lane [this is the oldest part of the city, site of the original Celtic monastery]. If you look at the early maps you will find a lot of courts all over the city – there's Foxton's Court and Thomson's Court and Florentine's Court and so on. I think there were a lot of hovels in these courts and they probably shared lavatories or there'd be a cesspool outside or a midden. They were trying to clean it up at the turn of the century, but the reports still comment on this.'

These courts were a throwback to mediaeval times and a common sight in the nineteenth and early twentieth centuries, not only in Ripon. The imagination of Charles Dickens, as a boy alone in London, his parents incarcerated in the Marshalsea debtors' prison, was set alight by 'wild visions' as he lurked around their entries and looked down into their inky depths. In Ripon, the city centre retained its mediaeval street plan right into the twentieth century, and the labouring poor were consigned to cottages in just such dark and dismal courts or yards, set behind the narrow streets. Very often at the top of them you'd find workshops – a blacksmith, bakery or slaughterhouse.

There was tremendous movement by the poor within them. In the first decade of the twentieth century, Edith's brother Joseph (Barbara's great uncle) moved at least four times in the space of four years through one maze of them. In 1907 he could be found at 2 York Yard, Skellgarths (a continuation to the east of Water Skellgate), having just moved there from 3 Millgate Yard. By 1910 he had moved to 1 York Yard, then to 4 York Yard. In 1911 he took up residence at 3 Johnson's Court, between 14 and 16 Low Skellgate (continuation to the west of the street), settling there and getting wed. Sadly, he was then almost certainly killed in the First War, for when records resumed in 1918 the sole occupant of 3 Johnson's Court was his widow, Ruth Matilda Walker. Within a year she remarried, her second husband a man called James Draper. And life went on.

These yards were private, often close-knit communities, safe from outsiders because few dared venture into them unless they had business to perform, but Beryl was right that conditions were grim. In 1902, a Ripon sanitary inspector reported: 'The really antiquated and disgusting sanitary arrangements now existing in the poorer quarters – where it is not unusual to find numbers of homes crowded round a common midden, which is constructed to hold several months' deposit of closet and vegetable matter, ashes and every sort of household refuse imaginable, and which remains in a festering and decaying condition, poisoning what pure air may reach the narrow courts . . .'

A Ripon Council report, dated seven years before Freda was born, records one domicile 'where ten human beings have been herded together in a space scarcely adequate for a self-respecting litter of pigs,' and it is recorded in *A Ripon Record 1887–1986* that in 1906, when Freda was two, increasing numbers of children were turning up at school without shoes.

The awful conditions in which unskilled working-class people lived in Edwardian England was so widely appreciated that in the hard winter of 1903, the New York *Independent* could find no more deserving case than England to cover: 'The workhouses have no space left in which to pack the starving crowds who are craving every day and night at their doors for food and shelter. All the charitable institutions have exhausted their means in trying to raise supplies of food for the famishing residents of the garrets and cellars of London lanes and alleys.'

As in London, so in Ripon. These horrors were to be found 'within a stone's throw of our cathedrals and palaces', as William Booth, founder of the Salvation Army, noted in his book, *In Darkest England and the Way Out* (1890). George R. Sims, a respected journalist writing a year earlier, had conjured up a picture that would not have seemed out of place in Dickens's *A Tale of Two Cities*, of 'underground cellars where the vilest outcasts hide from the light of day ... [where] it is dangerous to breathe for some hours at a stretch an atmosphere charged with infection and poisoned with indescribable effluvia.'

In Ripon, at precisely the time that William Booth

published his book about the slums of England being 'within a stone's throw of our cathedrals and palaces', life for the Walkers in Water Skellgate, a stone's throw from Ripon Minster, will have been hard by our standards today, but it would also have given Edith a keen sense of what life was like on the other side of the wealth divide, and an opportunity perhaps to dream of how to make the transition from one to the other.

When John Walker and his first wife first lived in the city in 1869 there would still have been water running openly through Water Skellgate – a section of the millrace already described – and one can imagine that the speedy brook provided a useful if smelly flush in the days before water sewerage systems. In 1875, however, the foetid stream was covered over, perhaps after pressure from the more well-to-do who had begun to frequent the area. For, by the time Edith was living there in the 1890s, Water Skellgate was masquerading as downtown Ripon, with its pubs and a musical hall, theatre and dance hall which attracted the nobs – all cheek-by-jowl with an intriguing mix of small businesses, dismal courts and low-rent accommodation in easy reach of a pawnshop in High Skellgate, and various charitable organisations, including the Jepson Hospital and Bluecoat School, the Girls' Friendly Society Lodge (run by a Miss Taylor) and a Wesleyan Mission Chapel to which Edith attached her allegiance whenever required to state her religion officially.

The leisure facilities in the vicinity included the Palace Theatre at the lower end of adjacent Kirkgate, and in Water Skellgate itself the Victoria Hall, a music hall and theatre, which later became the Opera House. Next door was the Constitutional Club, and then the Crown Vaults, a pub owned by a Mr Lavin, who was also a horse dealer. At one stage, in a yard set back from the main street, between Nos 8 and 16, there was even a covered casino, a skating rink, where young skaters would 'glide away to the strains of the Volunteer Band', and the delights of a permanent fun fair.

It was the Victoria Hall in particular that would have given young Edith an opportunity to see how the other half lived. In late Victorian and Edwardian England such places were accessible to rich and poor alike, and full to overflowing. Jim Gott recalled the Victoria Hall as a place that drew the nobility in droves:

See the carriages sway and whirl to the main entrance. In the long-necked brass candle lamps, the flames flicker and dance as the carriages trundle away.

Intermingling shadows appear and disappear into the Hall, amid the flickering yellow lights. Flashing gems highlight the colourful satins and silks swished by my ladies, echoed by the sheen of their escorts' black velvet toppers. This is their hour – the local nobility – as they vanish within the gaslit auditorium. Can we forget those Primrose League, Conservative, and Volunteer balls – sparkling and colourful? From a distance we

*watched these grand spectacles, with the Beck-
with orchestra playing music, soothing, simple
and haunting.*

Edith was living in the thick of it all, a few doors up
in Water Skellgate, and no doubt wanting it all too.
Did she have her first thrilling taste of theatre at the
Victoria Hall, and later did her daughter Freda come
bustling along in the wake of her mother and perhaps
some male escort, the little girl thrilling to the brief
suspension of daily care? 'Freda loved opera and she
loved all the musical things like Gilbert and Sullivan
and all of the things that I mention [that Audra likes]
in *Act of Will* . . .' Barbara told me. Had her mother's
love of it been sparked at the Victoria Hall?

The presence of local nobility on such occasions
meant, in Ripon's case, the presence of the Studley
Royal party. The Studley Royal Estate is set in a
secluded valley just four miles southwest of the
Market Place obelisk, a monument to one William
Aislabie designed by the celebrated London architect
Nicholas Hawksmoor in 1781.

Studley Royal, which Aislabie then owned, has
been called 'the Wonder of the North'. It is a World
Heritage site and contains over 900 years of history
with a twelfth-century abbey, a mediaeval deer park,
a Jacobean Hall, an eighteenth-century water garden,
and a Victorian church.

There are other stately homes close to the city.
Newby Hall, to the southeast, is an eighteenth-century
Robert Adam house with a magnificent tapestry room,

library, statue gallery and some of Thomas Chippendale's finest furniture, all of which leave readers of
Barbara's novels in no doubt as to the part played by
the Hall in her education at Freda's hands. Less than
three miles to the north lies Norton Conyers, claimed
as the original of Thornfield Hall in *Jane Eyre*,
although so too is Rydings in Birstall, five miles southwest of Leeds, the crenellated family home of Ellen
Nussey, one of Charlotte Brontë's two best childhood
friends. Charlotte did visit Norton Conyers, however,
and family pictures, furniture and costumes are on
display.

But neither was as influential in the lives of Edith
and Freda as Studley Royal, the Estate the most pervasive reminder of the influence of power, money and
politics on all Ripon's citizens since 1180. Studley
Royal reached into their lives as one of the city's
biggest employers, and owned many of the properties
in which they dwelt, particularly in the area where the
Walkers lived. For example, in February 1889 Lord
Ripon put up six houses for sale in Water Skellgate –
Nos. 18 to 23 – No. 20 including in its lot a blacksmith's shop, a joiner's, a brewhouse, stable buildings
and yard. These must have been leasehold sales
because Studley Royal tenants are still recorded as
paying rent on them through 1991, when records
stop.

Studley Royal's influence was so ubiquitous in the
city that on High Skellgate there traded a cycle-maker,
whose top-end product was 'the famous Studley Royal
model'. Almost certainly he was supplier by appoint-

ment to the Estate, where visitors – amounting to some 40,000 annually before the First World War – could hire bicycles, 'motors', or a bath chair. Even the front stage cloth at the Victoria Hall carried on it a painting of Fountains Abbey (part of Studley Royal since the eighteenth century), and Jim Gott writes about this with great reverence. The Estate was the unseen hand in everything, it impinged on life in Ripon at every level, as employer, as property owner, as political presence, and the male line of it no doubt also impinged on more than a few young girls' dreams, the Estate's very name seeming to recommend it in the matter of breeding.

The Aislabie family had succeeded to Studley Royal in 1664, when one George Aislabie, a merchant from York, married into the ancient, landed Mallory family. A long history led up to this succession. The estate is called Royal because the manor was originally held directly from Henry II, king from 1154 to 1189, its earliest owner being one Richard le Aleman. Succession was often carried by means of daughters from one family to another, the Mallory family getting it through marriage into the Tempest family in 1444.

The Tempests had themselves come into the Estate early in the fourteenth century when Sir Richard Tempest married a member of the Le Gras family who succeeded from the Le Alemans in similar fashion. The Tempests died out in the male line, as did the Mallorys in the seventeenth century, but it is perfectly in line with Barbara's interest in Ripon's history that names of these powerful, knightly Ripon families should live on in some of her fictional heroines. One thinks of Mallory Keswick in *Everything to Gain* and Katharine Tempest in *Voice of the Heart*, for example. The film of *A Woman of Substance* actually began shooting at Broughton Hall, near Skipton, which was once the home of the Tempest family.

Ten years after George Aislabie inherited Studley Royal, he was killed in a duel and the Estate passed to his son, John, who, twenty years later, became Member of Parliament for Ripon and rose to Chancellor of the Exchequer, only to be run out of office in 1710 following the most celebrated financial scandal in English history, the South Sea Bubble, a disastrous scheme for paying off the National Debt in which Aislabie appeared personally to profit. Aislabie was arrested and imprisoned in the Tower of London, and although at his trial he was unable to explain his great wealth, he somehow managed to keep Studley Royal, dedicating himself thereafter to improving its house and gardens.

The Tudor house, Studley Hall, had been partly destroyed by fire in 1716. Aislabie's eighteenth-century rebuild was never finished and much of it was said to have rather spoiled what was left of the original architecture, that it had been reduced by Aislabie to a grand architectural mess, a terrible muddle of styles. This and the fact that it had been fired for the second time when Barbara was a child, instantly recommended it to me as the model for Fairley Hall, where Emma works as a maid and which she later takes great delight in razing to the ground to avenge her treatment at the hand of Edwin Fairley, father of her illegitimate child. In particular, the passage came to mind when Blackie O'Neill, with his eye for perspective and line, surprises us with his condemnation of it as 'the most grotesque house he had ever seen ... it had no redeeming features at all ... an ugly, hodgepodge of styles.'

> *In essence, Fairley Hall was a hodgepodge of diverse periods that competed with each other to create a façade that was without proportion, symmetry, or beauty. The house was large, solid, and rich, a veritable mansion, in fact, but its architectural inconsistencies made it hideous. Blackie sighed. He loved Georgian houses in Ireland, with their fluid lines and classical proportions that gave them such perfect balance. He had not expected to find such a house on these rough Yorkshire moors, but not unaware of the standing and importance of the Fairley family, and their great wealth, he had anticipated a structure that had more taste and refinement than this.*

The four-hundred-acre deer park and garden were another matter. In 1726, one hundred men were at work making canals and waterworks at Studley Royal, and it is worth noting that while the formal geometric design and extraordinary vistas were the brainchild of Aislabie, the works were carried out by local labour under the direction of a man called John Simpson, almost certainly a member of a Ripon family that would one day play a significant role in Edith's story.

In 1768, William Aislabie took over the estate and purchased the ruined Fountains Abbey and adjacent Fountains Hall, unifying them with Studley Hall by landscaping the valley that stands between them. The terraced landscaping of the gardens, sweeping vistas and incorporation of the abbey ruins, make Studley Royal today one of the most romantic places in all England.

Barbara denies the original Studley Hall as model for Fairley Hall, but, as already mentioned, she did use the front façade of Fountains Hall as that of Penni-stone Royal in the six-novel Emma Harte series which leaves no doubt as to the call the Estate's very English-ness makes on her.

By 1901 Edith Walker was living and working a few miles away from the Hall as a domestic servant at No. 10 Skell Bank, which leads off the west end of Water Skellgate. Her father, John, had moved from 8 Water Skellgate to 9 Bedern Bank, a short walk to the east in the shadow of the minster, and a property owned by the Studley Royal Estate. He would live there until 1910, but the house would be leased to the family for years afterwards.

Here, with John and wife Elizabeth in 1901, are son Joseph (who has not yet set up on his own), grandson Gabriel Barker (aged ten) and various lodgers, includ-ing a builder called Leo Walker, a boy of nine called Chris (surname illegible) and a girl, Rebecca, who is thirteen. Next door at No. 8, John's eldest son

Thomas has reappeared and has followed in his father's footsteps as a slater. Thomas's wife, whose name is difficult to read but could be Frances, is with him, along with their son, Jamie, who is fifteen, and three daughters, Lillie, Elizabeth and Minnie, who are five, four and two respectively. Lillie – Freda's cousin – is the future wife of Joe Wray, with whom Barbara and Freda would later lodge at Thorpe Prebend House.

This ancient street of Bedern Bank, once called Betherom Bank, runs down the west side of the minster precinct, by the old cathedral graveyard, leading to the minster's south boundary at High St Agnesgate. The street was part of a localised area for census in Freda's time, which included thirty-two houses employing fifty-one servants – high density relative to the city as a whole, where only twenty-three per cent employed any servants at all. Nevertheless, Bedern Bank appears from a map of 1909 to have been made up of quite tiny cottages, except for an early Georgian brick house known as The Hall at the top of the hill by the minster. Very likely, Bedern Bank was where some of the servants of the area lived.

At the top of the Bank were '2 *cottages with yards and outbuildings behind*', described as such in a leasehold sale by the Studley Royal Estate held at the Unicorn Hotel on 29th November 1887. At that time these cottages – actually 8 and 9 Bedern Bank – were 'in the occupation of William Gott Senior and William Gott Junior', none other than grandfatherly relations (great-great and great respectively) of our witness of these times, Jim Gott. Thanks to him we have the following description of two dwellings inhabited by members of Barbara's family from the start of the twentieth century until (with one short gap) 1935, cottages that Edith and Freda knew particularly well:

> *On top of Bedern Bank, two low, yellow-washed cottages used to stand. One in particular was of great significant [sic] to me, being the residence of a great, great grandfather of mine – William Gott – who was a jeweller, clock and watchmaker ... The style of the establishment was unique itself, especially the front with its low window. The pathway continued the sill, and the gradient of the hill made it seem lower still. In fact, one had to bend down to see into the window. Steep steps led down to the inner doorway. From inside, one got a grand view through the window of feet and legs.*

So, in 1901, for the first time in her life, Edith was living independently of her father. Her employer, thirty-seven-year-old Richard Guy, hailed from Waterford in Ireland and lived in Skell Bank with his wife Annie and their four children. Richard Guy was a tailor; he had his own business and shop. His younger brother George also lived in the house and worked in the business with him.

You did not have to be rich to afford a servant in those days – they cost little to hire – but as early as 1897 Richard Guy was prosperous enough to pay for an advertisement in the West Riding edition of *Kelly's Trade Directory*, and by 1908 he had moved from Skell Bank to No. 6 North Street, to the north of the Market Place, a better address though nothing special. Jim Gott recalled Richard Guy's shop in North Street, and offers a rather unsettling glimpse of it, its contents seeming to carry the dust of ages: 'Day after day, year after year, I have gazed into the window of the clothier's shop [Mr Guy's] where time virtually stands still,' he wrote. 'The same old wax models in the same old place with their sweaty, sickly complexions tanned by the grime and dust of age, fixedly staring with death-like ghostly impressions. There they stand bedecked in the very latest – a la Fauntleroy; or the choicest design – the Norfolk pattern; or the *pièce de résistance* – the ever popular children's sailor outfit complete with wooden whistle. Surrounding these . . . are the well-known chicken chokers, dicky fronts, straw boaters and Beau Brummel bows.' Richard Guy was still at 6 North Street in 1936. By 1923 he carried the letter 'J' beside his name, indicating that he was respected enough to serve as a juror.

When I discovered the Guy family it occurred to me what a coincidence it was that servant-girl Edith will have been surrounded by the same kind of Irish cheer that servant-girl Emma Harte experiences in the close company of Blackie O'Neill at precisely the same period of her life, when she is kitchen maid at Fairley Hall. The Guys' home county even supplies the origins of Blackie's 'spectacular Waterford crystal chandelier', which hangs from the 'soaring ceiling' of his Harrogate mansion after he and Emma become rich. The Irish influence in the novels, particularly in *A Woman of Substance*, is completely in tune with the Irish influence in Ripon at this time. Nearly a third of the unskilled workforce (which, you will recall, represented nineteen per cent of all workers in the city) were born in Ireland. So, there were a lot of Irish about.

In the novel, Blackie is Emma's succour. His liveliness and gaiety, his distinctive character, an 'unquenchable spirit and a soul that was joyous and without rancour', transform her. From the start he calls her 'mavourneen', later telling her that it's the Irish equivalent of 'luv' in Yorkshire, an Irish term of endearment, which turns up time and again in the novels.

> *Blackie O'Neill was, in fact, an exceptionally handsome young man. But it was his manner and his attitude that were most intriguing and which, in many ways, set Blackie apart from other men. He exuded liveliness and gaiety. His face was full of vivacity, and it had great mobility and not a little wit. An easy, careless charm was second nature to him, and he was buoyant of spirit, as if he accepted life for what it was, and was constantly entertained by it. There was a lighthearted self-confidence inherent in him, and to Emma, observing him, he seemed untouched by the weariness and the fear and the hopelessness that haunted the men of the village, bowing them down and ageing them prematurely.*

Blackie and his Irishness are central to Emma's ambition, for it is of course he who opens Emma's eyes to the very idea that she can make a fortune. 'It was the magical word "fortune" that had made the most profound impact on her . . . Emma's heart was pounding so hard she thought her chest would burst . . . "Can a girl like me make a fortune in Leeds?" she asked, breathless in her anticipation of his answer.' It's the word 'fortune' that holds Emma spellbound. When she savours it, Blackie sees in her face 'ambition, raw and inexorable'.

It is not wholly fanciful to suppose that Richard Guy was similarly encouraging of Edith, that she, too, first considered she might make herself a fortune and lift herself out of the poverty into which she was born, buoyed up by an Irishman's blarney. Certainly Richard was on the 'up' and would have been full of his own ambitions, and for a girl like Edith (as for Emma Harte), dreams of success would have been measured in material terms, in terms of *making a fortune*.

In 1902, when Jack London came to England from America to conduct an investigation into the living conditions of the poor, he commented that they were as materialistic, indeed perhaps more so than the rich, and this is so important in charting the lives of Edith, Freda and, later, Barbara – the one life, the seed in the garden of Barbara's fiction, where success means money. In *A Woman of Substance* Emma Harte's purpose is money, 'Vast amounts of it. For money was power. She would become so rich and powerful she would be invulnerable to the world.'

Given the conditions of life for Emma, as for Edith and Freda in the real world, and other of Barbara's fictional heroines whose money 'arms them against the world', one can see why.

Emma knew that without money you were nothing, just a powerless and oppressed victim of the ruling class, a yoked and shackled beast of burden destined to a life of mindless drudgery, and an existence so wretched and so without hope, so filled with terror and despair that it was hardly worth the contemplation let alone the living. Without money you were susceptible to all the capricious whims and moods and fancies of the careless, thoughtless rich, to all the vicissitudes of life. Without money you were vulnerable to the world.

Barbara never knew the want and vulnerability she described, but, like Emma Harte, her grandmother Edith did. In the novel, as Emma becomes richer her hatred of the Fairley family, who have exploited and brought her down, diminishes, so that by the end of the book she can forgive and forget, and allow Jim Fairley, the last of the Fairley line, to become engaged to her favourite granddaughter, Paula. At that point, money no longer has the same status: 'Money is only important when you're truly poor, when you need it for a roof over your head, for food and clothes,' writes Barbara. 'Once you have these essentials taken care of and go beyond them, money is simply a unit, a tool

106

to work with.' But at the start, it is making a fortune that motivates her.

Barbara gave me a picture of Edith in her mid to late twenties wearing her hair in the Edwardian style and a lace-trimmed dress. It is impossible to date the photograph accurately, but it was almost certainly taken after she had ceased working for Richard Guy and was enjoying a period of uncharacteristic prosperity, to which we will come. It is, however, quite possible that a perk of working for the Guys was that Edith had access to far better clothes than she would otherwise have been able to afford. Mistresses often gave their maids cast-offs, so how much better to work in a tailor's. There are references to this practice in *A Woman of Substance*, where Emma discovers from Adele Fairley, 'the smell of expensive perfumes, the touch of good linens and supple silks, and the sparkle of brilliant jewels . . .' Such things fan the flickering flames of ambition in Emma to become 'a grand lady . . .' Having access to decent hand-made clothes would have made Edith feel better about herself too, showing her that there was more to life than the hopelessness she saw all around her, and perhaps also giving her confidence to dream of making something of her life.

For maidservants the dream was usually as far as it went, their only realistic hope being to find a man from a higher class, a prospect fraught with the risk of exploitation and one that invariably led to complete disaster. Not so for Emma Harte of course, whose exploitation by Edwin Fairley ironically gives her the guts, the fury, to claw herself up by her own efforts. The picture of Edith Walker in her mid to late twenties (see second photo section), with her hand set purposefully on hip, suggests that she might have had a similarly forceful character. She would soon have occasion to put it to the test, for towards the end of 1903 Edith became pregnant, and on 3rd June 1904 she gave birth out of wedlock to a baby girl called Freda.

Being an unmarried domestic servant, the birth could not take place at the Guys' house, and for some reason it did not take place at the house that Edith's father was occupying at 9 Bedern Bank. Freda was born at 9A Water Skellgate in that yard of dwellings between Nos. 8 and 16 already described.

In the 1901 census, the one most recently available to public scrutiny, there is a note that 9A Water Skellgate was leased to the Irish League. Perhaps the Guys had co-opted it for Edith out of kindness, though the census return suggests that the address was something of a secret hideaway. Normally an occupier's name is given for each address, but in the case of 9A Water Skellgate there is no name. Instead the words 'in occupation' are appended. This is unusual even for somewhere leased by an organisation, where occupancy might change frequently. There was frequent occupancy drift elsewhere in Ripon's yards and the census records names in those cases. It is not the purpose of census to establish permanent occupancy. Again, if the house was known to be occupied, an occupant's name would be available. Nevertheless, the name of the occupant has been withheld. It is an interesting anomaly or fudge, which would have needed explanation, or sanctioning by someone high up.

There are so many unanswered questions attending Freda's birth. Why did Edith not have the child at the family home in Bedern Bank? Was there simply no room? Or had Edith fallen out with her father, John Walker, over the fact of this illegitimate birth? Perhaps having it elsewhere was a mark of her independent will. Or was it at the insistence of Freda's father that Edith took up occupancy of 9A Water Skellgate, because it was in his gift?

Then there are the more interesting questions posed by Freda's birth certificate. The name of the father has been withheld. Edith retains her maiden name, Walker, and lines are drawn through the boxes headed 'Name and Surname of Father' and 'Occupation of Father'. Again, this is most unusual, and indicates a definite decision by Edith or the father or both to keep paternity a secret. In an official Ripon illegitimacy return dated 1857, where eight out of nine single mothers are granted five shillings per week for the first six weeks and one shilling and sixpence until the child is thirteen, there is *in every case* appended the name of a father, whether or not authentic. It was done even if the mother wasn't sure who the father was, because in those days illegitimacy was regarded as a terrible stigma, and a mother would do all in her power to alleviate the burden on the illegitimate child, inventing a name if necessary. In the case of the Tyneside novelist Catherine Cookson (born illegitimately only two years after Freda), the name of a man – Alexander

Davies – appeared on her birth certificate as father even though he (if indeed the name is genuinely that of her father) had known her mother for a very short time and had long left her in the lurch by the time Catherine was born. My contact at the Harrogate area registry confirmed that it is unusual for a name not to have been conjured up from somewhere, especially on three consecutive birth certificates, as was the case for Freda. For, as we shall see, Edith gave birth to three illegitimate children between 1904 and 1910, and in each case no father was named on the certificate.

We may safely conclude that a definite decision was taken not to name the father and that there was good reason not to name him. Very likely he was a married man with a position to uphold, a man whose reputation would suffer were his 'indiscretions' made known. Either the father insisted on it or Edith wanted to maximise her chances of keeping him by making paternity a secret.

Either way, not naming the father on three certificates in 1904, 1907 and 1910 suggests continuity, that the father was the same man in each case, that each birth was not a one-time fling. If Edith had been leading a profligate life with different men, there would be no reason not to name the children's fathers, or to invent names, as was the way in such cases. The three children are bound to one father by the very fact of his not being named on all three certificates, and most convincingly, as we shall see, by the choice of their Christian names.

Moreover, if one man fathers three children by the

same woman out of wedlock over a period of seven years it seems likely that love was involved in the relationship. Perforce money will also have been involved. Being pregnant so often would have made it impossible for Edith to hold down a job as a maid. No one would have hired her. And I have it from Barbara that Edith didn't work because – so Freda told her – she didn't need to. Edith's support would appear to have been bound up in the deal.

It is of course logically possible that the father was a working man who had Edith in thrall, a tradesman perhaps, like Richard Guy, her erstwhile employer. But this is, I think, unlikely. In the case of Guy, was he not busy enough building his own family, with four children under ten? Would he undertake a parallel family of three with a former maid? Would such a man – respectable but hardly wealthy – have been able to persuade Edith he was worth waiting for through three births and the passage of seven years or more, from at least 1903 to 1910? And would he have been able to afford to keep her during this time out of that dusty shop in North Street? How would any ordinary, working, married man have kept two families in this way?

If support was part of the arrangement, there would indeed have been a reputation to protect, and the very fact that Edith chose not to register a false name may even suggest a certain pride in who the father was, that *at all costs* the name had to be withheld from the record but that that also made it vital, on another less expedient plane, not to compromise the truth with a false name. Perhaps subconsciously this was her way of drawing attention to the secret, to what it was she was hiding. Perhaps, after all, Edith saw Freda's birth as anything but a calamity, rather as the first step to realising a dream of great fortune . . . If she could persuade the fellow to marry her.

All this takes us into the emotional epicentre of *A Woman of Substance* and *Act of Will*, where problems attached to illegitimacy figure strongly, and as we pursue the shadows of the past it is increasingly difficult to be sure where fact ends and fiction begins.

Barbara would register deep shock when she learned from my researches that her mother Freda was illegitimate, yet Audra Kenton in *Act of Will*, who Barbara admits is the fictional equivalent of Freda and has a mother called Edith, is herself born illegitimately. And when we look for who Audra's father was, he turns out to have been the fictional Edith's 'benefactor and protector'. Again, Audra is set apart from her working-class husband, Vincent, by her better birth. Writes Barbara in the novel (her italics): '*If the circumstances of her life had been different she would never have been permitted to marry him* [viz working-class Vincent].' The point, and it is a crucial one, is that what makes Audra different is her high birth of which she has been dispossessed. Is that what Freda believed made her different? Did she believe that her father had been a member of the nobility? If so, it would likely have infuriated Winston's mother, just as it did Vincent's mother in the novel.

So, was Freda, like Audra, dispossessed of some

great inheritance by the illegitimacy of her birth? 'Who leaves what to whom' is an enduring preoccupation of the Emma Harte novels. They are bound up with what is lost when a character is dispossessed, cheated out of the rights attached to their birth. In *Act of Will*, Audra has to remind herself who she really is and where she really comes from by going to her 'memory place', from which she can look out at the long, low, eighteenth-century manor house called High Cleugh, where she was born and brought up, and mourn what might have been.

High Cleugh attracts Audra 'like a magnet'. Barbara, for some reason unexplained, positions High Cleugh northwest of Ripon, instead of southwest, where in fact it lies. For High Cleugh, I discovered, is a real place. In reality, it is not a house at all, but a delightful, tree-lined green space on the bank of the River Laver, just before it melds with the Skell, as you exit the city by means of Mallorie Park Drive and Studley Road.

High Cleugh is so close to the Studley Royal Estate that when Lord Wemyss set fire to a butt on the Estate one hundred years ago during a shoot, and the flames took hold of the dry turf and spread out of control, a workforce was raised in Ripon and the flames were extinguished by means of buckets passed hand-to-hand from the river there. High Cleugh is, in effect, the *perfect* 'memory place' for Freda to sit and consider what might have been hers if she, like Audra, had been connected to someone there.

But Barbara doesn't know why she used High

Cleugh as a memory place. She was not trying to suggest that Audra/Freda was linked to Studley Royal by birth. She had no reason to do so. So, on the face of it, there can be no significance in High Cleugh ... except that there is.

Three years after Freda was born, on 21st July 1907, Edith had a second illegitimate child, whom she named Fred. Again, the father is unnamed on the official certificate. Transparently, the names of Edith's first two illegitimate children are diminutives of 'Frederick'. I am told by the Registrar of Births that it was common practice for a single mother to include the father's name as a Christian name of the illegitimate child. There is a desire to acknowledge the father's identity which the circumstances of the birth must keep hidden, and, perhaps for the child's sake, to establish its identity however clandestinely. In Edith's case it may even have been the compromise to which she had the unnamed father agree.

In *A Woman of Substance* there is a similar desire for secrecy over the identity of the father of Emma Harte's illegitimate daughter Edwina, the son of the lord of the manor, Edwin Fairley. Yet the girl is named after him in that case too. Emma wants no one to know who Edwina's father is. She imparts only half-truths about him to the man she later marries, Joe Lowther, and for brothers Winston and Frank she invents 'a nebulous gentleman of doubtful background ... whom she had met in Leeds'. Yet, as was often done, she uses the derivative of 'Edwin' to seal Edwina's identity, leaving the key to the secret for posterity as it were, or perhaps for her daughter to find when she is older.

In the context of common practice the names of Edith's first two illegitimate children being diminutives of 'Frederick' cannot be regarded as chance. In our search for Freda's father we are surely looking for a man in a prominent, wealthy, local family whose name is Frederick and with whom Edith could conceivably have come into contact.

Asking a local studies archivist, steeped in Ripon's history, whether she could nominate a prominent Ripon citizen called Frederick in Edwardian times turned out not to be too searching a request. Given the tidy nature of the city (no more heavily populated than some so-called villages), the fantastic amount of research available, the archivist's own knowledge and the fact that one prominent family is well-known even today for the sheer number of Fredericks in it meant that she did not pause for one moment before replying.

Frederick has been the family name of the Robinsons of Ripon since at least 1746, when one Frederick Robinson first drew breath. In 1782 a Frederick John was added to the family, in 1816 a Hobart Frederick and in 1830 a Frederick William. In 1832, Lady Mary Gertrude Robinson married into the Vyners of Gautby, Lincolnshire, and soon Fredericks began to litter their family records too – in 1836 Henry Frederick Clare Vyner was born and Frederick Grantham Vyner in 1847. Meanwhile, in 1827, Frederick John Robinson had a son named George

Frederick Samuel. And in 1852 George Frederick's son by (his cousin) Henrietta Ann Theodosia Vyner, was named Frederick Oliver Robinson. Both George Frederick Samuel and his son Frederick Oliver were contemporaries of Edith in Ripon. There couldn't have been a more visible or, as it turns out, more accessible family of Fredericks available to her.

The Robinsons' history takes us back to 1522, the year in which one William Robinson was born in the city of York. William went on to make a fortune in trade with Germany, became Lord Mayor of the city in 1581 and was subsequently its Member of Parliament. Like many a successful Tudor merchant, he invested in land, leaving estates both in Yorkshire and Lincolnshire, an inheritance which caught its first whiff of noblesse in 1660 when William's Royalist grandson picked up a baronetcy at the Restoration.

It was not, however, until 1761 that the transformation of the Robinsons from trade to aristocracy was made official, when a Thomas Robinson was rewarded for diplomatic services to the Crown with the Barony of Grantham. Subsequent Robinsons added to the family coffers, but now found themselves with a new opportunity to enhance the value of Robinson bloodstock by means of marriage into truer, blue-blooded veins of nobility, and it was on account of this that the family eventually came to Ripon.

In 1780, the second Baron Grantham took as his spouse one Mary Gemima Grey Yorke, daughter of the second Earl of Hardwicke, which brought within the Robinson orbit the de Grey earldom and, through a connection in Mary's line with one George Aislabie, a royal estate. In 1845, Miss Elizabeth Lawrence, the last of the Aislabies, died, and Studley Royal passed into the hands of Thomas Philip Robinson, elder brother of Frederick John Robinson, by virtue of his descent from a daughter of George Aislabie. By 1859, the way lay clear for George Frederick Samuel Robinson (nephew of Thomas Philip, son of Frederick John, who died that year) to inherit Studley Royal. George Frederick was a highly successful politician and would be rewarded with the title Marquess of Ripon by Gladstone for drawing up the Treaty of Washington. With his death in 1909, George Frederick's son, Frederick Oliver Robinson, inherited the title of Marquess and took up the reins at the estate to which Freda remembered Edith dragging her constantly when she was a child and on which Freda would have gazed, mournful of what might have been, if High Cleugh had been her memory place, as indeed it was in the fiction.

I have kept until now the name of Edith's third illegitimate child, a girl born on 18th February 1910. Again, no father is named. Edith called the child Mary. Frederick Oliver Robinson, Second Marquess of Ripon, had only one sibling, a dear sister who died in infancy. Her name was Mary.

Frederick Oliver was born on 29th January 1852, and when he fell dead in 1923 while out grouse shooting, he was, like Jim Fairley of Fairley Hall in *A Woman of Substance*, the last of the family line, the last legitimate

Robinson who could lay claim to Studley Royal.

Like his father he stood for Parliament. The Robinsons had quite a track record in Westminster. Frederick John, Frederick Oliver's grandfather, had even made it to 10 Downing Street as Prime Minister, succeeding George Canning in the summer of 1827, but earning the distinction of holding office for so short a time – the autumn and winter of 1827–8 – that he never once addressed the House as PM. His son, George Frederick Samuel, was a good deal more successful, entering the House of Commons as member for Hull in 1852, the House of Lords seven years later, and serving in every Liberal government for the next half-century, rising to Lord Privy Seal.

Frederick Oliver was a rather different kettle of fish. He took little interest in the affairs of the House of Commons and spent most of his time shooting on the Studley Royal Estate. A fantastic shot he made shooting his career; indeed, he had a reputation as one of the two best shots in Britain (the other was his friend Lord Walsingham). There are countless legendary stories of his skills, for example the speed with which he could change guns is supposed to have led to his accounting for seven birds dead in the air before any hit the ground. In 1905 he took 306 at Studley Royal, and that was small compared to the 576 out of 2745 partridges at a shoot in Austria. On Dallowgill Moor the best score ever made was 1216 grouse to four guns in 1915. Frederick Oliver personally took 588 of them. He expired while picking up his grouse after a drive on Dallowgill Moor, on 22nd September

1923. A month earlier he had killed 249 birds in one day. He was seventy-three.

Frederick Oliver will have called frequently at Water Skellgate, which at one time or another he or his father largely owned, and not only at the places of entertainment which were points of contact between rich and poor in the Ripon community, but to attend the Masonic Lodge there that bore his titles and to pursue his particular social concerns as patron of the Ripon Home For Girls close by. His father and mother had done a huge amount of social and philanthropic work in Ripon and were held in esteem by its inhabitants – Frederick Oliver was again very much in the shadow of his father in this, but he made the Ripon Home For Girls his special thing.

The de Grey & Ripon Lodge (No. 837) met first of all in the Town Hall on the city's Market Place. But in 1902, a Masonic Temple, a Studley Estate property built on the site of a stables they had also owned, opened on the corner of High Skellgate and Water Skellgate, opposite the Victoria Hall, the subsequent festive board being held in the nearby Unicorn Hotel, another property of Studley Royal, on the southeast side of the Market Place. The lodge still meets there today, in every month of the year except August.

The First Marquess had been a leading light in the Masonic Craft, holding the position of Provincial Grand Master for thirteen years, and then Grand Master for four years (that's top dog nationally, a most unusual appointment outside London), before resigning in 1874 after a sudden conversion to the

Roman Catholic Church, which he believed mistakenly to be incompatible due to some outstanding Papal Bulls against the Craft. He was received into the Church at the London Oratory on 4 September 1874. I have it from the secretary of the de Grey & Ripon Masonic Lodge that he did so 'after marrying a Catholic', in other words at Henrietta Ann Theodosia Vyner's behest. News of his conversion was received with astonishment. *The Times* launched a vicious attack, accusing Ripon of renouncing 'his mental and moral freedom. A statesman who becomes a convert to Roman Catholicism forfeits at once the confidence of the English people.' Such was the anti-Catholic feeling of the time, following the assertion of the Vatican Council of 1870 of papal infallibility.

The Masonic Hall on Water Skellgate still has the Marquess's Provincial Grand Master regalia on display. Ripon gave it to his gardener to burn, but the gardener, considering it was of value, disobeyed his instructions and the costume found its way to the local lodge.

Frederick Oliver would not himself have been deterred by his father's resignation, and there even seems to have been second thoughts on the First Marquess's part about quitting Freemasonry after he discovered that the Pope's position was not as intractable as he had thought. He helped bring the Prince of Wales (afterwards King Edward VII) to the Craft in 1870, and subsequently the other Royal Princes, the Duke of Connaught and his younger brother, the Duke of Albany. It was a period of unprecedented support for Freemasonry by the Royal Family. In the Marquess of Ripon's circle, 'to be a Freemason was to be the quintessential Englishman, a part of the establishment at the height of the British Empire.'

One crisp winter afternoon I walked in the freezing sunlight from Skellgarths through Water Skellgate, via High Cleugh, across the fields through Studley Roger onto the Marquess's estate. It was as crystal clear to me as the air I breathed that High Cleugh really is a window onto the past, a past that was, for Barbara's mother, the reality in which she truly dwelt. There are other points of circumstance, to which we will come, that recommend a liaison between Edith and Frederick, and in the final chapter I bring all of them together for the reader to judge. But even if one prefers to agree with Vincent in *Act of Will*, who says, 'Only Edith knows the truth,' in a sense it doesn't matter. For, if Freda mistakenly thought of herself as high-born – if she was given that impression deceitfully by Edith – her fantasy turned out to be just as significant as if it had been true. For the belief empowered Freda, as it did Audra in her relationship with her daughter in *Act of Will*, to lift Barbara out of her situation and enable her to succeed far beyond Edith's wildest dreams.

As biographer of the late Catherine Cookson, I am aware how important a belief in a genetic connection with the aristocracy could be in this business of rising in the world from humble origins in the first decade of the twentieth century. Catherine's conviction that she was the illegitimate daughter of a gentleman saw her through the entire process of her rise. Enormous self-belief was born of it, and even after she came to doubt the truth of it, the comfort the fantasy had provided stayed with her, because it shored up her sense of identity. Perhaps Studley Royal gave Freda an identity, just as the house, High Cleugh, gave Audra hers in *Act of Will*.

My walk there, which retraces one in *Her Own Rules* from the fictional Skell Garth Hotel to Fountains Abbey on the Estate, took me less than an hour, no distance at all in the days when a pair of legs was the most likely mode of transport. There is a public footpath between High Cleugh and Studley Royal to ease one's passage. Before you know it, you are walking through the gates of the Estate and passing along the '*stately avenue of lime trees*', the vista which leads up to 'Studley church', as Barbara writes in the novel. It is in fact the church of St Mary the Virgin, where all the Robinsons I have described lie buried, and which was built by Frederick Oliver's mother, Henrietta, from 1871–8, at a cost of £15,000. There is a monument to the Marchioness, a big white marble effigy on a tomb chest dated 1908.

It was she, according to my informant within Frederick's Water Skellgate Masonic Lodge, who persuaded Frederick Oliver's father to convert to Catholicism. In *A Woman of Substance* and elsewhere (for example in *Everything to Gain*) the Catholic attitude to divorce has a crucial bearing on Barbara's plot. In the first novel, wealthy, dashing Australian Paul McGill, with whom Emma falls deeply in love after Joe Lowther dies in France, cannot break free of his Catholic wife, Constance. It is as a direct result of this that Paul sires Daisy, Emma's second illegitimate child. A Catholic woman as strong as Henrietta clearly was, strong enough to have her husband George Frederick become a Catholic when it was politically a very unwise thing to do, would have been the best excuse a son of hers could find for not divorcing his own wife and marrying Edith Walker, or at least the kindest way of disabusing Edith of the notion that he did not love her enough to marry her.

A hundred head of deer crossed my path as I walked the route Edith, Freda and Barbara trod so many times. They came thundering past me in the crisp light as I gazed in awe at the sublime marriage of picturesque landscape art and wild nature that is Studley Royal. There are ancient, broken-down trees on which Edith's eyes would have rested when they were saplings. At the top of the rise, like Meri in *Her Own Rules*, I 'glanced over at Studley Church, so picturesque in the snow, and at the obelisk nearby, and then directed my gaze to the lake below, glittering in the sunlight. The River Skell flowed beyond it, and there, just a short distance upstream, was the abbey . . .'

Could this indeed have been the trip made so often by Edith to see the man she believed might one day leave his wife and marry her? Time and again the *grit* of the novels comes out of the speculative possibilities that will have haunted Freda as Edith's real-life illegitimate daughter, and which might solve the problem of her identity – possibilities which perhaps Barbara blanked out as a child, sensing that they were already a source of disquiet in the tight little unit in Tower Lane, Armley, and which were only to emerge years later when she was writing her novels.

The coincidence of fictional plot and real-life fact is too great to allow any other conclusion. Here was I caught up in a web of imaginative truth spun by three women at the centre of which was an incomplete birth-certificate dated 3 June 1904, exactly a century before I was writing.

One is bound to look for similarities between Freda and Barbara and the two Fredericks, father and son. George Frederick was described by M. Bence-Jones in his book *Viceroys of India* (1982) as 'a rather timid' fellow, 'serious-minded, a voracious reader of books . . . noted for his sincerity and moral earnestness . . . prosaic, endowed with neither grace nor sparkle . . . *Persistence* was Ripon's outstanding quality.' The character fits Freda to a T and introduces the key element of the woman of substance, of which Freda's 'iron will' was not short – *persistence*.

In photographs, his son, the Second Marquess – Frederick Oliver – looks a dapper fellow, fine looking and very well groomed. He is supposed to have inherited his father's serious, 'prosaic' qualities. In *The Big Shots* Jonathan Garnier Riffler writes that 'he could never have been described as good company.' But this needs deeper consideration, for clearly he was a man who, unlike his father, pursued his pleasures rather than his duties.

Studley Royal was the principal shoot in England at this time and in the Prince of Wales's Marlborough House set, Frederick Oliver was a popular figure. He may not have been much of a party animal, but that is not to say that he was dull. There was, for example, something of the poet in him. He had a real sense of the spirit of the Yorkshire moors, and loved to talk about the beauty of the birds of the moors in flight (albeit oblivious to the fact that he killed more of them than anybody else), once writing: 'Maybe a generation will spring up to whom all these things [the beauty of the moors, the colour and characteristic sounds of the birds of the shoot he knew so well] will be a closed book; but when that day comes England will lose her most attractive and distinctive feature, and one of her most cherished traditions. For the England of whom the poets have sung will have ceased to exist.'

Also, there was something in Frederick Oliver that attracted, and was attracted by, women of great vitality and vigour – in that sense women that were the opposite of him. On 7 May 1885 he married Constance Gladys Lonsdale, widow of the Fourth Earl of Lonsdale. In hindsight, commentators have wondered how this prosaic character had attracted her, and concluded that she must have grabbed him for the promise of a marquessate and 24,000 acres, to which, at that time, he was heir.

This may well have been the case, but it is unlikely to have been the whole story, for Frederick Oliver will have been in no doubt when he married Gladys, as she was known, as to what she promised him, and very often opposite poles attract.

Gladys Ripon was a bit of a Lillie Langtry figure. She knew how to have a good time, and had a reputation for living in the fast lane. Edward VII once referred to her as 'a professional beauty'. Her first husband, Lonsdale, himself once an ardent admirer of Lillie Langtry, the actress mistress of Edward VII, died in a brothel in 1882.

Gladys was away from the Ripon estate a lot, leaving Frederick to his own devices. She owned the lease of a house – Coombe Court, Kingston Hill in Surrey, on the edge of London, and when she died she breathed her last not at Studley Royal but at 13 Bryanston Square in London.

'Lady Ripon was the uncrowned queen of a smart, artistic, bohemian, and frivolous social set,' Donald Taylor reports in an article entitled, 'The Bohemian Mistress of Studley Royal'. The bohemian and artistic elements of her reputation were deserved. Oscar Wilde dedicated the printed edition of his play *A Woman of No Importance* (1893) to her (whether this was a wry comment on Gladys or a genuine compliment goes unrecorded). She became a close friend of the Russian dancer Nijinsky, attracted to him because of his poverty-stricken childhood, and managed him socially during the Russian ballet's first season in Covent Garden in 1911 – booking him into the Savoy and advising him on where to go and which invitations to accept. Later she would galvanise support for him when he was detained as a prisoner of war in Hungary.

The party atmosphere Gladys engendered was inspired by a reverence for art, which was spirited, idealistic and yet racy: 'When one begins to sacrifice Art to personal matters,' she once said, 'it takes away every wish to have anything to do with it.'

Art apparently justified anything, and as tireless fundraising patron of the arts she once had the puritanical Raymond Asquith, son of the Prime Minister, view 'with a jaundiced eye' her seduction of a millionaire neighbour of his at dinner: 'By the end of dinner she had got £35,000 out of him, and probably had more before she went to bed – or after,' Asquith was reported to have said.

When Gladys was around, you could expect a party, and often a noisy one. Her party-piece was to arrange a surprise smashing of quantities of crockery at dinner, an event which in fact guests looked forward to, and which was, according to the Duchess of Marlborough, originally precipitated by a real incident: 'Once a footman had dropped a tray,' she recounted, 'producing the amusement that the misfortune of others usually creates; since then the incident was repeated, with the china specially bought for making a noise.'

Gladys was as much at home in the company of royals as that of artists. Queen Alexandra, Edward VII's wife, became a close friend, and arranged for her to be on the house-party guest list of all the royal estates, another reason why she was frequently absent from Studley Royal. There was, however, no danger of Gladys sidelining her husband. As a result of her contacts, Edward VII became a shooting companion of Frederick Oliver's, and she brought her party-set lifestyle often enough to the estate for the gardeners to know never to mow the lawns until late in the day when she was in residence, owing to her 'delicate nature'. (Delicate she may have been the morning after, but not so by nature.)

It is, therefore, to Gladys Ripon that we can ascribe an exciting, *laissez faire* attitude within Studley Royal, which servants and employees clearly enjoyed and which was in line with her dropping of her first name, which spelled steadfast qualities she abhorred. She and Frederick were a childless couple and one cannot help but wonder whether during her many absences from the Estate, the sudden removal of her vivacity left her husband with expectations which he then pursued on his own account. Did Gladys create in Frederick Oliver a thirst for a good time that did not disappear when she withdrew? Or did she perhaps make him feel rather inadequate in company and in need of relationships in which he could exercise control? If he did, and Gladys knew about them, she was sufficiently a woman of the world not to object, having earlier come to terms with her first husband meeting his maker in a brothel possibly for similar reasons.

It is likely, as I have suggested, that a love of glamour and a natural vitality were defining elements in Edith's character, too, until the world finally buried her. In *Act of Will* Audra's mother is 'the beautiful Edith Kenton. That was how they always spoke about her hereabouts.' It was also how people spoke of Edith Walker. 'She was called "the beautiful Edith" by

128

members of the family,' Barbara said to Billie Figg in the mid-1980s. It is possible that this glittering something, which Edith had (and which Barbara probably inherited from her), and which Gladys Ripon clearly had in spades (and which attracted Frederick Oliver to her), was also what attracted the otherwise prosaic Frederick Oliver to Edith.

We have a possible match, access, and on both sides a need. It is of course possible that Edith came at length to be in the Studley Royal employ. Many from Ripon were. Sadly there are no records either to substantiate this or to rule it out.

What we do know is that the Estate had a special allure for her, which she passed on to her daughter Freda, and which Freda impressed upon Barbara in her childhood sufficiently for Studley Royal to play a central role in the novels, as in *Her Own Rules* when Meredith, who has come halfway across the world to discover her true identity, experiences the sense Barbara had there of déjà vu:

> *It was just turning nine o'clock on Tuesday morning. Meredith was bundled up in boots and a sheepskin coat, walking through Studley Park. The stately avenue of lime trees down which she hurried led to Studley Church, just visible on top of the hill at the end of the avenue . . .*
>
> *I'm almost there, Meredith told herself, as she finally reached the top of the hill at the end of the avenue of limes. She glanced over at Studley Church, so picturesque in the snow, and at the*

obelisk nearby. She then directed her gaze to the lake below, glittering in the sunlight. The River Skell flowed beyond it, and there, just a short distance upstream, was the abbey . . .

A strange sensation came over her. She stood very still, all of her senses alert. Instantly, she knew what it was . . . a curious feeling that she had been here before, that she had stood on this very spot, on this very hill, gazing down at those mediaeval ruins . . . She shivered again. Déjà vu, the French call it, already seen, she reminded herself. But she had not been here before; she had never even been to Yorkshire . . .

As she looked around, absorbing everything, her heart clenched, and she felt a strange sense of loss. So acute, so strong, so overwhelming was this feeling, that tears came into her eyes. Her throat closed with such a rush of emotion she was further startled at herself.

Something was taken from me here . . . something of immense value to me. I have been here before. I know this ancient place . . . somehow it is a part of me. What was it I lost here? . . . She closed her eyes, not understanding what was happening to her; it was as though her heart was breaking. Something had been taken from her . . . The only thing she really knew at this moment was that she was experiencing an immense sense of deprivation . . .

Pain, she thought. Why do I feel pain and hurt and despair?

CHAPTER FOUR

The Abyss

'Who are you, Meredith Stratton. And why are
you so troubled? Where does that deep well of
sadness spring from? Who was it that hurt you
so badly they've scarred your soul?'

Her Own Rules

If Edith meant to protect the father of her children by
withholding his name from the authorities, it was a
favour which, for one reason or another, was not – in
the last resort – returned by the man in question, who,
after an affair of around eight or nine years, appears
to have deserted Edith and consigned her to a fate
that was bound to scar their children for life.

Having an illegitimate child, with no partner to
bring in the money, was next to suicide in Edwardian
England. As I have said, Edith would not have been
able to go out to work. There was no crèche or child
support mechanism available, no State financial allowance that made any difference. That she managed to
keep her head above water financially between 1904
and 1910 must indicate that she was receiving support

from the father of her children. Her own father, John Walker, was in no position to help a family of four. Since his days as lamplighter, John (by 1910 a man of sixty-six years) had become a builder, working latterly for the Ripon Corporation.

It is interesting that the tenancy of 8 and 9 Bedern Bank, known to have been owned by the Studley Royal Estate, remained with the Walkers into the mid-1930s (except for one short but pertinent period). As the Walkers could not have afforded to buy them, could a lease have been in the gift of Frederick as part of his support for Edith?

There are two crucial dates in Edith and her children's lives, which coincide with crucial moments in those of the Robinsons of Studley Royal, and further support a connection between them. The first is the death on 9th July 1909, of the First Marquess, George Frederick, which heralded a long and terrible stint in the Ripon Workhouse for Edith, Freda, Fred and Mary.

As aforementioned, the birth of Edith's third illegitimate child, Mary, took place on 18th February 1910, which suggests a late spring/early summer conception in 1909, a few months prior to George Frederick's death. Did the First Marquess's death precipitate their incarceration, spelling the end of their protection? Barbara chooses the same year for the death of Adrian Kenton in *Act of Will*, which precipitates the fall of Audra – Freda's fictional self – apparently quite coincidentally.

Did Frederick foreclose on Edith in 1909–10? The

First Marquess's wife, Henrietta, had died two years earlier. With the removal of the heavy Catholic influence of his parents, Frederick Oliver's 'good reason' for not divorcing Gladys and marrying Edith had disappeared. Did Edith pile pressure on him to do the right thing by her, to the extent that Frederick decided to rid himself of the bind of his second family by withdrawing support? Or was he wiping the slate clean before taking on the onerous responsibilities of the Estate (which doubtless did not appeal to him)? Or had Edith's protection been in the gift of the First Marquess, and simply ended with his death?

Interestingly, the electoral rolls show that no person eligible to vote lived at 9 Bedern Bank from 1910. John seems to have disappeared, yet we know he was still alive until at least 1912. Does his sudden absence and Edith's simultaneous fall in 1910 suggest that the lease on 9 Bedern Bank had been withdrawn from the Walkers during the period of Edith's despair in the workhouse?

Ripon Workhouse records, handwritten at the time, are contained within half-year periods. They show that in the first half-year of 1910, Edith, Freda, Fred and Mary spent continuously 52, 49, 49 and 41 consecutive days in the workhouse respectively, that the four of them then spent the entire 184 days of the next half-year there, and fifteen days into the first half-year of 1911.

Edith arrived at the workhouse gates on her own in May 1910, three days before Freda and Fred, who were six and three years old respectively, and eleven days before Mary, who was only three months old, the children's late coming suggesting that an arrangement to look after them had fallen through. What this means is that Barbara's mother was not only illegitimate, but was delivered into the care of the workhouse when she was a child of six.

It is difficult to imagine truly what this meant to Edith, Freda and her siblings. The picture we have of the workhouse generally comes to us from Dickens, and the illustrations of Cruikshank or Phiz. Today, it is all too easy to admire the art with which Dickens writes almost at the expense of the agonies of the workhouse he depicts. The ironic tone he adopted as Oliver Twist faced the Workhouse Board for the first time may suggest that he greatly exaggerated the situation, though he did not.

> 'What are you crying for?' inquired the gentleman in the white waistcoat. And to be sure it was very extraordinary. What could the boy be crying for?
>
> 'I hope you say your prayers every night,' said another gentleman in a gruff voice, 'and pray for the people who feed you, and take care of you, like a Christian.'
>
> 'Yes, sir,' stammered the boy . . .
>
> 'Well! You have come here to be educated, and taught a useful trade,' said the red-faced gentleman in the high chair.
>
> 'So you'll begin to pick oakum tomorrow morning at six o'clock,' added the surly one in the white waistcoat.

For the combination of both these blessings in the one simple process of picking oakum, Oliver bowed low by the direction of the beadle, and was then hurried away to a large ward, where, on a rough, hard bed he sobbed himself to sleep. What a noble illustration of the tender laws of this favoured country! They let the paupers go to sleep! . . .

The members of this board were very sage, deep, philosophical men, and when they came to turn their attention to the workhouse, they found out at once what ordinary folk would never have discovered – the poor liked it! It was a regular place of public entertainment for the poorer classes; a tavern where there was nothing to pay; a public breakfast, dinner, tea, and supper all the year round; a brick and mortar Elysium, where it was all play and no work. 'Oho!' said the board, looking very knowing: 'we are the fellows to set this to rights; we'll stop it all, in no time.' So, they established the rule, that all poor people should have the alternative (for they would compel nobody, not they) of being starved by a gradual process in the house, or by a quick one out of it. With this view, they contracted with the water-works to lay on an unlimited supply of water; and with a corn-factory to supply periodically small quantities of oatmeal; and issued three meals of thin gruel a day, with an onion twice a week, and half a roll on Sundays. They made a great many other wise and humane regulations having reference to the ladies, which it is not necessary to repeat; kindly undertook to divorce poor married people, in consequence of the great expense of a suit in Doctors' Commons; and, instead of compelling a man to support his family, as they had theretofore done, took his family away from him and made him a bachelor!'

The Ripon Union Workhouse that Edith, Freda and her siblings knew was built in 1854 to the north of the city at 75 Allhallowgate. Twenty years earlier the Poor Law Amendment Act had brought an end to 'outdoor relief' (top-up wages when earnings fell below a certain level). Henceforth, only asylum within the workhouse, in exchange for work, was on offer and all claimants had to prove themselves paupers. If a vagrant possessed even a shilling he would be turned away. The pauper test, along with the conditions of the new residential workhouses – made awful to deter claimants – were the demeaning aspects of the law that caused such a furore.

The declared purpose of the Act was to encourage unemployed, able-bodied men to get a job and all employers to pay at least a subsistence wage; while the asylum aspect would, it was felt, prevent paupers from breeding because once in the workhouse a man would be separated from his wife. Also, as shown in a report on the West Riding of Yorkshire, it was expected that 'the separation of husband and wife would have a beneficial tendency in rousing the indolent to exert themselves.' Records depict firm discipline and terrible sorrow. In reality, the agonies of the receiving wards, where husbands were separated from wives, and children from parents, were devastating.

What had also been overlooked was the effect upon the *needy*, that the unemployed and vagrants were not all shirkers, that unmarried mothers were not all prostitutes, that orphans were not a lower order, and that if you lived into your sixties you could easily become destitute because there were no state pensions in those days. All had effectively been criminalised by the Act. Adding to their burden, workhouses were made to take in 'lunatics', mentally defective children and the physically sick. Guardians displayed their patronising attitude by lumping their charges – 'idiots and lunatics, bastards, venereals, the idle and dissolute' – together. Yet segregation was by gender and age only.

Today, visitors to Ripon Workhouse – part of it is open to the public – will approach the same nineteenth-century portico through which Barbara's mother passed in 1910. The entrance to the Grubber, as it was known, is a low, one- and two-storey, brick-built construct with a stone gateway and imposing twelve-foot doors, behind which lie a village-sized collection of buildings within very much higher walls. There were adult wards (into which sane and insane intermingled) and receiving wards, where the separations – male/female, child/adult – took place, and bodies were stripped, disinfected and clothed in workhouse attire before being taken to segregated dormitories, exercise yards or casual ward cells barely big enough for a bed.

If inmates wanted to eat they must work: breaking stone, chopping wood (there was a chopping shed built in 1903), weeding, lifting potatoes (Ripon Work-house had its own garden), or – as in Dickens – picking oakum, the loose fibre obtained by unravelling old rope. Respite was only given after the task was com-plete. Inmates would dine in gender-segregated areas, sitting on benches at long tables, all facing the same way and eating in silence. Edith's daily diet consisted of less than half a pint of milk, just under a pound of flour (bread was baked on the premises until 1916), a few potatoes (equivalent to four small new pota-toes), a little sugar, butter and cheese (about 3 oz a week), a quarter of a pound of meat, and a cup full of oatmeal. Coffee was not introduced until 1917. Bedtime was '8.30 p.m., rising in summer at 6.15 a.m. and in winter at 6.45 a.m.'

There were also children's nurseries and at one time a schoolroom, and a hospital block (male and female wards, and a special maternity ward) and mortuary. The maternity or lying-in ward was available to un-married mothers and others who, in the days before National Health Service hospitals, could not afford hospitalisation. Edith, perhaps because she had had a difficult birth with Freda, availed herself of the facility in 1907 and 1910 for the births of Fred and Mary. She would have been in and out as quickly as possible, for the ward was notably without frills: 'Traditionally the noisiest and worst-behaved part of the workhouse was the "lying-in" ward,' writes Beryl Thompson. Mostly the women in the ward were regarded as of 'low moral character'. Some were youngsters in their teens expecting their first baby, generally frightened and apprehensive, but most were 'regulars' with a lifetime of prostitution behind them. Quarrelling and fighting often broke out and the workhouse staff found these inmates resentful and uncooperative.

Jack London's famous book, *The People of the Abyss*, gives us a fascinating glimpse of conditions in a workhouse at around the time Barbara's mother and grandmother were suffering the one in Ripon, its relevance accentuated by Barbara's own choice of 'The Abyss' as title of Part Two of *A Woman of Substance*, where she introduces us to the poverty in which Emma Harte's own mother lived in Fairley Village. Here, on the title page of the latter, a quote from John Milton leaves us in no doubt that clawing herself out of it was no mean achievement:

> *Long is the way*
> *And hard, that out of hell leads up to light.*
> Paradise Lost

Jack London actually lived among the homeless of the East End of London. This he did over seven weeks in the summer of 1902, repairing regularly to a safe house to recover. Immediately in his book there is a sense of division between two worlds, of Light and Dark, of Hope and Despair, and of the one-way passage between them. For him, the workhouse casual ward (for vagrants) was the pit. Interestingly, the inmates there were of the opinion that the metropolis workhouses were better than those in the countryside, for less food was offered in rural parts. Here he describes his first night:

Many hours passed before I won to sleep. It was only seven in the evening, and the voices of children, in shrill outcry, playing in the street, continued till nearly midnight. The smell was frightful and sickening, while my imagination broke loose, and my skin crept and crawled till I was nearly frantic. Grunting, groaning, and snoring arose like the sounds emitted by some sea monster, and several times, afflicted by nightmare, one or another, by his shrieks and yells, aroused the lot of us. Towards morning I was awakened by a rat or some similar animal on my breast. In the quick transition from sleep to waking, before I was completely myself, I raised a shout to wake the dead. At any rate, I woke the living, and they cursed me for my lack of manners.

In Edith and Freda's ears the children playing in the street might well have included Jim Gott, who was a thirteen-year-old lad living in Allhallowgate when the Walkers passed through the workhouse gates for the first time. In his memoir he gives a sense of how children on the outside would be lured towards the workhouse walls in the hope of the odd glimpse of an inmate. How the imagination would take flight when so rewarded – as when Tommy Jackson suddenly bobbed his head above the side gates: 'It was like a nightmare in the daylight. He used to stare with eyes like lemonade glass alleys set in the circular rings of raw liver; and when he laughed it was like the opening of the Mersey Tunnel on a wet day.' Then there was Tommy Coates with his 'one upper molar', and 'Bill Sykes cap . . . perched on his thin, worn head . . . He always reminded me, when he walked, of those jointed wooden dolls, his every movement stiff and mechanical as though he had to be wound up like a clockwork model.'

One who had not actually witnessed life within the Ripon Workhouse walls assured me that, 'This was a small, rural workhouse. Forget Charles Dickens. There would be gramophone evenings from people in the city, special treats at Christmas, they even went to the theatre.'

It is true, as specialist Anthony Chadwick points out in an excellent booklet on the subject, that 'some Yorkshire workhouses were reprimanded by London for allowing such comforts as tobacco or seaside trips,' and Ripon's own records point to a Magic Lantern Entertainment for aged inmates in 1884, a mayoral tea and concert eight years later, a pint of beer and an ounce of tobacco on the occasion of the marriage of the Duke of York in 1893, and outings to the Victoria Hall (I have a note that in November 1912, inmates were treated to a production of Gilbert and Sullivan's *Pirates of Penzance* there), Studley

Royal and Fountains Abbey – what would Edith have made of these! But they were very occasional and anyone who has braved the Ripon Workhouse museum, housed in the old male casual wards, on a chilly autumnal morning, as I did, will beg to differ. The tiny vagrant cells, one complete with restraining chair for rowdies or lunatics, were as cold as stone. The ignominy, the uncertainty and fear, the absence of warmth of any kind, love and comfort, the loneliness, the sheer despair are missing from any equation that delivers a pleasure verdict to a child on such a place as this. And unaccounted for is the authoritarian and patronising attitude of such a system in respect of the poor, and the stigma and humiliating aspect of being in receipt of charity. As Jack London wrote: 'It is the way of the world that when one man feeds another he is that man's master . . .'

> *Poverty, misery, and fear of the workhouse, are the principal causes of suicide among the working classes. 'I'll drown myself before I go into the workhouse,' said Ellen Hughes Hunt, aged fifty-two. Last Wednesday they held an inquest on her body at Shoreditch. Her husband came from the Islington Workhouse to testify. He had been a cheesemonger, but failure in business and poverty had driven him into the workhouse, whither his wife had refused to accompany him.*

As for the view that Ripon Workhouse was a place of entertainment, Dickens's 'brick and mortar Elysium', let Jim Gott give us the benefit of actual experience, for he was once an entertainer there:

> *Years ago, when I was throng in the entertainment world, I appeared at No. 75 Allhallowgate ... and really the memory of the night will always be with me. I remember I sang one of my compositions, 'Down at Fishergreen'. I've often wondered since what were their thoughts as I reminded them of their early days.*
>
> *Many old familiar faces were before me – some that I had thought had passed on. How strange to see them there like a long-forgotten community cut off from the rest of the world. Not that I am decrying the administration of those in charge, but through my eyes, the inmates seemed so lonely with a pitiful hunger for the warmth of their own kith and kin ...*

The stigma and the fear lived on. The stigma of being a workhouse child was burned into the child's very soul. However solicitous some may have been in lightening the burden, 75 Allhallowgate was the gateway to hell, as the endless lists of those who died there bears terrible testimony. Ripon Workhouse was no more independent of the system that Dickens was set against than any other.

If Edith had been let down by Frederick it would have been very difficult for her to make enough of a rumpus to put a stain on his reputation. It would have taken time to make accusations stick or raise much credibility from inside the workhouse. Yet this would have been her only hope.

In Barbara's novel *Three Weeks in Paris*, we have a similar scenario to the Fairley family's cruel disassociation of Emma Harte in *A Woman of Substance*, but wound on a few years and with the male suitor as more obviously predatory from the start, and ending in the same desperate situation for heroine Kay Andrews as for Emma, and as, in reality, for Edith: pregnancy, with no man to support her.

Kay Andrews goes with her mother to run the house of a titled member of the aristocracy in magnificent grounds just outside Edinburgh, on the Firth of Forth. Kay is molested by 'his lordship', their relationship beginning at so young an age that she does not protest until such time as she becomes pregnant, when she tells her mother what's been going on. The squire arranges for an abortion for Kay and three weeks' severance for Kay's mother, who, far from accepting the situation, sits down and considers her options.

> *Suddenly she understood she was holding all the cards. His lordship sat in the House of Lords, he was a businessman, and very well known socially. He moved in all of the top social circles, and so did her ladyship. It struck Mam very forcibly that the last thing he wanted was a scandal . . .*

So she demands money, and, 'frightened out of his wits', his lordship pays up. 'It was blackmail,' confesses Kay to her aged school headmistress Anya Sedgwick. 'My mother saw an opportunity to help me, not only then, but in the future. And so she blackmailed him.'

> *There was a silence.*
>
> *Everything was very still in the garden. Not a leaf stirred, nor a blade of grass. Nothing moved at all. Even the birds were quiet.*
>
> *But Anya's head buzzed with all that she had heard.*

Echoes of the past inhabit Barbara's fiction in an almost uncanny way. Secrets abound around every corner, the only question is which flight of fancy to follow in pursuit of them. The facts in Edith's case are that on 15 October 1910, she was taken from the workhouse to Ripon Minster and married to one John Thomas Simpson, a labourer six years her junior, and then she was returned to 75 Allhallowgate to resume her 'sentence'. Who was this John Thomas Simpson? He describes himself on their marriage certificate as a labourer, and gives his address as 8 Belle Vue Yard, Somerset Place, where we know his father, Thomas, lived (though the son is not included on the return).

John Thomas Simpson was born in 1886 and had three brothers: James, Arthur and Alfred. He was only twenty-four when he was married. Edith's sister-in-law, Ruth Matilda Walker (wife of Edith's brother Joseph), was one of two witnesses to the wedding.

What seems so strange is that Edith returned afterwards to the workhouse. What kind of marriage was this? Had Simpson stepped forward to rescue her from the abyss? It seems unlikely, in that a twenty-four-year-old labourer offered little financial security. Had she known him before entering the workhouse and fallen in love with him perhaps? Again, unlikely, given that Edith returned to the workhouse rather than joining her new husband.

Edith finally left the workhouse in January 1911, three months after the marriage. On 3 February 1912 she produced a second son, Norman. On the birth certificate, Simpson is named as the child's father, but gives his residence as 9 Bondgate, Ripon, while Edith gives hers as 9 Bedern Bank. Why the two addresses if she and Simpson were husband and wife in the normal way? Furthermore, from the electoral roll we also know that from 1913, Freda's cousin Gabriel Barker was also living at Bedern Bank. What sort of circumstances could have suddenly made the Bedern Bank address available once more to the Walker family?

Increasingly, the whole thing feels like a put-up job, a marriage of convenience and not one that necessarily involved any emotional input on Simpson's part. Could he have been suggested as a safe way forward? Perhaps he already worked on the Studley Royal Estate. Consider the ramifications. Simpson would be guaranteed employment. Edith would have her respectability, and as soon as the keys of Bedern Bank could be returned to her, she could quit the workhouse and repair to her own home. As far as Frederick was concerned, he was off the hook. So long as there was a husband registered on the birth certificate, his name – the Robinson name – was in the clear. Edith was at last a married woman.

It was a solution that appealed to everyone for their own reasons, and it is quite possible for it to have been cooked up in the workhouse. Ripon Workhouse records for the period show various Simpsons as inmates. One Elizabeth Ann Simpson had an almost permanent residence there – could this be Edith's elder sister who had also married a Simpson? And there's a Thomas Simpson (born 1845), who is in and out of the Grubber constantly – could this be John Thomas's father (he would be the right age)? Also a Joseph Simpson crops up time and again, as does a labourer called James Simpson – could this be John Thomas's brother, James?

Furthermore, just as Edith had contact with the Simpson family through the workhouse, so there is a distinct possibility that Frederick had contact with the family too. At the time that Edith married John Thomas Simpson, a branch of the Simpson family had a gardening business at Kirby Road in Ripon and, among other duties, looked after the cemetery gardens. Edith's husband described himself on the marriage certificate as a labourer, but later at the birth of Edith's first child after their marriage, he was more specific, calling himself a 'grocer's waggoner'. This commercial gardening connection cries out for us to make the link between the time-honoured gardening

Simpsons of Ripon and the Studley Royal Estate, one John Simpson heading the gardening workforce there when the main works were done. Ripon was a very small city, people did not move around like they do today. The Simpsons of Ripon that Edith knew may well have been that same family, further down the line.

Other facts also suggest a connection between Simpson and Studley Royal. Records show that on 3rd July 1914, Edith had her fifth child, called Frances, a child who, quite clearly, Barbara knew nothing about. Nor was it easy to find out much about her. The only Frances Simpson born in 1914, the year recorded as the year of her birth in a later workhouse record, to which I will come, was indeed registered as born to John Thomas Simpson and his wife, Edith Simpson (née Walker), but baby Frances was born in Millar's Lane, Morpeth, in Northumberland, not in Ripon at all.

Had Simpson taken his wife on holiday? Not very likely. Given paucity of funds and general inclination, holidays eighty miles away to the northeast are an unlikely part of the agenda. Could it be that work had taken him up there, possibly at the behest of the Studley Royal Estate? I rang the local library at Morpeth and asked a helpful young lady whether she knew of any connection between the Ripons of Studley Royal and any estates in the area. 'Funnily enough,' she said, 'there is a connection. In my village of Swarland, just north of Morpeth, Commander Clare Vyner [who would take up the reins of Studley

Royal after Frederick Oliver Robinson died] had an estate there, where workers could relocate, live in their own house and work a piece of land.'

In fact, the Swarland Settlement itself, as the Vyner project became known, didn't happen until 1934, but the land ownership is a fact and it evinces the particular character of the Ripons of Studley Royal: land ownership and social conscience is what engaged them, which is evident at other times and which is clearly consistent with the notion of Edith being 'looked after' there and kept out of the way.

The Studley Royal Estate had land holdings in the area at least as early as 1575 and the specific connection between Morpeth and Ripon goes as far back in time as the twelfth century when Ranulph de Merlay, Second Baron of Morpeth, financed the monks of Fountains to build a replica of their abbey, calling it Newminster Abbey, in a similar position southwest of the town. In Victorian, Edwardian and more modern times there were ever-closer collaborations. Frederick Oliver, being one of the two best shots in England, would have enjoyed fraternisation with the other big grouse and pheasant shooting areas, of which Northumberland is key. And Commander Clare Vyner would seal the connection by marrying into the Northumberland aristocracy. In 1923 he married Lady Doris Gordon Lennox, who was the niece of Helen, Duchess of Northumberland.

This has strange echoes in *Act Of Will*. Lady Doris and Helen, Duchess of Northumberland were grand-daughter and daughter of the Duke of Richmond and

Gordon, and their maiden names were both Gordon Lennox. In *Act of Will*, Matron Lennox is a women's libber of the old school – 'she was of a new breed of woman, very modern in her way of thinking, some said even radical. She was well known in the North of England for her passionate *espousal of reforms in woman and child welfare*, and for her dedication to the advancement of women's rights in general.' Matron Lennox is willing and able to pull strings for Audra at a time when work was becoming difficult to find. Was Edith's Northumberland sojourn perhaps a sign that she was a beneficiary of the Lennox family social conscience?

Was Frederick Oliver Robinson's reputed interest in the social welfare of females – as patron of the Ripon Home For Girls – Edith's ticket to this otherwise unlikely destination? Did the Ripon Masons smooth the path to the Edith Simpson 'solution' perhaps? The question is relevant because in Morpeth, at Winton House, was the headquarters of the Freemasons in the North. The Robinsons of Studley Royal were leading lights in the Craft, not only in Ripon but nationally, and will have been hand-in-glove with the Morpeth Masons. That Winton House had previously been the home of the famous suffragette, Emily Davison, may be deemed coincidence even in the light of the Lennox/Robinson interest in women's welfare, but it is perfectly consistent with practice elsewhere at this time that the Masons would have been involved in welfare projects of this sort.

The Morpeth Masons would first and foremost

have included in their membership the local landed gentry, the most visible of whom in the town was one J. R. Blackett-Ord. Just as Frederick Oliver Robinson owned Fountains, so Blackett-Ord had the Newminster Abbey Estate among other significant holdings in Morpeth. He employed an estate manager called John Sadler who looked after Newminster and owned various properties in the town on his own account. We know from an assessment undertaken in 1910 following the Finance Act, who owned and occupied every property in England and Wales. For a few years afterwards, in localities up and down the country, copies of the assessment were updated as land or properties changed hands and new occupiers moved in. The 1910 names were simply crossed out and new names added. Imagine my surprise to find the name J. Simpson replacing that of the 1910 occupier of a small house in a yard in the same block as Winton House. The humble abode was owned by Blackett-Ord's manager, John Sadler. Was Simpson working for Sadler/Blackett-Ord? It seems likely.

If so, this was surely an ongoing protection strategy of Edith of an extraordinary kind, and one that, for Frederick, happily distanced his little problem geographically from Ripon. But whatever the reason for their going there, the Northumbrian experiment came to an end around 1916, and the couple returned to live not in Bedern Bank, which Edith had probably sublet, but at Yorkshire Hussar Yard. The Yorkshire Hussars was an inn, marked on the 1909 map on the east side of the Market Place, by what is now the archway entrance to the main city car park. There, on 14th August 1917, Edith gave birth to her sixth and last child, a girl, also called Edith.

It is odd that Simpson had not been called up. At the start of the First World War, married men were not required to serve in the forces, but by 1916 the killing fields of France were not so choosy and men avoiding the draft would be shamed with white feathers. From that time it would have been very difficult for Simpson to remain in Morpeth, which was headquarters of C Squadron of the Northumberland Yeomanry and of A Company of the 7th Battalion of the Northumberland Fusiliers. Perhaps that is why they returned. Ripon was, by Freda's account, also busy with soldiers, but the situation may have been more manageable there under the Marquess's personal protection.

In 1918, Freda, who had experienced life without Edith during her mother's Northumberland sojourn, struck out on her own. Perhaps she had begun to form her own opinions about the helter-skelter ride which had been her life to date and decided to take it into her own hands. What we know is that Freda began working at the Ripon Fever Hospital in Stonebridgegate, off Allhallowgate – the workhouse and fever hospital were in fact neighbouring buildings. Erected in 1878 and enlarged in 1916, it provided for twenty-five patients.

Although it was to one side of the Ripon Union Workhouse, the Fever Hospital was not part of it, and the workhouse had its own hospital. It features, of course, in *Act of Will*, where Audra, like Freda, is beset by 'all the gruelling work ... the endless scrubbing and cleaning and washing and ironing, the terrible drudgery ... [but] there was something very special in Audra Kenton, call it stubbornness, that made her stick it out until she could graduate to a nurse's training ... she had unusual stamina, as well as mental energy and toughness of mind ... inner resources which she was able to draw on for inner strength. And so she had valiantly continued to scrub and clean and polish endlessly ...' It is, now, easy enough to believe it. One might even call it *persistence*.

No. 9 Bedern Bank had by this time been let to a couple called John and Lily Taylor. With the First World War coming to an end, and with the Taylors suddenly entering upon the scene, it is as if one generation is handing over to the next. Could John and Lily be related to the Taylors of Armley, the family into which Barbara would be born? When Freda eventually found her way to Leeds looking for work, did she travel with an introduction to John and Lily's big-city relations? Is this how Freda met Winston? It is possible, although when Freda first left Ripon she did not go immediately to Leeds, as we shall see.

During this period, when Edith is listed as living at Yorkshire Hussar Yard, Freda was almost certainly living at No. 8 Bedern Bank, next door to the Taylors. Women were eligible to vote from 1918, but Freda was not yet of voting age and is not listed as resident there on the electoral roll, although another member of the Walker family is ... a woman called Frances

Walker, who might well have been looking after Freda. Who was Frances Walker? Could she have been Edith's elder brother Thomas Walker's widow, whose name was a scrawl in the earlier records, but just could have been read as 'Frances'?

Frances Walker is, I discovered, yet another name to emerge from the shadows between fact and fiction, where truth so often lies in our story. In *Act of Will*, a certain Frances is the mother of wicked Aunt Alicia, who has Audra's brother and sister transported to Australia after their mother Edith's death. In real life, Freda's brothers and sisters were similarly transported, as was the way in those days, not only in the case of orphans but in any case where proper care was deemed inadequate.

While unaware of much of Edith and Freda's story, Barbara did know that her uncles and aunts had been so dealt with, believing the event to have been precipitated by Edith's death. Indeed, she made the whole heartless practice of child deportation the wellspring of *Her Own Rules*. Early on, Barbara said to me: 'Freda had, I think, two brothers, Frederick and Norman, and two sisters, Mary and Edith [she was unaware of Edith's fourth-born child, Frances]. One brother and two sisters were sent to Australia. One brother to Canada. I think only Norman went to Canada. Australian emigration could have had something to do with the scheme, the emigration of thousands of orphaned children in the 1920s. There was a Granada TV film about it – *The Lost Children of the Empire*.'

Later she would also tell me that there had indeed been an Aunt Alicia figure in real life – different name and not as heartless, but someone who ultimately handed over Freda's brothers and sisters to the authorities, and that Freda had been given the choice whether to go or stay, and that being older and with a job at the fever hospital, had opted to stay.

It was a wrenching moment for the three young Kentons when Frederick and William took leave of their sister on that bitter winter morning. Before setting out for London and the boat to Sydney, they had huddled together in the front hall, saying their goodbyes, fighting back their tears.

Act of Will

In the novel, the children's 'fiercest protestations and anguished pleadings to stay together had made no impression. They were helpless in the face of their aunt's determination.' And so, against their wishes, and those of Alicia Drummond's mother, 'Great-Aunt Frances', they had been forced to do as Alicia had said. Now, I was wondering, could that fictional Great-Aunt Frances be one and the same woman as Frances Walker, listed as living at 8 Bedern Bank in 1918?

Barbara gave me the answer before I knew even to ask for it, in a note on a letter I faxed to her at the start of my research when I queried what her childhood friend Margery Clarke had told me about Edith

– Freda's mother – being still alive and living in Bedern Bank when Barbara was a small girl. Barbara appended a note to my letter and faxed it back: 'NO,' she wrote in capitals. 'She's thinking of Great-Aunt Frances.'

Searching for confirmation of the transportation of Freda's siblings, I came up against all kinds of problems. Records of a practice that sometimes amounted to child deportation are jealously guarded, no one denying that many were taken without parental consent if their mothers were sick or otherwise deemed incapable.

The official justification for the scheme had been that it would relieve Britain's overcrowded cities of orphans and children at risk, while the receiving nation would benefit from the cheapness of labour these children promised. The Barnardo migrations to Canada began around 1870. For seventy years, over fifty British childcare organisations sent 100,000 children aged between four and fifteen to work as indentured farm workers and domestic servants. Later there was also a scheme to Australia and New Zealand, the scheme persisting until the mid-1960s.

Allegations of abuse and exploitation have been rife. In the case of Barnardo's, one of the main vehicles for the emigration of child victims of poverty, illegitimacy or broken homes to Canada, there was an employer agreement with the receiving farmer, which covered the period of 'adoption', stating that the child would be provided with sufficient and proper board, that he or she would attend church and school, and a wage was agreed, which was remitted to Barnardo's in trust. In addition a fee was paid by the Canadian government to Barnardo's for each child that emigrated to Canada. Each child had a trust account with the Bank of Commerce in Canada, but the passbook was sent to Barnardo's office in Toronto and no withdrawal could be made by a child without Barnardo's permission. At the ages of eighteen and twenty-one respectively, Barnardo's boys and girls could withdraw money from their account.

There was also a system of inspection to protect a child from abuse, but 'rewards for endurance' were given to those who remained on Canadian farms for long periods of time, and very few if any children were ever removed for reasons of abuse or neglect. Meanwhile, many reports reached the ears of the public, and Barnardo's employees admitted that there were employers 'who are far from desirable guardians or associates of young children.'

Newspaper articles of the period proclaim only a positive message about the opportunities the colonies provided: 'Open Door to Canada – free loans to nominated immigrants . . . No Exploitation . . . cooperative policies of Great Britain and Canada.' In Ripon, the *Gazette* urged locals to rally to an 'Australia Calls' slogan, which heralded the arrival of a certain Mr Stabler of the Australian Immigration Office. At the YMCA Lecture Hall, Stabler waxed lyrical about 'the splendid opportunities afforded to young men of this country desiring to emigrate to the far-distant colony of Australia'. On 12th February 1925, a party of

Barnardo's boys were promoting the organisation in the YMCA Lecture Hall in Ripon, as the *Gazette* reported: 'A very delightful entertainment was given by the boys, who exhibited remarkable skill in the manipulation of the different instruments, the playing of the handbells being especially good.'

Just one year earlier, however, Dr Barnardo's bells tolled a more mournful note at 'the verdict of a coroner's jury, which heard evidence [in Ontario, Canada] in connection with the suicide of a Barnardo boy, John Payne, on the farm of Mr Charles Fee . . . The evidence showed that Payne had read in the news-papers about the suicide of another boy from the Marchmont Home, and the jury found that this, com-bined with an alleged threat of Mrs Fee that he would be sent back to the Barnardo Home if he did not mend his ways, was the only cause that they could find from the evidence . . . On the day he killed himself, Mrs Fee had given him a slap in the face for calling her a liar.' Such suicides were not infrequent.

On 13th June 2002 a British Home Children Class Action Law Suit was commenced against Barnardo's on behalf of the class of persons whom Barnardo's emigrated to Canada. It was moved by one Harold Warneford Vennell, who was left destitute as a boy with his mother and older brother after his father left them. Around 1923 he contracted the pauper's disease – rickets. Taken in by Barnardo's, he claims that records show he was denied visits from his mother, and that without her permission, and despite the pro-visions of a contract she had signed, Barnardo's sent the fourteen-year-old boy to Toronto, and thence to a farm in Pakenham, Ontario, where he undertook hard farm labour eighteen hours a day (with no schooling or church). Harold tells of meagre food, poor clothing, neglect and mistreatment, even assaults by the farmer and his wife.

This, then, was the fate to which the real-life equivalent of *Act of Will*'s wicked Aunt Alicia – the daughter of Great-Aunt Frances of No. 8 Bedern Bank – had consigned Freda's brothers and sisters. For Freda herself it must have been a terrible blow. In the novel, Audra tells Vincent of 'the endless, endless miles of ocean stretching from here to Australia. And quite suddenly I did miss William and Frederick so, it was like a tight pain in my chest, a terrible constriction . . .' In reality, Barbara told me that 'Norman Simpson did come back and see us during the Second War,' but by then the past must have seemed to Freda like another world. At the time, the pathos of their departure cannot have failed to touch her and perhaps hardened her will further to get out and make something of her life, which we see Audra attempting to do in *Act of Will* before she finds her purpose in her daughter.

I got nowhere with Barnardo's on a search for Freda's siblings – they will only deal with family members and Barbara did not want to jump through the hoops. But my search was rewarded by chance with the saddest of all entries appertaining to Edith's family in the records of the Ripon Workhouse: on 22nd December 1924, just three days before

Christmas, Norman, Frances and Edith Simpson (twelve, ten and seven respectively) were admitted *on their own* to 75 Allhallowgate by order of the Children's Act 1908. They were held there until 10th February 1925, when they were discharged into the care of the NSPCC '*for removal to Dr Barnardo's Homes*', and onward transportation to the colonies. It is to be assumed that Fred and Mary went with them.

Whatever the level of treatment, the terrible psychological effect of enforced removal from one's roots and country emerges from the Granada TV film aforementioned by Barbara, *The Lost Children of the Empire*, as a lasting problem. Leslie Shaw was sent to Halifax, Nova Scotia, on 23rd March 1927, and a lifetime later asserts that the problem this set in motion was one of identity, still needing solution: 'It is important to know who I am,' she said, even at this late stage seeing the TV team as an opportunity too good to lose. An eighty-year-old grandmother says that in all the years she has been in her adopted country, 'my mother was never out of my mind.' The migration scheme was Freda's own sorrow writ large. Accusations of sexual abuse fly in the film, as terrible memories lift the veil on indignity, degradation and suffering. But beneath it all there is this sense of dispossession, of loss, lost identity, which can never be made good. 'I love my children,' says one woman. 'But even they don't completely fill that gap. I feel as if I was robbed . . . Even today I am very insecure, deep down. I feel a nobody.'

In 1925, at the very moment that the Barnardo

boys were being applauded at Ripon's YMCA, all three Simpson children were rubbed out of the city for ever, and, as far as Barbara is aware, so were Fred and Mary too. Only Freda escaped, she being twenty in 1924 and making her way on her own.

Barbara was always told that the children were sent abroad because Edith died, but if this terrible act was due to their mother's death I can find no record of it. If Edith was still alive at this stage, she would only have been forty-four.

It is possible that the children were taken from Edith without her permission, for this was a common-enough occurrence, especially if, as is the case in *Her Own Rules*, the sole charge of the children – the mother – was ill when the 'care-takers' swung into action.

Edith, as ever, remains a mystery. I searched for records of her demise, either as Edith Simpson or Walker, from 1917 (the year in which she gave birth to her last child) until 1942, and came up with a list of possibles but no clear claims. The only Edith Simpson to die during the period in Ripon did so in 1934, but she is a farmer's wife, quite distinct and aged forty-three, whereas Barbara's grandmother would have been fifty-four. There are other Edith Walkers and Edith Simpsons listed who are the same age as our Edith, but they are in other places: Dewsbury (1917), Spilsby, Lincoln (1922), Halifax (1927), Barnsley (1929), Birkenhead (1935), Marylebone (1937), Leeds (1939), and none matches on other grounds.

Could it be that, like Meredith's mother in *Her*

Own Rules, Edith had not in fact died when her daughter supposed? Could it be that she married again and moved on, perhaps even abroad after her children, or even changed her name after the devastation of losing them? In 1924 when the last three children were put in care, Edith was only in her mid-forties, which is young to die, though of course TB was an early killer of many.

There is one compelling possibility other than Edith's death in explaining how Freda's brothers and sister were brought to this pass. It is the second date that points to a connection between Studley Royal and Edith's fortunes, for in 1923, one year before the children were taken into care, the Second Marquess of Ripon died.

If Edith and the children had been living under his protection, then for sure, now, it had come to an end, and who else could afford to look after so many children? Not John Thomas Simpson, the putative father of three of them, that's for sure. Edith's husband was still alive in 1924, but when he did go, he perished in penury in Ripon Workhouse from cardiac arrest after a bout of pneumonia and lies buried in Ripon cemetery. He was only forty-four.

Secrets, there were so many in our family . . . I never wanted to face those secrets from my childhood. Better to forget them; better still to pretend they did not exist. But they did. My childhood was constructed on secrets layered one on top of the other.

As I write, I am left with no other possibility as to Edith's demise, unless the death records are incomplete (which, I am told, can be the case). It sometimes seems that she simply disappeared.

At Bedern Bank, following the children's enforced emigration, Frances Walker was joined for a while by an Elizabeth Walker – could this be her daughter? (She and Thomas had three – Lillie, who married Joe Wray, Elizabeth, and Minnie.) Could this be the real-life Alicia Drummond? Then, in 1933, the year that Barbara was born, there is no sign of Frances, and in 1935 no sign of 8 Bedern Bank itself, which is appropriate, for by then the focus of the action, both in fiction and in reality, had switched from Ripon to Leeds.

And yet the chapter is not quite ended, because there is a question mark that hangs over Freda, who seems to me so private a person. She must have shown tremendous inner strength. She had known real loss, real deprivation, real destitution. Barbara, though quite unaware of the enormity, recognised as much: 'I believe that my mother always had a great sense of loss, in fact I know that she did.' Fate – her age and independent streak – had saved her from the Migration Scheme, she was able to choose not to go, but Freda knew what it was to feel robbed, insecure, and – fatherless – uncertain deep down of who she was. Yet, I have this feeling about Freda, however private, however difficult she may have been with people, that incredibly she was always in control. It was an essential element of her character, which Barbara, when I put it to her, recognised too.

In *A Woman of Substance* revenge is a major theme. The gentry get their comeuppance. Emma Harte ruins Edwin Fairley's family and razes Fairley Hall to the ground – 'I do not want one rosebud, one single leaf left growing,' Emma orders. Emma has been hurt so deeply that she cannot bear even to smell the perfume of roses (symbolic of romance and Freda's favourite flower), which filled the air when Edwin dumped her. Strange as it may seem, in reality the Robinsons' house – Studley Hall – was also razed, first in 1716 for reasons sadly lost to us, though arson was suspected and the finger pointed at a woman, a local, one Anne Gill – 'so divilish a woman that there is no mischief she could invent'. Could this act have been born of vengeance too? One could be forgiven for speculating. Two hundred and thirty years later, on unlucky Saturday, 13th April 1946, when Barbara was in her first year at Northcote Private School and her mother Freda was, according to her account, working her fingers to the bone to send her daughter there, Studley Royal was set on fire again . . .

> *Studley Royal, the home of Commander Clare Vyner and Lady Doris Vyner, was until a fortnight ago being used by the Queen Ethelburga School of Harrogate. Commander and Lady Vyner were expected to return from Ross-shire at the weekend to arrange for the mansion's redecoration before taking up residence.*
>
> *Within half an hour of the outbreak the whole length of the two-storey building was ablaze, and*

the light of the fire could be seen thirty to forty miles away. Firemen from eight areas in the North Riding were called out. Water had to be pumped about three-quarters of a mile from a lake in the grounds and an adjoining reservoir. An eye-witness stated that valuable paintings, tapestries, and furniture were saved by villagers, estate workers, and police, who formed themselves into a chain and passed the articles from hand to hand.

The Times, Monday, 15th April 1946

In the middle of May, Emma made a second trip to Fairley Hall. She walked along the terrace, which still remained intact, and regarded the great tract of rough, bare ground where the house and stables had formerly stood. Not one brick was left and the rose garden, too, had disappeared. Emma felt an enormous surge of relief and an unexpected sense of liberation. Fairley Hall, that house where she had suffered such humiliation and heartache, might never have existed. It could no longer hurt her with the painful memories it evoked. She had exorcised all the ghosts of her childhood. She was free at last . . .

A Woman of Substance

PART TWO

CHAPTER ONE

A New Start?

'Yesterday was now. The past was immutable.'
A Woman of Substance

Precisely when Freda Walker upped and left Ripon is not clear. Barbara says that like Audra in *Act of Will*, 'Mummy wanted to be a nurse. After working as a ward maid [at the Ripon Fever Hospital] she became a trainee student nurse, then she went to Bradford to be a nanny.'

On her marriage certificate in 1929, Freda would describe herself as a domestic servant, which allows service as a nanny. In Bradford she worked for a short time for a family of mill owners, looking after their son, before moving to Leeds where she was employed in the posher part of Upper Armley (in the direction of Hill Top), as is Audra in *Act of Will*.

In the novel, Audra's Leeds employer is a Mrs Irene Bell, a suffragette and modern thinker and an important influence on Audra. Irene's son (Audra's charge) is called Theophilus, actually the name of the boy that Freda looked after in Bradford and one that fascinated

Barbara after she discovered it meant 'beloved of God'.

In reality, Freda's Leeds employer was a Mrs Ellwood and quite unlike Irene Bell, though her son, Tony, always believed he was the model for Theo in *Act of Will* and surprised Barbara one day in the mid-Eighties by stepping out of the shadows while she was over from America signing copies of the novel.

'I was in Leeds at one of the bookstores. They had this enormous queue of people,' she told Billie Figg in 1986. 'It being my home town, all sorts of people turned up, girls I was at school with ... Then this man suddenly appeared and he looked at me, and I looked at him, and he said, "You don't know who it is, do you?" And I did immediately, I said "Yes", and said his name, and then he said, "These are my grandchildren and I *had* to come and buy your book." It was the child my mother had brought up! He said, "Freda would be so proud of you." I was so touched my eyes actually filled with tears.'

Barbara and Tony saw each other again: 'He always said he had the best nanny in the world, and his daughter said, "That was your mother." After that, Tony Ellwood and Janice, his daughter, always came to my book signings and he always managed to make me cry.'

When Freda emerged from Ripon and went to Bradford she would have needed to be at least in her early twenties in order to be offered these responsible child-caring positions. In which case she probably left Ripon around 1926–7, aged twenty-two or twenty-

three, just two or three years before she met and married Winston Taylor. As Barbara confirmed, 'She was
actually working in Upper Armley for the Ellwoods
when she met my father.'

It is difficult to imagine Freda's frame of mind.
She had lost everything, her father, her mother, her
brothers and sisters. She was alone, stigmatised in her
own mind by the calamity of life that had destroyed
her family. Yet she did not hold her mother Edith
responsible for the mess she'd got the family into.
Barbara insisted: 'Freda missed her mother a lot. She
loved her mother a great deal and spoke about her a
lot. She was *very* close to her.' This can only have
exacerbated the loneliness Freda now felt.

In her stints of nannying in Bradford and Leeds,
Freda poured into her boys the love she needed so
much to feel. Tony Ellwood recognised this in speaking so lovingly of Freda. It was why Barbara nearly
cried whenever they met, though of course neither
Tony nor Barbara knew the half of it.

In *Act of Will*, Irene Bell, with her modern politics
and feminist principles, gives Audra tremendous confidence to stand up for herself and move forward, and
it may be that there was someone like this in Freda's
life, possibly her matron at the Fever Hospital, with
whom she will have remained in touch if only to
supply references to her new employers. Freda would
have appreciated the support. In the end, of course,
she met Winston Taylor, who swept her off her feet,
just as Audra meets Vincent in the novel, and, like
Vincent, Winston proved his value.

Freda found the love she needed in Winston, but, as we have seen, she couldn't accept it. She neglected him and turned instead to their daughter, pouring her whole life into Barbara. I was at first surprised to learn that Freda had not blamed Edith for what had become of her family. But if she had, she would very likely not have turned to Barbara in the way she did. On the contrary, she may even have spurned and neglected her daughter rather than her husband. Instead, Freda re-created in her relationship with Barbara the strong bond she had had with her own mother. Freda was Edith's first child, they would have been always together, there being no father around. They too would have been 'joined at the hip' in the early years. Now, with Barbara, she would revivify that bond and relive the period of her childhood when Edith was living her dream and Freda had enjoyed the most security.

As a child Barbara was so bound up in Freda's will that she only allowed herself to see the positive aspects, her father's anguish coming to her only occasionally as a missed step in the night when she worried what had become of him.

Others saw a different woman. So withdrawn and shy did Freda become as a result of her childhood experience that Billie Figg found it 'very hard to associate her with the input to Barbara's success with which Barbara credits her', even harbouring a suspicion that Barbara might have been adopted: 'She [Freda] was a very quiet woman, not one that you would expect to be behind such a powerfully driven woman like Barbara,' Billie explained.

The map, dated 1909, shows Ripon when Barbara's mother, Freda, was five. To the south, Water Skellgate, where Freda was born to Edith Walker on June 3, 1904. A few minutes walk east, in the shadow of the Minster, Bedern Bank, where members of Edith's family lived in two low-lying, yellow-washed cottages until the mid-1930s. To the north of the Market Place, Allhallowgate and Ripon Workhouse.

Above: Ripon Minster at the north end of Bedern Bank, was founded in 1175. Barbara's grandmother, Edith Walker, is first recorded as resident in the city in 1891 with her father, John, a lamplighter, and her five brothers and sisters.

Below: Ripon Market Place as Edith knew it, the huge obelisk testimony to the commanding presence of the Ripons of Studley Royal. It carries an inscription by Frederick Oliver Robinson, Marquess from 1910–1923. Note the Lawrence Hotel to its right, where Barbara and her friend Margery Knowles would dance in the 1940s.

Ripon, redolent of times past. The Wakeman Hornblower *(right)* still announces the watch each night at 9.

Water Skellgate in 1904, the year that Edith Walker gave birth there to Freda, Barbara's mother – in poverty, but with great expectations.

The stepping stones on the Skell where Freda fell and dripped duck-egg blue all the way home.

Below left: one of Ripon's ancient courts off Water Skellgate, not unlike the one where Freda was born in 1904. *Below right:* Freda dressed in her best at 14, a decade after her workhouse experience and the year she took her life in her own hands and began working at the Fever Hospital.

Studley Royal Hall, home of the Marquesses of Ripon. The hall was mysteriously burned down in 1946.

Fountains Hall was made part of the Studley Royal Estate in the 18th century. Barbara used it as Pennistone Royal in the Emma Harte novels. It is the one place in which Emma finds peace.

Edith Walker, Barbara's grandmother, an Edwardian through and through, with the fashionable hairstyle of the day, lace trimmings to her collar and cuffs, a diamond brooch blazing at her neck, and no small amount of determination in her hand-on-hip stance. But Edith's appearance belies her situation, a domestic servant who fell into the same trap as Emma Harte in *A Woman Of Substance* and gave birth to an illegitimate child. This was no one-night stand, however, her comfortable position suggesting a long-term lover of distinction. Two more children would follow, their birth certificates and pattern of their fortunes pointing the finger ever more obviously at the father.

The one clear favourite *(right)*: Frederick Oliver Robinson of Studley Royal, 2nd Marquess of Ripon, the estate to which Freda remembered Edith dragging her constantly when she was a child and to which Freda took Barbara repeatedly from as early as she can remember.

The Grubber, Ripon Union Workhouse, to which Edith and her children were reduced after the death of the First Marquess of Ripon, which left them destitute. Edith arrived first, in May 1910, three days before her children Freda and Fred, six and three years old respectively, and eleven days before three-month-old Mary was delivered to its doors. The stigma of being in the workhouse was burned into a child's very soul.

Adult Barbara became aware of their different personalities, once saying to me, 'My mother might have irritated you because she was very self-effacing, shy.' Knowing what it must have meant to have been fatherless, to have suffered the indignities of the workhouse and other terrible uncertainties from six years of age, to have lost all her brothers and sisters as a teenager, and then to have lost a son, I should have expected nothing from Freda, but I have a feeling I would not have left empty-handed. For, like Audra in *Act of Will*, Freda could say, 'There was a time in my life when I had absolutely nothing and no-one.' Yet she, a mother, had made something out of her nothing, and given it to her daughter.

Certainly, Freda was not the driving personality that people who feel they know Barbara might expect of her tutor in life, and yet Barbara herself knows she has achieved everything as a result of her mother. What went on between them went on below the line – no one else was a party to it. Their union ran very deep and was in a real sense a continuation of the best part of Freda's earlier experience.

However different, Freda and Barbara were one, and that was Freda's doing, her loss the vital ingredient in Barbara's success. When I said, 'She may have been shy, but she was also single-minded,' Barbara was already ahead of my thoughts: 'Single-minded about her daughter, about me . . . A sweet woman.'

'She was never going to be happy, though, was she?'

'My father used to say, "Freda, you cross your

bridge before you get to it. You are always worrying."
My mother was the biggest worrier.'

The thought flashed through my mind that Freda
had kept her past from Winston, that even the love of
Freda's life might not have known the depth of her
suffering. Later Barbara told me that she was sure
Winston didn't know. If so, one can only marvel at
the fortitude of a woman who could hold so much to
herself, and not be surprised that the effect of such
extreme repression should be felt in the obsessional
nature of her relationship with Barbara, which had
Freda telling her every day of her life how much she
loved her and that she was the 'most beautiful and
the cleverest and the most talented and the most
charming and the most wonderful person in the
world', and which was entered into at the expense of
her own marriage. Years later Freda confessed to her
daughter that she had sidelined Winston because, ' "I
couldn't have given you everything if I had had
another child. And *I wanted you to have everything* . . ." My mother was even glad I wasn't a boy
because she felt that a boy would go off with the
father, you know, but that I was hers. I am conscious
of her always saying to me, "I prayed for a girl and
my prayers came true, my prayers were answered."'

The loss of Freda's first child, a psychological catas-
trophe in the making for any mother, must surely have
finally triggered this extreme reaction. The boy who
contracted meningitis is called Adrian Alfred in *Act
Of Will*, Alfie for short, and everybody loves him. As
for his mother, 'she had never known such happiness

as this tiny person gave her.' Then one day the fever is upon him, delirium, coma, and he is gone. Billie asked Barbara whether Freda ever got over it. Barbara replied, 'Yes, I suppose she did. She didn't discuss it much.'

In the novel Audra suffers depression after Alfie's death, and this was probably the state in which Freda found herself leading up to Barbara's birth. Says Vincent: 'Audra was so odd, she was like a stranger to me.' His friend, Mike Lesley, concedes she is in a bad way, 'but a lot of women react as she did when they lose a child, especially when it's the first baby. They're demented for a while. And her loss was a terrible one, in that she's had so many other losses in her life already.'

Winston Taylor left the Navy on 16th July 1924, and married Freda five years later. He was working as a general labourer at the time. Barbara says that when they married, Freda ceased working, as was often the way, but she went back to work before Barbara was born in 1933, which is when we get the proud outburst from Vincent in the novel: 'No wife of mine is going out to work and that's that!' Freda went to work anyway, of course, because Winston, along with many others, had lost his job.

She was at work all Barbara's childhood. So what was life like as the child of a working mum? 'Lovely, because she was so special, and later when I was older I used to come home from school and always turned on all the gas rings, you know, [for] the pots and pans. And then she'd get home for tea, she was working in nursing ... and Daddy took me to my grandma's every day for lunch. Yes, he'd have lunch too, and try to get work. So I never felt deprived because my mother worked. Oh no, she taught me everything ...'

In selecting for her daughter's education every aristocratic seat and museum of antiques and *objets d'art* in the neighbourhood to which Barbara might aspire – from Ripley Castle to Middleham, from Temple Newsam to Harewood House, from Newby Hall to Norton Conyers, and in particular Studley Royal, where her own identity lay buried – Freda was of course holding up a mirror to the life of which Edith, and by extension Freda herself and Barbara, had been dispossessed. By earthing her daughter's adolescent emotions and natural ambition in values inherent in the literature and history of Yorkshire and fusing them in the landscape – noble values that would, in the end, characterise the novels – Freda also ensured a strong sense within Barbara of her own destiny.

Freda's focus may have seemed to be wholly an educational strategy – the trips to the theatre, the ballet, the reading of books – and at one level it was. But as important was her introduction of Barbara to fine things, beautiful and, above all, expensive artefacts, and to the aristocratic lifestyle that spoke of her loss. Manners were 'a very important part' of Freda's strategy – table manners and social etiquette. Though apparently there was little money being earned, Barbara's clothes, other than hats and coats and shoes, were all professionally handmade. This was most unusual in working-class Armley, as was calling her parents Mummy and Daddy rather than Mam and Dad. She was given shoe-trees as a child and hangers for her clothes, which she noticed others didn't have. All of it spoke of Freda's need to realise a purpose in the rubble of her childhood, to resurrect the dream that Edith had shared with her when she was a child.

In Daphne du Maurier's *Rebecca*, the ruined Manderley is the sepulchre of the unnamed heroine's dreams. They lie buried in the burned-out shell, and will remain so for ever. But in Freda's case there was a determination that *there should be a resurrection* ... She and her daughter would roll away the stone on her past, on Edith and what might have been. Freda's project was, as it turned out, a success, for Barbara went on to tell it as it might have been, and to live the life that Edith saw and so nearly attained, but which she lost to the damnation of her six children.

This is why Freda drew Barbara back to Ripon time and again. Appropriately, resurrection was the theme of Barbara's remembrance of it: 'Easter Sunday. My mother used to *love* to go to Ripon Cathedral on Easter Sunday and she used to take me there.' Good Friday was spent in Armley, and Barbara would busy herself with comforting food. 'Good Friday I always think of hot cross buns, at home with mother and father, for tea. I used to go and get them and I see this long-legged skinny little girl of ten running down

177

to the local baker my mother liked in Town Street.'
Then it was off to celebrate Easter, the Feast of the
Resurrection, in the very sepulchre of Edith's dreams
– Studley Royal: 'I loved to be outdoors all the time
and especially when we went to Ripon,' Barbara said.
'We (mother and I) would go for long walks picking
flowers in the hedgerows. We would especially go to
Studley Royal. But Studley Royal House burned down
during the war years, some accident ... it always
fascinated me.'

They would take picnics, home-made sandwiches,
and there is a 'Manderlay moment' in Chapter Two
of *Act of Will*, where Audra comes upon High Cleugh,
not unlike the way du Maurier's heroine comes upon
the house of her dreams in *Rebecca* – 'Last night I
dreamt I went to Manderlay again ...' Audra sits
down upon the grass and looks at High Cleugh from
a distance. The house 'appeared to slumber in the
brilliant sunshine as if it were not inhabited.'

A peacefulness lay over the motionless gardens.
Not a blade of grass, not a single leaf stirred ...
Audra's gaze became more intense than ever.
She saw beyond the exterior walls to the inner
core of the house. She closed her eyes, let herself
sink down into her imagination, remembering,
remembering ...

As in *Rebecca*, Barbara's heroine imagines herself
inside the house: 'She closed her eyes, let herself sink
down into her imagination, remembering, remember-

ing...' and there SHE is. Edith standing before her. Freda, as Audra, is a little girl again, mindful of...

> ... *her mother's laughter, the swish of her silk gown, as she joined her by the fire. The Beautiful Edith Kenton. That was how they always spoke of her hereabouts. Sapphires blazed at her throat, on her cool white arms. Blue fire against that translucent skin. Hair the colour of new pennies, an aureole of burnished copper light around the pale heart-shaped face. Warm and loving lips were pressed down to her young cheek. The smell of gardenias and Coty powder enveloped her. A slender, elegant hand took hold of hers, guided her out of the room ...*

This was Edith's style. Barbara was born to it, which is why she acquiesced in Freda's strategy so readily. In *Act of Will*, Gwen sees the hallmarks of it in Audra. This style – if not aristo blue blood itself – ran in Audra's veins, even if she (like Freda) can only avail herself of it in the limited environs of the little place she shares with Vincent:

> *'The place does you proud, lovey.'*
> *Audra beamed at her. 'Thanks, Gwen, and I am glad you like it. The room's small, of course, but that makes it cosy and comfortable, don't you think?'*
> *Gwen nodded, then let her eyes roam around.*

'And what did you say the name of this funny green on the wall is?'

Audra laughed. 'Eau-de-Nil.'

'What a strange name.' Gwen made a face.

'It means water of the Nile in French, and it's a very popular colour at the moment ... in fashion, I mean.'

'Oh is it. Fancy that. Well, you always did keep up with the latest trends in clothes, lovey, didn't you? I keep telling Mum that you're the expert on fashion and styles and fabrics and all that kind of thing. I hope you realise how much I value your advice. Yes, you've got the best taste of anybody I know.'

Gwen accepted the drink from Audra. 'Thanks, lovey,' she said. The two women clinked glasses and Audra stepped up to the fireside, sat down in one of the Chippendale-style chairs which had belonged to her mother. 'I'm glad you think so – that I have taste, I mean.'

The novelist Muriel Spark, who, like Barbara, creates characters 'dizzy with power', once said: 'You can't separate style from the person. You bring that package into the world with you.' Barbara's novels explore this as a theme. Time and again we see the mother figure nurture what is inherent in the daughter. For example, *To Be the Best*, the third novel in the Emma Harte series, asks how Paula's PA, Madelana O'Shea, a poor Irish-American Catholic girl from the South, has so many things in common with 'an aristocratic

Englishwoman, heiress to one of the world's great fortunes and a noted international business tycoon'. The answer is that she has been born with a certain inherited style, which amounts to a potential to succeed, but she has been beset by loss: 'her parents are dead, her brothers have been killed in Vietnam, her little sister died when she was four from complications following a tonsillectomy. Loss, loss, loss . . .' But then a new mother figure emerges, Sister Bronagh of the Sisters of Divine Providence at the Catholic hostel on West 24th Street in New York, where Madelana lives. The nun tells her that the courage was 'with you, already part of you then . . . If I did anything at all, it was to show you that it was there.' And Madelana is defining Freda's role in Barbara's life when she says to Sister Bronagh: 'Your belief in me has been so important . . . it has mirrored the belief my mother had in me. She encouraged me the way you have. I'll try never to let you down.'

Also significant in terms of Barbara's inherited style, it is the grandchild who inherits more completely than the daughter, as if the qualities actually skip a generation. In *A Woman of Substance* it is granddaughter Paula who inherits Emma Harte's style, and not Daisy, Emma's second illegitimate daughter and Paula's mother.

Edith's vanity and vivacious style seem to lie dormant in Freda (or have been knocked out of her), but are evident in her granddaughter, so that Freda plays nurse to what she sees and recognises in Barbara: 'My mother saw in me something she felt had to be cultivated.' And cultivate it she did – in effect nursing Edith's ambition in her with all the persistence that allied her, perhaps, to her natural father.

I once asked Barbara why she thought her mother took her to these historic houses with their things of expensive beauty. She said: 'She loved those places, she loved to see *furniture* – it was seeing beautiful things. She used to say to me, "Barbara, you must always use your eyes, you must always look."'

'She was saying this to you because she wanted you to be a writer, or to draw or to be a painter or – ?'

'No. She wanted me to *reach* . . .'

'Were any of your friends taken to these places?'

'Not with us.'

'No, but by their parents?'

'I doubt it. I don't think Margery was ever taken . . .'

'So this was most unusual for a girl from Armley or Ripon.'

'My mother exposed me to a lot of things. She would say to me, "I want you to have a better life than I've had."'

The style of the places to which Freda introduces her daughter *becomes* Barbara because the style is endemic, and what encouraged Freda, I believe, is that she saw other qualities in Barbara that were endemic, too, and would enable her daughter to succeed where Edith had not; qualities of persistence but also of self-discipline. 'I know a lot of talented people who fail because they don't have that kind of focus or determination or discipline . . .' said Barbara when discussing the legacy Freda gave her to excel. Freda knew that Barbara would have to work hard for success, but that the inclination to do so was also in her.

In another child, without the genetic inheritance that I believe Barbara had, Freda's ambitions, sourced as they were in the dysfunctional aspects of her childhood and in repression, would very probably have been revealed as fantasy and remained unfulfilled.

Confidence and stability came, too, from the very closeness of her relationship with her mother. 'When your mother tells you all the time that you are loved and that you are the best at everything you do, you gain tremendous self-confidence.'

The only child may be a spoiled child, and getting one hundred per cent of her mother's attention and approbation there was a danger of this for Barbara: 'I was very spoiled, I was a very adored child,' she freely admits, but her character was not weakened by Freda's strategy. On the contrary, on account of the educational and disciplinary aspects, it empowered her. It made her unstoppable.

The discipline told first in little things at home. 'I always made my own bed, was always taught to hang up clothes and put my clothes away ... and from when I was six or seven had my chores at the weekend. ... I had to help with the washing up, scraping the potatoes and taking the eyes out, and I was allowed to dust the sitting room as long as I was careful with her ornaments and things. I went on errands, went to the corner shop and things like that. And I used to scour the steps. I had to do a line around the steps. My most favourite thing was helping my mother to bake, weighing the fruit, and I always got a bit of dough which was filthy when it went into the oven and it came out terrible, as hard as a rock.'

Marking the edges of front steps of a house with a donkey stone (light brown chalk) is an ancient ritual dating back to Celtic times to ward off evil spirits, though in commentaries on the working-class North it is generally taken to be a token of respectability, hard fought for in the terraced streets of industrial England.

Later, sometimes as often as twice a week, Freda took her to the Picturedome: '. . . she wanted to go, and had no one to leave me with. I think I learned a lot from the movies. I know that I thought Nelson Eddy was the greatest thing since sliced bread – wonderful musicals.' Eddy had a hugely successful partnership in the 1930s with Jeanette MacDonald. By the mid-1940s there were more than fifty cinemas in Leeds, all changing their programmes twice a week. Barbara was 'absolutely blown away in the cinema, watching people like Cary Grant and Ginger Rogers and Fred Astaire,' admitting in 2003 on *Desert Island Discs*, 'I think I fell in love with glamour then, because it was a time when movie stars really were glamorous and elegant and beautiful, and where are they today?'

The programme's presenter, Sue Lawley, was on absolutely the right track when she followed up Barbara's comment by asking, 'Fell in love with it in the sense that you wanted to write about it, or that you wanted to *have it to yourself* . . . ?'

Barbara stopped in her tracks and said only, 'I'm not sure . . .'

Movie glamour was a contemporary extension of the aristocratic world to which Freda was introducing Barbara in the Yorkshire stately homes. It was presumably bound up, too, in the acting element of her theatrical education. Very quickly, moviedom was integrated into her image of self and that of people who mattered to her, especially the man in her life – well-groomed Winston Taylor – who may not have had an aristocratic drop of blood in him, but could *be* the part as well as his namesake, Robert Taylor – another of Barbara's movie heroes – and was the idealised measure against which all her boyfriends would be assessed:

His looks dazzled.

It was his colouring that was so sensational. The gleaming black hair and the black brows were in marked contrast to a light, creamy complexion and cheeks that held a tinge of pink like the bloom on a peach; he had cool green eyes, the colour of light, clear tourmalines, fringed with thick black lashes. His eyes and his skin were the envy of his sisters – and most other women.

Matched to the striking colouring and handsome profile was a superb athletic body. He was exactly five feet nine and a half inches tall, well muscled, firm and taut and without one ounce of fat or flab on him.

Immaculate at all times, Vincent considered

himself to be a bit of a dandy, loved clothes, wore
them with flair and elegance. He cut quite a swa-
the wherever he went, especially on the dance
floor, where his easy grace and good looks
showed to such advantage.

Act of Will

Barbara's love of movies took Freda's strategy on, modernising it, giving it roots in a world beyond the fantasy bubble her mother had created and within which they dwelt, by connecting it to popular culture. This became her period. In the late Fifties and Sixties she would avoid pop culture like the plague, and the Forties and early Fifties would remain her period for the rest of her life, because it fitted her style. It was a modern extension of Frederick's style, which Freda nursed in her and which was Barbara's identity long before her contemporaries had found theirs.

Other elements of popular culture of the period conspired to influence her self-image. In her early teens, Barbara read Kathleen Winsor's *Forever Amber*, in which heroine Amber St Clare is prepared to go to any lengths (lying, stealing, even whoring) to get what she wants. 'I remember that I could not put it down,' Barbara wrote in a foreword to the Penguin edition in 2000. 'In fact, I read it so quickly that I immediately reread it to be certain I hadn't missed anything important.' What transfixed Barbara when she read it as a teenager, besides the detail of Restoration England, was that Amber *reached* for what she wanted, as Freda encouraged Barbara to reach. 'As a teenager, I was determined to get ahead. There was no way I was going to end up slaving in some textile factory, married off and perpetually pregnant like so many Yorkshire girls of my generation.'

By this time the Taylors had left 38 Tower Lane, the bucolic sanctuary of Barbara's earliest years, and moved a quarter of a mile east to No. 5 Greenock Terrace – 'One sitting room and kitchen, two bedrooms upstairs and an attic,' said Barbara as we approached the house. 'I remember it very well.' Greenock Terrace is in the thick of the brick-built terraces where Alfred and Esther Taylor dwelt, a stroll away from Christ Church School and the church, and still a long way from the low end of Armley, the prison with Wortley Cemetery.

When we got there she was astonished that the house had only a few small steps leading up to the front door – how had donkey-stoning them so preoccupied her? The reality, a rundown terrace sadly unloved, disturbed comfortable memories and was dealt with instantly with the observation that at least No. 5 was well kept. It was the only one in the street that was. 'There was a fish-and-chip shop in the next street,' she said. 'My mother used to say, "Run around to the fish-and-chip shop." And next door lived another family called Taylor, and a girl called Barbara, no relation!'

I told her that when Graham Greene travelled the world, he was habitually met with the news at hotel receptions that another Graham Greene had just left, as if he were constantly one step behind his doppelgänger. The difference here was that Barbara was confronted by hers every day; she even attended the same school. 'They called her Barbara "Poppy" Taylor because she was born on Poppy Day. She had a disabled sister in a wheelchair, damaged at birth. She went to Thorsby Girls High School, I remember, got married and moved to some seaside place.

'Oh, but none of it looked like this, because everyone was so proud of their front steps and so on. I'm glad our house looks nice. It was a community then. I'll tell you something, we played in all these streets, and they all had window boxes and they were all pristine. I used to run down this way [via Ridge Road] to my church . . .'

A couple of years after the move, in 1945, Barbara left Christ Church School and enrolled at Northcote School on nearby Town Street, a private establishment independent of the State system. We find our way to the site, but look in vain. 'It *was* on Town Street and it was facing Keene's Dairy. What a memory I've got, Keene's Dairy! The school was an old house with a garden behind a wall, a high stone wall, a little like a manor house. There were trees. They must have knocked it down! Is that the Barley Corn? My father used to go there for a drink. These shops didn't look so garish then, they didn't have all the signs outside, they were very old-fashioned, you know. It was *all* more like a village then . . .'

The absence of the school building was soon forgotten in the search for another. Barbara attended Northcote for three years, between 1945 and 1948, following which she and her parents moved from Greenock Terrace to a house next door to the school, and Freda cooked meals for the teachers. So now we were looking for No. 148. 'This is the house! My mother used to take those lunches into the back door of the school. You see, a door opened from the school into our backyard. And it didn't look so shabby! Ours was all one house, and I think they have made it into two – 148 and 146. It was all one house, surely, or have they built one on? That was the front room and you entered there where it says 146. That was the sitting room and the dining room, with the kitchen at the back. There were three bedrooms upstairs. It was all brick, not all concreted over like this . . .'

Not brick but grey pebbledash confronted us. It seemed that from somewhere an apology was in order, but the scene did not bend to her will. Barbara was twelve in 1945. The decision to go to Northcote was all Freda's of course, but had not been taken easily. A private school meant fees, a uniform. When Barbara's grandmother, Esther Taylor, rebuked Freda for suggesting such a thing, telling her it would give Barbara 'big ideas', Freda had retorted: 'Nothing's too good for our Barbara.'

I asked her what the school brought to mind. 'We wore green gymslips, yes, a green gymslip with a white cotton blouse, a green tie with a yellow stripe, and a green coat; and in summer green dresses, cotton, green and white (I don't know, maybe it was striped) and panama hats, cream panama hats with ribbon – green with yellow – and we had green skirts and white cotton shirts, if we wanted with the tie. Oh, I remember things like the little plays, the parties, the church service and the present-exchange we used to have before Christmas when the senior classroom smelled like a perfumery from all the pot pourri and scented presents we used to give each other. Lots of people come up when I'm signing books in Leeds and say: "Hello love, you don't know who I am, do you, but we know who you are." And I'm looking at a woman who used to be at Northcote School with me.'

June Kettlelow sat next to Barbara at Northcote: 'Exelby was my name then. Barbara didn't live next door at that time, she lived at the Greenocks. We were the same age, her birthday was a week before mine. The school took children in from five, but the boys could only stay in the primary department, they left at eleven or something like that. We stayed until we left at fourteen or fifteen. It came in just at that point that you had to stay at school until you were fifteen. The morning was General Studies and then in the afternoon was typing and shorthand, and French. The headmistress was Mrs Harrison. Miss Smith taught the commercial subjects. Our form teacher was Mrs Cox. I didn't go until I was eleven, until I failed my eleven-plus. That's when I went. I think there were three classes from then on, probably fifteen or something in each class.'

Shirley Martin, another contemporary of Barbara's at Northcote, told me: 'It was a lovely little school, a very small prep school and commercial college, from five upwards. A particular friend of Barbara's, Alma

Franks, lived across the road. At eleven, if you were a boy you might go to West Leeds High School or somewhere like that. From eleven or twelve everybody mixed together, all ages. You weren't divided up into grades. You'd do General Studies in the morning and then in the afternoon you'd do commercial, short-hand, typing certificates. In those days it went up to fifteen. Barbara left at fifteen and so did I. You could go on after fifteen, but if by then you already had 100, 120 words a minute shorthand and typing, why bother?'

Shirley, who works for solicitors Irwin Mitchell in Leeds, also remembers the Taylors living next door to the school, because her family lived next door to them. She remembers in particular how proud Barbara's mother was of her. 'I remember our mothers talking in the garden, over the fence, and it sticks in my mind her mother always talking about "*our Barbara*". She was a lovely person, very, very friendly, and it was a lovely school. I cried my eyes out when I left. No shortage of jobs secretarial-wise, but you needed good qualifications.'

Barbara, however, had no intention of becoming a secretary, nor indeed would Freda have countenanced it. Barbara is adamant that Freda had only university in mind for her, and although I first saw that as a measure of the dangerous level of fantasy in Freda's plans for her daughter, there being no precedent for a child going to university from Northcote, changes in education at the time might well have suggested to her that it was within Barbara's reach.

Post-war, the concepts of a vocational training and academia were no longer mutually exclusive, and higher education for families who would not earlier have been able to afford it, or indeed have it in their sights, was becoming a reality.

The 1944 Education Act had made secondary education compulsory and available free to all, and there evolved three categories of secondary school. Alongside grammar schools came technical schools (including those biased to commerce – like Northcote – or art) and so-called secondary modern schools (for pupils who had failed the eleven-plus and did not elect to go to one of the technical schools).

The notion of schools with a commercial bias had arisen out of a London-based network of 'central schools' established as early as 1911. When these were transformed into technical schools in 1945, a number of recognised secondary schools (many girls' schools among them) followed suit, offering thirteen- to fifteen-year-olds a two-year course that included shorthand, typewriting, bookkeeping and commercial practice. Northcote was one of these, and although the practice never became widespread (and Northcote itself would not survive), Freda's opinion that Barbara might go on to university was perfectly feasible in this context of change, the chief consequences of which lay in a socio-economic spread of university applications, and a massive increase of state scholarships and local authority awards towards that end.

Alan Bennett benefited from the latter, as he writes in *Telling Tales* (2000). Acceptance by a university meant that 'a boy or girl was automatically awarded a scholarship by the city . . . My education – elementary school [Christ Church], secondary school [West Leeds High School], university [Exeter College, Oxford] – cost my parents nothing, their only sacrifice (which they didn't see as a sacrifice) that by staying on at school beyond sixteen, I'm not bringing in a wage.'

Between 1900 and 1909, six new universities – Birmingham, Liverpool, Manchester, Sheffield, Bristol and Leeds – had been created. Three of them, including Leeds, had come out of science colleges, where training for jobs was uppermost. As early as 1900 Joseph Chamberlain inserted into the charter of Birmingham University (created in that year) a faculty of commerce, and now Leeds, Manchester, Durham, London, Bristol and Southampton had followed suit.

As it happened, none of this would matter to Barbara, who had journalism, not university, on her mind, as indeed did another youngster living elsewhere in Leeds – Keith Waterhouse – with whom she would shortly be meeting. Waterhouse was born in 1929, four years before Barbara, and still writes his award-winning column for the *Daily Mail* today. His first considerable literary success came with *Billy Liar* (1959), a loosely autobiographical novel about a North Country undertaker's clerk who lives in a world of fantasy in preference to bleak reality. In collaboration with his friend Willis Hall, who also grew up in Leeds, Waterhouse made it into a play starring Albert Finney, and then a film starring Tom Courtenay and Julie Christie. The work reached far beyond the industrial North that spawned it, but no doubt found many sympathetic northern ears for the very reason that Billy himself, and others who suffered the traumas of a northern childhood, needed the fantasy element just to survive.

Like Freda Walker's, Waterhouse's family had fallen into the hands of the Board of Workhouse Guardians when he was a young boy. His father, a costermonger, died penniless after borrowing money to start a business and spending it instead on drink and the horses. The bailiffs stripped the family home of furniture, and his mother was reduced to hiding her prized possessions – a pair of fairground vases and a harp zither – from the means-test man in the coal-hole and airing cupboard. Later, the family was moved to a council estate on Halton Moor, not far from Temple Newsam. In *City Lights* (1994), Waterhouse tells us that he, like Billy, did work for an undertaker's – J. T. Buckton & Sons of Leeds – 'whose motto was "We never sleep", to which the sniggering rejoinder from everyone who heard it was, "Maybe not, but the customers do."'

He'd seen the job listed at the College of Commerce in Woodhouse Lane, Leeds, which he attended after failing the entrance exam to Cockburn High School, 'Leeds's answer to the grammar school on the other side of the tracks,' he calls it. The school ran courses like those that Barbara was studying at Northcote. The shorthand and typing would serve Waterhouse well in journalism, but he excelled in particular at commerce, because it was taught by making use of real-life, Leeds-based example: 'We were talking about the actual arrival of actual bales of wool on actual barges on the River Aire and the Leeds and Liverpool Canal, and their progress through the named mills of Leeds, such as the Perseverance or the Albion, to the named clothing factories of Leeds, like John Barran's, who invented the ready-made tailoring industry, or Montague Burton, the Tailor of Taste, to known retail outlets like Marks & Spencer, who had got their start in Kirkgate Market, or the Mutual Clothing company.'

Barbara will have learned all this too at Northcote, and readers of *A Woman of Substance* will appreciate how she put to good use her knowledge of the clothing industry in Leeds and the great Leeds landmarks of the industrial era (such as the multi-national retailer Marks & Spencer, which began here as a penny bazaar), and also how the entrepreneurial spirit of the times tied in with her burgeoning desire to get on in the world on her own account and not as a slave 'in some textile factory', a desire she made plain in the character of Emma Harte and in the character of Leeds, as she saw it:

Leeds was then, and still is, a lusty and vital city, and the streets on this busy Friday were, as usual, crowded with people rushing about their business. Tram-cars rumbled out from the Corn Exchange to all parts of the town and outlying districts. Fine carriages with prancing horses carried elegant ladies and gentlemen of distinction to their destinations. Prosperity, that sense of self-help and independence, nonconformity, hardheaded Yorkshire shrewdness and industriousness, were endemic, were communicated most vibrantly to Emma, so that she was instantly infected. And the rhythm and power of the city only served to consolidate and buttress these very same characteristics so intrinsic in her, for with her energy, tenacity, and zest, her obstinate will and driving ambition, she was, without knowing it, the very embodiment of Leeds. This was undoubtedly the place for her. She had always felt that to be true and now she was absolutely convinced.

She made her way decisively to Leeds Market in Kirkgate, an enormous, sprawling covered hall composed of an incredible conglomeration of stalls selling all manner of merchandise imaginable — pots and pans, kitchen utensils, china, fabrics, clothes, foodstuffs to be bought and taken home or eaten there, including jellied eels, meat pies, mussels, cockles, cartloads of fruit, fancy cakes and toffee apples. She stopped at the Marks and Spencer Penny Bazaar, her attention riveted on the sign: Don't ask the price, it's a penny! Her eyes roved over the goods on display, so easy to view, open to inspection, so well organised in categories and so cheaply priced. She tucked the information at the back of her mind, her eyes keenly thoughtful. The idea of this Penny Bazaar is simple, yet it is exceedingly clever, she said *to herself. Emma lingered for a moment longer, inspecting the goods, which included almost everything from wax candles and cleaning products to toys, stationery, and haberdashery, and then, still reflecting about the bazaar, she moved on. It was well turned two o'clock and she was conscious of a growing hunger gnawing at her. She bought a plate of winkles and mussels from the fishman's stall, lavished them with vinegar and pepper, ate them with her fingers, dried her hands on her handkerchief, and set out for North Street, where the tailoring shops were located . . .*

A Woman of Substance

'Mummy and I used to go to Leeds market, the famous covered market burgeoning with fruits and flowers, cockles and mussels, on Saturday mornings,' Barbara told me. 'We used to go on the tram from Armley. I would buy daffodils and narcissus. It's near the Corn Exchange, the tram took us right there. A great treat for me was to go to the shellfish stall. Mussels, winkles, oysters and all sorts of shellfish like that with vinegar. Pickled vinegar. The first Mr Marks [of Marks & Spencer] was a pedlar and he peddled his goods on a cart and then he had a stall in Leeds market, which had the sign: "Don't ask the price it's a penny". So I had Emma go into that market.'

In *A Woman of Substance* we learn that Michael Marks was a Jewish immigrant, who came to Leeds from Poland. The idea of the M&S Penny Bazaars spreading from Leeds market all over the city and to other cities, making it a national chain, sets Emma's ambition alight.

There is a popular misconception, which fills readers' letters to Barbara, that Emma's flagship store in *A Woman of Substance* is modelled on Harrods in London. 'It is most definitely not,' stresses Barbara. 'I borrowed the building, but not the family story . . . But we did film two books there, *A Woman of Substance* and *Hold the Dream*.'

The description that links Emma's store to Harrods in people's minds comes relatively early in the novel and concerns the food halls: 'To Emma, the food halls would always be the nucleus of the store, for in essence they had been the beginning of it all . . .' Anyone who has been to Harrods Food Hall will likely conjure up an image of it as they read on.

However, anyone who knew Kirkgate Market in Leeds as Barbara and Keith Waterhouse did, will prefer to bring the food halls in Emma's store to ground there. Waterhouse's father, Ernest, sold fruit, vegetables and unskinned rabbits from a horse and cart, so Keith knew this massive Victorian market well, and worked out early on that it was laid out in the form of rows or avenues, each with its own speciality. 'On one row,' he writes in *City Lights*, 'I could find the crumbly Cheshire [cheese] that my mother always bought . . . On another would be hams swinging from brass rails and stuck with cloves like mapping pins; and below them white enamel trays piled high with chitterlings, polonies, Yorkshire ducks, stand pies, Aintree pies, whist pies, pork sausages, black pudding, white pudding, boiled ham, tongue, corned beef, sliced roast beef, salt beef, brawn, pigs' trotters – the same robust fare, in short, as could be found in any of the dozens of pork shops dotted around the city, which then as now could rival any Soho delicatessen or even Harrods Food Hall itself.'

Interesting, because it is Emma's fascination for the charcuterie department that brings her back to Leeds and the very roots of her ambition: 'When she came to the charcuterie department, a sudden mental image of her first shop in Leeds flitted before her, at once stark and realistic in every detail. It was so compelling it brought her to a standstill.'

Waterhouse claims that his desire to become a journalist, which he rehearsed in a paper of his own making as a very young boy, was moved by an image of himself as Edgar Wallace, the writer of such thrillers as *The Four Just Men* (1905), *The Crimson Circle* (1922) and *The Green Archer* (1923). Wallace was a journalist through and through, beginning his working life on Fleet Street (until the late 1980s the nucleus of British journalism) at the age of eleven, selling newspapers at Ludgate Circus. Waterhouse maintains that he was only three years old when he saw the picture of Wallace that so influenced his future. It showed his hero 'wearing the peaked cap of a Reuters' war correspondent when covering the Boer War.'

Barbara was also determined to be a journalist and had in her mind's eye a strong journalistic image to which she aspired: 'At different times, depending on what movie I'd seen with Mummy at the Picturedome,

I thought I was Rosalind Russell in *Front Page* or Jimmy Stewart in *Call NorthSide 777*, which was a newspaper story. I wanted to be a foreign correspondent or maybe a crime reporter.'

Freda, who so wanted her glittering prize to go to university, knew she had lost Barbara to journalism when she turned up wearing what looked like a brand-new raincoat that had been dragged around the back garden in an effort to confer on her something of the status of dogged reporter.

Being a journalist was not her principal ambition, however, more a means to an end. 'What I wanted to do was write books. I remember saying to my mother – whatever the words were – I want to write novels, I want to write books, I want to write stories when I grow up; and she smiled. And that was after I sold my first short story when I was ten to a children's magazine. I don't think I meant to sell it to them. Mummy sent the story in and they bought it. They paid me seven shillings and sixpence. I bought Daddy some handkerchiefs and Mummy a green vase, and put the rest in my moneybox.

'Daddy was always saying to me, "When I'm rich I'm going to buy you a pony." I don't know why he said it. I didn't want a pony actually, but he was always saying it. Anyway, he was never rich, so I never got the pony. But I wrote the story about a little girl who does get a pony. It was only about three or four pages, and three months later we got a letter and a postal order for seven and six. I said to my mother, I don't care about the money, I want to see my name there. So there was obviously that ambition and ego about writing already in me, wasn't there? I think my destiny was sealed that day. I said to my mother, "I'm going to write books one day." And she said, "Oh, that'll be nice." And then she said something to me that has always remained in my mind. She said, "You have to live life a little before you can write about it." She was right. Where better than in the reporters' room of a newspaper to do that? So the next best thing to writing novels, in my mind, was to become a journalist.'

Barbara loved reading, writing and telling stories – 'I was a big library girl. I had three library cards at one point' – and she had been writing them since she was seven: 'I always told stories – to my mother, to my doll – and wrote a lot of stories and poems and things, which my mother kept and I now have in New York, all yellowed with time.' Then, when she was twelve, her father bought her a second-hand type-writer. 'Now I wrote all sorts of stories and put them in a folder and stitched the folder so that they were held together firmly, then hand-painted the name of whatever book it was. I say "book", I mean just a dozen pages typed very badly.'

Soon, 'from about thirteen to fifteen I was taking books on journalism and on Fleet Street out of the library.' Barbara began writing little bits and pieces for the *Armley & Wortley News*, one of a group of newspapers within the Leeds Guardian Series, which also included the *North Leeds News* and the *Leeds Guardian* itself.

The *Armley & Wortley News* was published south of the river. The editors seem to have taken a leaf out of Fagin's book, encouraging gangs of city kids – budding reporters all of them – to deliver news on a daily basis, often for free. The papers were at a lower level than the three main Leeds papers, the *Yorkshire Post*, the *Yorkshire Evening Post* and the *Yorkshire Evening News*, and, not unlike the freebie papers of today, ran on a shoestring. On the *Leeds Guardian* the editor was also the compositor, wearing an apron and lining the characters up on the hot metal printing machine, as well as being the main reporter, advertising executive and sub. This was the paper for which Waterhouse reported as a lad, after he heard that someone else at his college was doing it. Eventually he was offered a regular job for the princely sum of ten shillings a week. Unfortunately, his mother needed him to earn more, so he took that job in the funeral parlour instead.

These editors were willing to consider for publication any items that their reporters might bring in. Waterhouse's editor gave him some good advice – 'Remember that names make news.' When Barbara went to see the editor of the *Armley & Wortley News*, he was non-committal but encouraging to the fourteen-year-old. 'I said, "Can I do some local stories?" and he said, "Well you can, love, but I don't know if I'll use them."' It was enough. Barbara's uncle and aunt, Don and Jean Taylor, remembered taking her to a fair in Armley one time, and her running up to them to ask for change to make a telephone call. She had just witnessed a crash on one of the rides and wanted to file her story to the *Armley & Wortley News*.

Then one day at Northcote, her typing and short-hand teacher, Dorothy Smith, told her that she could get her an interview with the *Yorkshire Evening Post*. 'She knew the woman from the typist pool.' Barbara went home and told Freda that she had an interview on the *Post*, but not what job it was for. This was 1948, and Barbara was fifteen. Her mother still had it firmly fixed in her mind that she would get her daughter to university, but this was an interview with the respected *Yorkshire Evening Post* and Barbara played her cards tight to her chest. 'So it was sort of like, "Well if I don't like it – let me go and see if I like it." You know, she wanted to go to the interview *with me*! I said, "You can't! My mother cannot go with me to a job interview!"

'And then of course I got the job. I came back and she said, "I can't believe they've given a fifteen-and-a-half-year-old a job in the reporters' room." I said, "Oh, Mummy, it's in the typist pool." Well that did it, she was furious! To cut a long story short, I don't remember any rows about it. I remember long discussions and me pleading, and me finally convincing her to let me at least try the job. If I didn't like it, if it wasn't working out, I promised that I'd go back to Northcote and then go to Leeds University.'

Freda was not happy. Barbara had begun to place her own hand on the tiller of her fortune. With her love of glamour reflected in her passion for

Hollywood movies she had given her mother's 'educational programme' a contemporary twist which may have seemed frivolous to Freda and possibly even reminded her of the pitfalls of her own mother's ambition. Her insistence on Barbara taking the contrary, academic route should be seen in that context of concern. Also, within the immediate family, Barbara's new outlook seemed to be associated not at all with Freda, but with Winston, and the way he looked and dressed and organised his priorities. Barbara was already beginning to operate outside the bubble Freda had made for them.

Barbara's awareness, whether conscious or not, of this subtle movement of relationships and ideas within the family, and her mother's feelings about it, can be seen in the central issue of the relationship between their fictional counterparts in *Act of Will*, where Audra's deep desire is not university but that her daughter Christina, who is a talented artist, realises her God-given gift. When Christina takes the commercial option, starting a fashion business instead, Audra accuses her of compromising her 'gift for creating beauty', and unfairly reminds Christina of the sacrifices she has made for her, while Vincent tells her, 'You've just broken your mother's heart.'

The interview must have caused quite a stir at school because June Exelby remembers it to this day. 'I remember her going for this interview to the *Yorkshire Evening Post* and Mrs Cox saying, "You make sure you take the job in the typing pool, because once you are in, you are in."'

Mrs Cox was right, but it really didn't matter what anyone said about taking or not taking the job. Barbara was showing that at fifteen she could handle herself, she was able to determine the best strategy to get what she wanted, in particular steering clear of confrontation at home. 'I talked my mother into it; I talked them both into it. There weren't rows because I was a little scared of my father; I would never argue with my father because he was very strong-willed.'

Barbara had decided she was going to work on the paper, she was confident that she would soon rise out of the typing pool. More significantly, she had shown that once her mind was made up, nothing and no one could stop her.

CHAPTER TWO

Getting On

> '*And where's all this scribbling going to get yer?*'
>   '*On to a newspaper . . . Maybe even the* York-
> shire Morning Gazette *. . . Stick that in yer pipe
> and smoke it, Emma Harte.*'
>
>   A Woman of Substance

Barbara's job on the *Yorkshire Evening Post* took her
daily into the centre of Leeds, to Albion Street, the
then site of the newspaper group the Yorkshire Conservative Newspaper Company. Later, the entirely
fictitious Yorkshire Consolidated Newspaper Group
would figure in Emma Harte's empire, but in the real
world, the editor of the *Yorkshire Evening Post* was
one Barry Horniblow, his name almost ridiculously
apt in the context of a tabloid revolution to which he
lent no small endeavour. 'He had come up from Fleet
Street,' Barbara recalls. 'The *Yorkshire Evening Post*
in those days was a broadsheet and he turned it into
a tabloid like the London *Evening Standard*.'

Top newspaperman Arthur Brittenden recalls
Horniblow as 'the whiz kid who had come from

London. Horniblow was going to come and set the place alight and I suspect he got bogged down by Yorkshire conservatism. He was succeeded by Alan Woodward [an in-house alternative: Woodward was the news editor when Barbara arrived]. But the paper had an amazing circulation. It made all the money that kept the more prestigious morning paper, the *Yorkshire Post*, afloat.'

Keith Waterhouse, a reporter on the *Evening Post* when Barbara arrived, describes Horniblow as looking like 'an unusually bright bank manager', but notes that he was also one for giving youngsters a chance. The conservative daub might well owe something to his mode of dress, which demonstrated an attention to appearance applauded, as ever, by Barbara: 'They didn't like him because he was Savile Row from top to bottom,' she told me. 'Obviously if he was in the newsroom he was in shirtsleeves, but his clothes were impeccable, while the others were tough newspapermen from the North with their sleeves rolled up. Barry was white-haired, well-dressed, always impeccably dressed.'

As typist on the *YEP*, Barbara worked mainly for the advertising and circulation departments and was expected to take dictation. Her first day was a disaster, 'something I would never care to live through again. Not only could I not type the letters because I was so nervous but I couldn't even read my shorthand back. Fortunately, all were standard letters for the advertising department, so the other girls helped me. However, I was still typing away at seven o'clock and everybody had gone home and finally, after the tenth time on the last letter, I sighed with relief. Then, as I was leaving I saw the wastepaper basket full of very expensive notepaper engraved with the Yorkshire Conservative Newspaper Company – never mind printed, it was engraved! And I thought, I'm going to get fired for wasting all their stationery. So, I took a handful, went into the ladies' room, put a match to it and threw it down the toilet. Well, the blaze was so enormous I didn't know how to put it out. I kept flushing the toilet, and finally I put the blaze out. I then thought, well, I might get fired for wasting their stationery, but that's better than getting fired for being an arsonist. So I took the rest of the paper, smoothed it out and made what was a full wastepaper basket seem much less, before hiding the rest in the bottom drawer of my desk! I went to that drawer every night of the week, transferring paper from it into one of my mother's shopping bags, and brought it home and burned it.

'I hated that job, loathed it. I wanted to leave, I really did, in spite of my ambition. But I couldn't because I had this paper there in the desk. I thought they'd come and get me. What they'd do to me I couldn't imagine. I was very young and naive . . .'

In time, as the whirlwind in the typist pool began to settle, Barbara turned her mind to developing a strategy that would make her a journalist as soon as possible. Part of the week every girl in the typing pool had to spend time in the copy room, sitting in a little booth with a typewriter and headphones, taking down copy phoned in by *YEP* reporters. 'Suddenly, the telephone would ring,' said Barbara, 'and the telephonist would say it was Keith Waterhouse, or whoever – Keith had brilliant red hair, very unruly – and I would type his dictation. You sat there typing as he dictated. You just put Keith Waterhouse at the top and when he'd finished he'd say goodbye and you'd take off your headphones and go into the newsroom and drop the article on the sub-editors' table, which thrilled me because it meant that I got to see the reporters sitting nearby.'

One day, Barbara realised that there was nothing to stop her feeding her own stories through the sub-editors in the same way. 'So I came to write my stories, used the same paper, put my name at the top – Barbara Taylor – and dropped it down on the sub-editors' table. And they ran three or four, and when it came to payday the question went up as to the identity of the writer of these stories and where to send payment. The Accounts Department said, "Barbara Taylor. Is she a stringer that we have in Doncaster or Harrogate or somewhere?" Suddenly, the penny dropped and they realised that I was the new girl in the typing pool. And so it all came out, and the editor was intrigued by this girl whom nobody knew, and he sent for me. This was when I first met Barry Horniblow.

'He said to me, "So, you want to be a journalist?" I replied, "Oh, yes sir, but I don't just *want* to be, I am *going* to be." This amused him. This was a man from Fleet Street and he liked that in me. I was about sixteen. Fools rush in where angels fear to tread . . .

I was so nervous I worked my toe into the carpet and lost my shoe, and had to ask whether I could retrieve it from under his desk. He said, "What have you written?" and I told him I had written for local newspapers and all of that. He said, "Oh, some time bring me your cuttings book." Then I said, "Thank you very much, sir," and off I went.

'Then, at lunch time, I ran all the way to City Square, took a tram home to get my clippings book, dashed into the house and my mother said something like, "Oh, good, you've been sacked!" She didn't want me on this paper, she wanted me at Leeds University. Panting, I got the clippings book, took it back and went to his office. Mr Horniblow, who could see I was out of breath, said, "Barbara what is it?" and I told him what I'd done. He was intrigued, and that was the beginning of my journalism career.'

The editor made her assistant to his secretary, and within six months she was a reporter, graduating to women's-page assistant and then women's-page editor at eighteen. She was barely a woman herself, but she wrote the lot anyway: cooking, fashion, personalities. Two years later, 'Fleet Street beckoned!' as Barbara put it.

So meteoric a rise would not have been possible without a large dose of journalistic skill, which she crafted painstakingly with the help of Keith Waterhouse, as well as a personality to carry it off. Also, as we shall see, her rise coincided with an unprecedented media interest in women as a consumer force, in their attitudes and opinions, and by women's own interest in the kind of thing she was writing. It was a mixture of talent, style and publishing environment, which would set her fair into the third millennium and not only in journalism. Immediately, what was most striking to those around her was Barbara's style, the way she carried herself off.

Arthur Brittenden, nine years older, was working for the *Yorkshire Post*, same building, same group of newspapers, when in 1948 the fifteen-year-old Barbara appeared on the scene. Brittenden would rise to become editor of the *Daily Mail* (1966–71), then director of Times Newspapers and later director of Murdoch's News International. He has seen her only once since she left Leeds for London, but managed a crystal-clear recall of the winning spark in her. 'She was very winning, very appealing. I think people who are going to get on tend to show it at some time along the way, and she most certainly did. When she was there in 1948 and '49, I was on the *Yorkshire Post* – it was the prestigious morning paper of the group until it lost some of its character when it absorbed the *Leeds Mercury* [the paper, incidentally, on which Emma Harte gets her brother Frank a job in *A Woman of Substance*]. Barbara was a secretary then. We had these "moments", which I still remember nearly fifty years on, when we came upon each other in the canteen . . . very romantic. That was how I first remember her. We used to sit at a table having a cup of tea, but there was always something *different* about her. Of course, she was very attractive. Unbelievable. But she had this something different about her and it was very appealing. I suppose, looking back, she must have been – I mean one reads about how ambitious she was and so on, but there was never anything aggressive or unpleasant or whatever about her. It was always terribly likeable. I think we were *all* in love with her probably.

'One other encounter stays with me – actually the last time I saw her. I was on the *News Chronicle* in Fleet Street. She had only recently come to London, and I remember coming down in the lift one day and going through the front hall, and there she was, sitting for some reason in the front hall with another girl. Why on earth would I remember with such clarity walking through the front hall of the *News Chronicle* fifty years ago and seeing Barbara there? But this was the thing about her, that you *did* remember. There was something always special about it – electric!'

I asked Leeds-based Bobby Caplin, a friend of Barbara since 1949, to describe her as she had been when they first met. 'She was a beautiful girl, absolutely *beautiful*. If you can imagine Barbara at sixteen years of age, a size eight or ten, slim, long hair –'

'Dangerous lady?' I teased.

'Very, very,' Bobby laughed. 'She was at the *Yorkshire Evening Post*, ended up on the women's page. In Leeds in those days there was a meeting for coffee on a Saturday morning at Marshall and Snelgrove, one of the top Leeds stores, a miniature Leeds Harrods in those days. There was also a lovely bar called Powolny's, a college bar in the centre, and we all met in there.

'Barbara had ambition, nothing wrong, but she had a good time, Barbara did. She was always very ambitious and she liked the nice things in life, as we all did, and she went out and got them. She never hurt anybody intentionally. I say that because at that age we are young, we want the nice things.

'But in those days it was a different life. The places weren't there to go to in Leeds, and we didn't have the money either. There was the odd coffee bar, but it was a different era. I mean, the trams were still running and I can remember when the cinemas were allowed to open for the first time on a Sunday evening, but had to close at nine thirty. So there wasn't much social life; well, there was a social life but it was in people's homes rather than going out.'

'She'd have been very popular with the boys, then?'

'Very. She was very, very attractive and she's always demanded the best. Even at that age. She went out with a very close friend of mine, came from a wealthy family, very good-looking, born with two golden spoons in his mouth, lovely guy, that was the sort of guy she went out with. Ronnie [Sumrie] is two years older than me. At seventeen these girls didn't want to go out with an eighteen-year-old, they wanted to go out with at least a twenty- or twenty-one-year-old. I mean we didn't have cars in those days, but Ronnie had a car, and he was a catch. He was known as one of the top catches in Leeds. And he took Barbara out, but then she moved, went to live in London.'

Barbara would need all of her feminine wiles to establish her position in the male-dominated *YEP* offices, especially after whiz-kid newcomer Horniblow backed her. 'After he'd seen the stories in my clippings book, he promised to get me shifted [out of the typing pool], and when he didn't, every time I saw him in a corridor I said, "It's Barbara, when will you move me?" So, one day I was told that I was going to be a part-time secretary. I was to help his secretary, Marion Greaves, and she hated my guts. An older woman, she resented me, she didn't want me there. I used to help out in the mornings. I had to be there in the morning and I had to be there when she took her lunch. The minute she'd gone to lunch Mr Horniblow would come out and say, "Everything all right?" and I'd say, "Oh yes."'

But in fact Miss Greaves was only giving Barbara letters to type, when the editor had wanted her to get experience on the women's page, known as the Kay Boughton page. Why it was so named has been lost to time. As Barbara explained, 'There was no such person. It was a name, and the secretary, Miss Greaves, did it. It was really only a column. After probably about a month or two, he [Horniblow] said, "You're not getting any experience, are you, Barbara?" And I said, "No, I'm not." And he said, "Well things are going to change." I would say I'd been on the paper eight or nine months when he said one day, "Instead of coming here to work and help Miss Greaves, I'm going to have you in the reporters' room. I think you'll get some better training there."

So, suddenly I was in the reporters' room, and one or two people were a bit suspicious . . .

'Edgar Craven was the chief sub-editor then, and they [the subs and reporters] thought Barry Horniblow was fancy pants. So, when he took this young girl under his wing, can you imagine? It never occurred to me at the time, but looking back I realise they had suspicions about him. They must have had. No? Wouldn't you think?'

'Were you having an affair with him?' I asked.

'No I wasn't. I know enough to know myself, I was not silly like that and he was a much older man. It was like a professor that you would adore. He was enchanted by my attitude. More than thinking it was sexual, they [in the newsroom] thought I was his spy. I know that because I've laughed about it with Keith. Barry loved young people, he was very focused on Keith so he put me with him – his desk butted up to mine, that's how they were arranged. So Keith was always helping me with my copy. He taught me to write for newspapers . . . Working on a newspaper at the age of sixteen and not a little village newspaper . . . a major, tough, provincial newspaper, a daily, being in that newsroom with a lot of newspapermen on the police beat, at court, inquest court, as a junior reporter. It was a great experience.

'Stanley Vaughan was the crime reporter, he used to drag me with him. I tagged on behind him – he spoke with an American accent and never took his hat off. I grew up in that newsroom. The nature of the work gives you exposure to life, sometimes life in the raw. Also, one has to have the human element in a news story. You can't just write about the landscape or a room setting in a novel and not have it peopled with real people. I became conscious of the human element in stories when I was a newspaper reporter because that's what it's about, isn't it? A newspaper story is only interesting if it's about people, their tragedies, their dramas, their heartbreak – that's what I'm dealing with [in the novels]. I'm dealing in human emotion and, according to my French publisher, I am able to put it down on paper in such a way that I touch a nerve in the reader.'

The newsroom was L-shaped. To the right of the door was the long side of the 'L', a long table big enough to seat around six sub-editors: 'waistcoated or cardiganned figures, alternately red-faced or sallow-complexioned, pot-bellied or concave-chested according to whether they drank Guinness for strength or milk for their ulcers; but all of them chain-smoking . . .' as Waterhouse described them. Opposite the door sat the news editor, and beyond were the face-to-face desks of the reporters. The passage of copy was from reporter to deputy news or news editor, who having read and passed it would shout, 'Boy!', bringing the copy boy over to take it to the subs' table, who would prepare the copy for press.

'I was very much in love with newspapers,' says Barbara, 'and being a newspaperwoman, a newspaperman I should say, even down to wanting a dirty trench coat, which indeed I got. My mother accused me of having taken it off in the garden and rolling it around in the dirt to make it look used, but I didn't, it just got dirty.' The raincoat episode appears in another guise in her novel *The Women in His Life*, where Teddy shouts to her young charge Maxim, 'Don't trail your new raincoat on the ground!' as he is saying his sad goodbyes to the most important woman in his life.

Waterhouse recalled Barbara as 'an ambitious sixteen-year-old . . . apt to burst into tears from time to time when bawled out for not yet knowing her job to perfection, and I became her hand-holder-in-chief. Little did she know that it was a case of the blinded-by-tears leading the blinded-by-tears.'

'Keith was very sweet to me,' Barbara says. 'We'd go to the Kardomah Café and have beans on toast. I remember he told me not to cry in the newsroom, to cry in the ladies' room instead.'

Being slapped down by Ken Lemmon, deputy news and later news editor, would have been a new experience for Barbara, perhaps a salutary one, and the tears that flowed, which Waterhouse mopped up with such care and attention that it won him Barbara's hand at a Press Ball at Leeds Town Hall 'in a dinner jacket hired from Rawcliffe's where my mother had bought my school cap', might have damaged a less purposeful girl. There is a clear line between self-belief and delusion, and Barbara kept herself on the right side of it by sheer hard work, determination and discipline. She often stayed late in the office because she liked to get her desk cleaned up. And later, if she went for a drink with the others at one of the pubs favoured by

THE WOMAN OF SUBSTANCE

the *YEP* reporters – the Pack Horse, say, or Whitelock's – she showed her self-discipline by not staying long. 'Frank Shire, deputy news editor at the time, said: "You're smart, Barbara, you stay for one drink and then you leave." I'd have a drink, buy them a round and then go.'

Other characters among the *YEP* journalists included 'whimsical' Con Gordon, the feature writer, and the leader writer, Percy, 'who kept a cottage piano in his office which he would play for inspiration in his ceaseless fight against the Attlee government,' according to Waterhouse. Idly I mention to Barbara that Waterhouse is a socialist – odd then that he worked for the Yorkshire Conservative Newspaper Company and writes now for the *Daily Mail*, also a right-wing paper. 'Yes,' said Barbara, 'and do you know what he sang walking through the Yorkshire Conservative Newspaper Company? "The Red Flag"! He did all these crazy things. He walked once from Land's End to John O'Groats for a story. And on the other evening paper – the *Evening News* – was Willis Hall [Waterhouse's collaborator on *Billy Liar*, and most famous perhaps for his play *The Long and the Short and the Tall* (1958)]. And do you know who else was on the *News*? Peter O'Toole! I didn't know him well. Keith says I did and that I don't recognise him because he had acne in those days and didn't look so good, and that this big movie star, this gorgeous hunk with blond hair and bright blue eyes used to say, "D'you want to come t'pictures, Barbara?" in his Yorkshire accent, but that now he's very posh and he

218

speaks like *this* . . . and he's Lawrence of Arabia. Keith used to say all these terrible things to me when *Lawrence of Arabia* came out. He'd say, "Oh, you really blew it when he wanted to take you t'pictures." By then we were both in Fleet Street, [and we] went to a party given by Sam Spiegel for *Lawrence of Arabia* and met Omar Sharif . . . but I don't remember Peter well, though I do remember there was a sort of pimply youth that used to hang around. It may have been Peter O'Toole.'

The Leeds newspaper scene does indeed have an extraordinary history of turning out famous people. Former *YEP* trainee Nick Clarke of BBC's *World at One* recalls a colleague being bawled out for poor timekeeping. 'The editor warned him: "You idle bugger – you turn up on time or one day you will have to make music for your living."' He couldn't have been more prescient: the poor timekeeper was Mark Knopfler, who would found multi-million-pound rock group Dire Straits.

At seventeen or eighteen, Barbara's social life tended to revolve around the friends she met regularly on a Saturday morning at Marshall and Snelgrove on Commercial Street: 'You could go through the circulation department, and there it was across the street. I would go across at 11.30 a.m. when I took my lunch hour. I'd meet Bobby Caplin and Ronnie Sumrie and various girlfriends. I didn't think of these boys as Jewish.' But they were among the second-generation Jewish clothiers who now ran Leeds industry. Many of the families had fled west out of Russia and Poland to escape persecution and stayed rather than continuing on to America, their original destination. It was a father–to-son inheritance.

Today, Barbara's readers will recognise this strain in her fictional account of the Kallinskis, a family of Russian Jews from Kiev. In *A Woman of Substance*, Emma rescues the patriarch of the family, Abraham, from a gang of hooligans in a Leeds street and he becomes a stalwart friend.

In the earlier twentieth century there were indeed Jewish ghettoes, and hooligan attacks on Jewish people, but Barbara developed a particular personal interest in the persecution of the Jews during the controversial and highly publicised trial of Adolph Eichmann in 1961, shortly before she met Robert Bradford, by origin a German Jew, when she was a journalist in London. In *A Woman of Substance*, after his rescue, Abraham takes Emma into his household, where she meets his wife, Janessa, and their sons, David (who will later propose to her) and Victor. He tells her that most of the Jews in Leeds came 'to escape the terror and harassment of the pogroms directed against us,' an event which Barbara alludes to in her second novel, *Voice of the Heart*.

Meanwhile, in Emma's company we get a description of the Leeds ghetto, and naturally of the Kallinski tailoring shop, where she will come to work, and altogether it is one of those moments in Barbara's fiction for which she became famous, because it is researched with intricate precision. In this case we end up with a complete knowledge of the divisional labour-system invented by Jewish tailor Herman Friend, whereby a suit would be made up in parts by different tailoring outfits, according to the dictates of a factory. Friend worked with, and made famous, the John Barren factory, 'the first ready-made clothiers to start in Leeds after Singer invented the sewing machine'. He wrought a revolution in the industry, we learn, 'and helped to put Leeds on the map as the biggest centre of ready-made clothing in the world.'

Discussing all this with Abraham's son David 'on that hot August night in 1905', a friendship is born that will endure through the Emma Harte series: 'Together they would climb, in their own individual-istic ways, struggling out of grim poverty, fighting all manner of prejudices, reaching for bigger and better things, and in their rising and their reaching they would carry the city with them.'

All of this was bred in the bone of the lads of Leeds, boys like Bobby Caplin: 'We were hard-working people in those days,' he remembers. 'I have an elder brother who was a little bit cleverer than me, who ended up as a project director at the World Bank in Washington, helped to design the first-ever computer in the UK. My late father started the family business and it was up to me to go into it. I was never good at school . . . I was struggling, I was never an academic and I can honestly say that the happiest day of my life was the day that I left school. But I was never the boss's son. I went in to the factory at ground level and had to go to Technical College to get my City and Guilds. Ronnie [Sumrie] was also in the clothing business. Sumrie Clothes of Leeds was one of the finest clothing companies in the country, very famous. He never had to work. He was a good-looking guy, sat in the showrooms when people came.'

Alan Bennett mentions Marshall and Snelgrove in *Telling Tales*, but never felt at home there like Barbara did. He writes that he feared 'imminent exposure' when dragged in there by his mother: 'Marshall and Snelgrove's is a provincial outpost of a store in London's West End, so has a certain metropolitan grandeur, the carpets thicker, voices more hushed and fur coats much in evidence, and though the menu caters to Mam's core requirement of tea and toasted tea-cakes, tea-cakes come under an EPNS dish-cover, the proper manipulation of which is an additional hazard to the terrors of eating out.'

Bennett describes the 'floor show', which was a fashion feature of the restaurant, 'resident manne-quins prowling the aisles between the tables modelling outfits on offer on the floor below in the couture department.' This was perfectly in tune with Barbara's love of glamour and also with an opportunity that had lined up for her. When Horniblow made her a reporter, he also hired Madeleine McLoughlin from the *Manchester Evening News* as women's page edi-tor, and soon Barbara was to become her assist-ant. 'Suddenly Kay Boughton's column became Kay Boughton's Women's Pages, and the secretary was the secretary and no longer writing her page, or her little bit, and there was Madeleine installed as women's page editor instead.'

Barbara remembers that 'A lot of the fashion was how to make six dresses out of two pieces of curtain or fabric or towel.' And Billie Figg showed me a photograph published in one of the Amalgamated Press women's magazines of her in a hat made out of a man's old tweed coat. 'It was still war-time "make-do-and-mend" days even in the early 1950s. Rationing went on for quite some considerable time after the war, food rationing until 1954. Isn't it funny,' said Billie, 'what was inculcated in us then never leaves you. I cannot waste the ends of soaps, I have to dig them into the next end. When I see youngsters in offices throwing away huge reams of paper that these machines spit out I'm appalled because I keep every sheet of paper that's got a plain white back to write on. You just can't get over it.'

No wonder Barbara had been so frantic at the paper wastage on her first day. Now she had justified her self-confidence, however, and found herself in something of a growth industry. What enabled Barbara's rise, what got her out of the North, with its relative lack of opportunity, was not only her singular desire to excel and a developing journalistic skill, but a combination of these and the opening up of the women's market, of which Horniblow's enhanced Kay Boughton women's page on the *Yorkshire Evening Post* was but one sign.

In the early 1950s, Billie was working on the PR side of an advertising agency – Napper, Stinton, Woolley in Great Chapel Street, off Oxford Street in London – with women as her main target. She recalls:

'There was this terrific feeling for the first time that women could get somewhere. People talk about the early 1950s as a depressed time – grey – but it wasn't. Things could only get better. Also, suddenly, women were being listened to. Women were the new market. Their opinion was being sought.'

Billie had professional experience of the old regime, when being a woman held considerably less promise. She cut her journalistic teeth on the Amalgamated Press in the mid-1940s, a group of magazines, 'all of them now defunct – *Woman's Pictorial, Mother and Home* and *Woman's Journal*. It was the company that the famous publishers Cecil King and Hugh Cudlipp later bought up and made into IPC. It was a marvellous place in Farringdon Street, with this rather ornate doorway and attendants in uniform.'

What is first relevant is why, in 1946, Billie left the company. 'The thing was that I got married and it was still the time that it wasn't done for the wife to work. As a matter of fact, until a very little way beforehand you weren't *allowed* to be married and work at the Amalgamated Press if you were a woman. There was a woman there then who was still pretending she was unmarried!

'Jack and I got married in 1946 and the practice must have been relaxed pretty soon after that. I was there in '44, '45, and right up to our marriage that woman was still masquerading under "Miss". I think it was a protection of men's jobs really. I remembered accepting at the time that once you've got married you've got a bit of support behind you and you mustn't occupy a job that could be given to a man. I remember accepting and understanding that,' said Billie.

Interesting, then, that Vincent's objection to Audra going out to work in *Act of Will* was not just a North Country thing. Indeed, Billie's husband Jack, who was brought up on a working-class estate on the edge of London in Dagenham, home of the Ford car industry, said, 'My mother never went to work except later on in the war when a lot of people did. I don't think any woman up and down our road went to work.'

'It was still part of the culture that the wife stayed home,' confirmed Billie. 'After a little while I got very restive and took a part-time job locally, over the road. Even so, one asked permission in those days,' she said, cocking an eye at her husband.

Realising too late what a career prospect she'd let slip at Amalgamated Press, Billie became determined to get back into journalism and found it almost impossible. 'I had to do it by steps . . .' and the job with Napper, Stinton, Woolley was an important one of these. 'I thought, I'll try and get in sideways. I couldn't get straight back into magazines, it was really tough. I'm talking 1950 . . . you couldn't easily get into magazines then.'

All of which attests to Barbara's ingenuity in landing a position as fashion editor on *Woman's Own*, though she had what was required, a column on a paper whose banner read 'Largest Circulation in the Country' – and a respected Fleet Street referee in Horniblow, if indeed they called upon him to provide one, for Barry Horniblow left Leeds some time before Barbara. There was also clear precedent for transfer from the Yorkshire newspaper group into Fleet Street. Arthur Brittenden had moved to the now defunct *News Chronicle*, and Waterhouse to the *Daily Mirror*, a move he describes with great wit in *Streets Ahead*, the compulsive sequel to *City Lights*. Fact was that a successful spell on the *YEP* was as good a setting-off point as any for a journalist, and had even been seen by Horniblow, of course, as anything but a step back in an already booming Fleet Street career.

Billie, on the other hand, was scuppered: 'My record was terribly broken, I hadn't got the cub reporter thing, had missed university because of a bout of TB and didn't even have much freelance. I'd very little and there didn't appear to be any vacancies. But I got in to the agency as secretary to Leslie Stinton, then I drove him mad. Bits of copy for baked beans, on anything the agency was selling, he'd find on his desk each morning.'

She soon realised, however, that she had in fact landed herself in the right place at the right time. 'The office had a woman doing what they used to call "editorial" then, and they decided that they'd like to expand, and they brought in a chap named Ted Jones.'

It was through Ted that Billie and Barbara first met. 'Oh, Ted was quite significant in our lives. He came from J. Walter Thompson, a journalist who'd got into advertising and PR. He just had a *sense* of a story and we did such exciting things.'

Finally worn down by these bits of copy coming

from this girl who was supposed to be his secretary, Leslie Stinton decided to despatch Billie to Ted Jones's department. 'We had one hell of a lot of fun. As I said, women had become a market; people wanted their opinions. Suddenly women were being listened to. They'd actually say things like, "Let's have a meeting and get all the women in and hear what they say about it." I was made head of a women's section in the PR department.

'Now, Ted, when he'd been at J. Walter Thompson, had had something to do with fisheries and he'd been up to Hull and Barbara had covered a story for the *Yorkshire Evening Post*. It so happened that Ted had an eye for a pretty girl and he and Barbara had obviously struck it up, so she'd got his name. Barbara was sharp on getting her contacts ready for when she was going to come down to London, and so she'd arranged to call on Ted at his advertising agency when she came down. So, he brought her into the office at some time around 1951, 1952 – before she worked for *Woman's Own*. She would have been eighteen, nineteen.

'Barbara and I had already had dealings, without knowing each other, because she'd been using my stories in her column – the Kay Boughton column. I'm eleven years older than Barbara, so there was quite an age gap, but a friendship blossomed.'

I asked Billie whether she could remember the day Barbara first walked into Napper, Stinton, Woolley. 'I can picture it very easily. What I remember is someone very slim and pretty, and with laughing eyes, and my thinking, what a Scandinavian-looking person.

My knowledge of Barbara now is putting her in a skirt to calf-length, but leaving me very conscious of very slim legs and . . . would it have been stiletto heels?

'Barbara Goalen was the great model at that time, and Barbara dressed to look like that. We wore hats and little white gloves. Couture ruled fashion, the ready-to-wear and the prêt à porter hadn't yet exploded. It was couture, Givenchy and the people that dressed Audrey Hepburn – those were our fashion icons then, and in London people like Victor Stiebel, and Hartnell, out of our reach but they were the icons who set the style you copied. You've made me realise that in those days Barbara dressed at a lower price-level than the couturier, but in those terms.'

The Kay Boughton page in early 1952 demonstrates Barbara's by then energetic but easy journalistic style: readable, well-informed, it captures her preference for elegance, sophistication and the feminine, well in advance of the more youthful, individual influences of the ready-to-wear revolution of the later 1950s.

These were the days when the public looked to royalty as well as Hollywood to set the tone. Long before she made spicier column inches in her regal Mustique period, with flamboyant villain John Bindon and other riotous crew playing court, Princess Margaret was about to become one such fashion muse, and Barbara was well on top of it. 'A new note in the Spring trends,' she writes, 'a hint of *the Princess line*, who is so much in the news just now. She was one of the first to adopt the flowing fan line used in

228

coats and suits, and to favour velvet ... Some say
Princess Margaret will be the new leader of fashion,
following in the footsteps of her much-admired aunt,
the Duchess of Kent. With an engagement in the air
that is more than possible.' Perceptive stuff. When
Anthony Armstrong Jones plighted his troth shortly
afterwards, the couple became the Prince Charles and
Princess Diana of their day.

By 1952, a year before she left for London, the
fashion scene had taken Barbara far from the hum-
drum realities of home. On 6th February 1952, she
was on the case at soon-to-be-crowned Princess
Elizabeth's couturier Hardy Amies's London show,
introducing us to 'the pyramid silhouette', and re-
commending 'wider hemlines worn over stiffening
petticoats ... for fun and games'.

The job also took her to the Paris Collections,
and a surprise meeting with Barry Horniblow. 'I
remember going to Paris for the first time when I was
about seventeen. I went with the WPE [Madeleine
McLoughlin] to cover the fashion shows. Paris totally
overwhelmed me, I thought it was one of the most
beautiful cities – it's still one of my favourite cities –
and I came back and sat down at my typewriter and
started to write the story of this ballet dancer [she
called her fictional heroine Vivienne Ramage] who
lived in a garret in Paris and was very poor. It was all
very dramatic and I think actually it was probably
something like *Camille*. I got to about page ten and
thought, No, I have a feeling I've read this somewhere
before.'

Camille had been filmed in 1937, starring Greta Garbo and Hollywood heart-throb Robert Taylor, who reminded Barbara of her father. The name of her heroine, Vivienne, was the feminine form of that of her older brother, who had so tragically died as a baby.

'Madeleine McLoughlin wanted to take me to the Paris shows because some boyfriend she had was going to be there, and I could do some of the work. I was quite happy to go, but I realised what she was up to when she said, "You'll have to sit in for me at times", and I said "Why?". And she said her boyfriend was coming. I think I was quite smart even then because I remember saying to her, "Well, I don't know if my mother will let me go. I could talk her into it, but you've got to promise me that we'll go and see Barry Horniblow when we go to London. So she said, "Yes," but on the way there we didn't. So I black-mailed her – if we didn't see him I'd want my name on what we'd written, and of course I'd written most of it.

'On the way back, she said we'd go. I think Barry was on the *Sunday Sketch* or one of those Sunday tabloids, and I *kept* saying to her (I can be a bit of a nag), "Did you make the appointment?" I remember she finally said, "No, but don't worry, it'll be fine." And I said, "How are we going to get in?" She said, "We'll go through the Circulation Department." Circulation, two girls. I was seventeen so she must have been twenty-seven, maybe a bit older, and an Irish woman – from Manchester. She's chatting, "Hello, how are you? How are you chaps?" They just let us in as if we owned the place – in and up the stairs. She kept saying, "We've an appointment with Mr Horniblow, which is the way?" And finally we were outside his office door with some woman trying to put us off . . . and he came out. And I said, "Oh, Mr Horniblow!"

'There he was, white-haired and elegant. And he said, "Barbara!"'

Fade and cut. 'You *must* have been in love with him,' I said.

'No I wasn't, because . . .'

'A crush?'

'No, it wasn't a crush, it wasn't romantic, it was like . . .'

'Adulation?'

'Yes, a good word, adulation.'

At the start of 1952, in spite of a keener focus on the women's market generally, prospects for manufacturers in the fashion industry were far from rosy. In January that year the Kay Boughton column reported that women's clothing manufacturers were facing gloomy trade prospects – eighty per cent had had to cut staff in the last three months. Barbara blamed this on 'world conditions . . . depression in the seven and eight o'clock BBC News bulletins . . . enough to put any woman off a day's shopping.' The saviour would be her hero, Winston Churchill. He, having been ousted by Labour in 1945, when all fell quiet on the Western Front, had, in 1951, been welcomed back as Prime Minister, and would continue to serve until

1955. '. . . On Mr Churchill's talks in America, the fashion industry's future lies,' Barbara told her readers. Meanwhile, if you couldn't find the money to dress yourself properly, you should 'Make the most of your voice! . . .

'An attractive voice is as important as appearance,' she wrote. 'While you will be admired for your clothes, you will be *remembered* for your voice . . .' It is an interesting thought, apt coming from Barbara, whose voice one does indeed remember. To broadcaster Richard Whiteley, who met Barbara for the first time in the autumn of 1979 when he interviewed her for Yorkshire Television's magazine programme, *Calendar*, her voice speaks of integrity: 'What I found most refreshing was that she hadn't adopted a transatlantic accent, despite having lived in the States for much of her adult life. She has retained a very crisp and rich English speaking voice.'

Barbara is skilful with her voice: she understands that it is a key instrument of style and she will modulate it accordingly and instinctively, so that she is probably not even aware she is doing it. In a crowded room at one of her book launches she wears its formal tones with all the confidence of a sophisticated woman of the world. Then, one-to-one, it can soften to reveal the vulnerable woman beneath. Sometimes – perhaps when she relaxes into her old self or is speaking to a rootsy Northern journalist like Michael Parkinson – the Yorkshire accent appears, as three years ago Simon Hatterstone of the *Guardian* ungallantly reported: 'The longer we talk, the flatter BTB's vowels become,'

232

he wrote. 'As the hours pass, I lose sight of the huge-haired New York caricature and find myself talking to Barbara, the bluff, likeable Yorkshirewoman.'

Barbara had worked her voice strategy out years earlier. In the Kay Boughton column, in her youth, she developed a seven-point strategy for an appealing voice: avoid bad thoughts, read aloud for ten minutes every day, control the breathing, make it even, flowing, low, sonorous. Copy a voice you admire, but don't mimic the voice – 'Avoid artificial accents, they are unconvincing and insincere!'

It is a mark of the style of Emma Harte in *A Woman of Substance* that she relinquishes her Yorkshire accent as soon as possible, and the girls at Kallinski's Leeds tailoring shop tease her about it: ' "Talking like cut glass," they called it.' Emma smiled and didn't take offence, so eventually it stopped, though they never quite became accustomed to her beauty or her air of breeding.'

Today, journalists are wont to assume that Barbara's mode of speech – 'the pleasing tones of the cosmopolitan,' as one put it – are 'the result of having lived her life in many different countries', but Billie Figg recalls that Barbara did not have a pronounced regional accent when they first met in London in 1950–1, though you could 'hear it softly behind'.

Regional accents were not part of the requisite accoutrements of success in the early 1950s, before *Angry Young Man* 'anarchism' took hold, domestic realism came in and working-class values were fêted in so-called kitchen-sink dramas, popular later in the decade.

When Barbara set forth from Leeds in 1953, it was unthinkable that anyone should read the news on radio with other than an arching, upper-crust English accent. But soon Alan Bennett would make a living partly out of the multifarious working-class characters that a Yorkshire accent suggests to him. Bennett does admit, however, that in the Fifties when he went to Oxford University, he, too, made an attempt to hide it. 'Then it came back, and now I don't know where I am.' In *Telling Tales*, he recalls a particular problem he had in a public recitation of a sentence by Oliver Goldsmith:

> *Of praise a mere glutton he swallow'd what came*
> *And the puff of a dunce he mistook it for fame*

Bennett died when the last line came out first as 'the paff of a dunce' and the second time as 'the poof of a dance'.

Barbara has been known to indulge her Yorkshire accent when returning to her roots, and at other times has been described as – and alternately accused of – putting on a 'power-packed Alexis Colby accent' (this was in 1997) and having 'an almost stagey upper-class English accent'. The fact is that different accents can be called on to send definable signals to different audiences. Empathy is a powerful tool in communication; why not use such a tool if you have the confidence and credibility to do so?

Barbara might say that her experimentation is a sign of the actress in her, but her husband Bob, who was pulled up by the roots from his home culture at five years of age and can claim a more cosmopolitan life-history even than Barbara, makes no attempt to experiment in this way. Born in Germany, he was brought up in Paris, lived for many years in America and has an accent which encompasses every stage of the hybridisation process, relieving any possibility of confusion with a sardonic twinkle in his eye.

None of this is of idle curiosity, for accents have traditionally been connected with identity, and, as we have seen, identity is the 'problem' at the root of Barbara's novels, slipped subliminally to her by Freda as the one to solve. It is significant, but not surprising, that Barbara's range of accents should attest this.

Uprooting from a home culture as strong as that of Yorkshire took guts for a twenty-year-old girl in 1953, but had a clear rationale. Roots not only feed a plant, they tie it down. Keith Waterhouse also left but took his Yorkshire roots with him, wearing them like a badge. He was still alluding this year to his childhood job in a Leeds undertakers in his column in the *Daily Mail*, and has retained, perhaps even built on, his Yorkshire accent, with its very particular, honest-working-class reference points.

On the other hand, Freda made a point of taking Barbara out of the local, post-industrial terraced world of Leeds as a child and into the rural landscape of North Yorkshire, where Barbara mined ideas, lessons of history and values with a wider relevance, ideas which set her up for the incredible international journey on which she would embark. In particular, she mined the abstract idea of beauty – the special spirit of places like Middleham, Studley Royal and Haworth – which impart a sense of the sublime that the industrial revolution had squeezed out of the urbanised working-class in the North with almost Judgement Day finality.

Keith Waterhouse avoided any opportunity to visit the countryside as a boy, his preferred environment being one with 'not a blade of grass in sight'. When called up to National Service at an RAF base at Wombleton he likened the North Yorkshire moors to 'Noel Coward's Norfolk, very flat,' as if he had never set eyes on the real moors, often precipitous. 'The North Yorkshire moors,' he writes, '. . . even in the driest summers give out such an impression of being marshland that one expects Magwitch staggering across them through the mist.' The fictional setting, where the escaped convict Magwitch appears and terrifies Pip in *Great Expectations*, was in fact based by Dickens on Cooling in Kent. Nothing could be further in imagination from the wild, expansive Yorkshire moors.

Again, Alan Bennett casts a few frogs, a crayfish and the sight of a lizard on a rock as '*it* as far as nature in my childhood is concerned', concluding that 'with nature, as in other departments, adults *pretended* . . . [in order to] conceal the fact that nature is dull.' Both Bennett and Waterhouse made their way in the wider world still spiritually confined within the cobbled world of bricks and mortar in which they had been brought up, trading on it sometimes ironically, sometimes to point of caricature.

The Albion Street home to *The Yorkshire Evening Post*, where Barbara got a job.

'And where's all this scribbling going to get yer?' says Emma Harte to her brother in *A Woman Of Substance*. 'On to a newspaper,' Frank replies. 'Maybe even the *Yorkshire Morning Gazette…* Stick that in yer pipe and smoke it, Emma Harte.' The *YEP* had an amazing circulation. It made all the money that kept its sister, the more prestigious morning paper, the *Yorkshire Post*, afloat. This was 1948, Barbara was only fifteen, but she was on her way.

Within six months she was a reporter, graduating to Women's Page Assistant at 17 – shown here at that age, standing in for a professional model who hadn't shown up for a fashion shoot.

Barbara at 19 and already Woman's Page Editor. She was barely a woman herself, but she wrote the lot anyway: cooking, fashion, personalities.

Barbara's meteoric rise would not have been possible without a large dose of journalistic skill, which she crafted painstakingly with the help of Keith Waterhouse, also on YEP at the time, shown here with Willis Hall (left), who worked on the Leeds *Evening News* and with whom Waterhouse adapted his first novel, *Billy Liar*, for stage and screen, the film starring Tom Courtenay and Julie Christie.

Barbara in 1953, aged twenty (just before she went to London to work as a Fashion Editor on *Woman's Own*), wearing a grey taffeta dress – 'Look at the pleating! It came from a very expensive gown shop in Leeds.'

Peter O'Toole with Omar Sharif in Lawrence Of Arabia. O'Toole was another who worked on the Leeds *Evening News* before getting his break. Barbara met Sharif at a party in London given by Sam Spiegel, but any relationship with O'Toole was only ever alive in Keith Waterhouse's imagination.

Barbara met film producer Robert Bradford (pictured on location in Hong Kong) in the London home of screenwriter Jack Davies in 1961. They were married in '63, and suddenly she found herself in Beverly Hills, New York and Paris.

The irony was that, through marriage to Robert Bradford, Barbara no longer needed the ambitious drive that had set her apart. She needn't have bothered with a career at all.

Barbara's mother, Freda Taylor, a long way from home on Fifth Avenue, New York, during one of her visits to her daughter, and with friends of Barbara, Ruth and Leslie Leigh – 'What was very nice,' says Billie Figg, 'was that she took her mother to all the places she frequented … whether she appeared to fit or not.'

Barbara, the writer. It was, in the end, an imaginative return to her roots in the landscape of Yorkshire that enabled her to write *A Woman of Substance*, the novel that defined her.

In her forties, Barbara was going back into her roots more, but it was an enlightened return: 'I remember her coming back to do research into the old mills for *A Woman of Substance*,' says Leeds-based Bobby Caplin. 'She had gone away a provincial girl and come back a very, very smart and intelligent person. It was great to see. But basically she was still Barbara.'

The Yorkshire countryside to which Barbara's mother turned her was something else. It awakened in her daughter an appreciation of landscape as character – as if it were overwritten with the exploits of its history and the emotions and values redolent of those who had steered it. Being part of this landscape was Barbara's birthright, it reflected something in her and became part of her identity long before she saw the narrative potential and returned to it to articulate her woman of substance.

Imbued with the character of the sublime Yorkshire moors – indestructible, everlasting – her self-belief heightened by Freda's conviction that she was capable of anything, that there were no limits to what she could achieve, she moved out of childhood and shed her working-class skin with the courage and vanity of a Neville, the persistence of a Ripon, and the vitality of her maternal grandmother, Edith Walker, to press her game to the end.

The industrial revolution was over. If rising in the world was flying in the face of the working-class rubric, there was no longer a sense of it in Barbara. Prevarication went against her instincts and against everything her mother had told her. Freda had led her back in time to eighteenth-century William Hazlitt's idea that self-belief is the mother of opportunity.

CHAPTER THREE

The Jeannie Years

'There's nothing you can't have if you try hard enough, work hard enough and strive towards a goal. And never, never limit yourself.'

Audra in *Act of Will*

The Fifties were an unforgettable era. The decade saw the exploding of the H-bomb, the coming of TV to the masses, the first exploration of outer space, the beginnings of the affluent society and the start of a period of teenage-powered rebellion against existing attitudes to sex, class, authority and good taste. It was the time of Elvis Presley, Marilyn Monroe, James Dean, Burgess and Maclean, and the papers were full, too, of Khrushchev, Castro and Suez. Feminist writer Simone de Beauvoir used the term 'women's liberation' for the first time in 1953, and, two years earlier, Irish writer Leslie Paul wrote *Angry Young Man*, providing the soubriquet for a radical school of writers that included John Osborne, Kingsley Amis, Alan Sillitoe, Colin Wilson, John Braine and others.

In fact, as we shall see, there were large parts of

this Fifties agenda that Barbara never experienced, partly because the 'good taste' and elegance elements that were up for replacement were endemic to her style, which it never occurred to her to change. Nevertheless, the era was an unforgettable experience for her, if quite unlike most people's. It began in austerity and finished up with a Hollywood liaison.

In 1950, twenty Dunhill cigarettes cost three shillings and sevenpence (about 17.5p in modern coinage); a large loaf of bread, two shillings and a penny (10p); a pound of cheese, a shilling (5p); and a bottle of gin, thirty-three shillings and ninepence (about £1.70). On the face of it, that sounds like a cheap shop, but of course salaries were far less then too. A political columnist on the *Sunday Pictorial*, a national newspaper, was earning £1500 in 1950. Would he be earning forty times as much today? If so, his shopping bill today, at 1950s prices, would be £7 for the packet of Dunhills, £4 for a large loaf of bread, £2 a pound for cheese, and £68 for a bottle of gin. Quite clearly the whole product-cost balance is different today, and there are many more things to spend our money on, but clearly, too, things were not cheap more than half a century ago.

When Freda delivered Barbara to her small flat at 44 Belsize Park Gardens, NW3, between the Finchley Road and Haverstock Hill, she was going to find it hard to make ends meet on a salary that will have been considerably less than £1500 per annum. Typically, the burden was eased by Freda. Like Christina in *Act of Will*, the rent was paid by her mother: 'My parents supported me when I was in London,' Barbara has said.

This might be assumed to have had an effect on the frame of mind in which Barbara began her decade in London. Indeed, she makes plain in *Act of Will* that there is a price for Christina to pay for Audra's self-sacrifice on her behalf. Christina is driven by what she now perceives as 'the crucial debt she owed her mother ... She must repay it. If I do not it will weigh heavy on my conscience all the days of my life, she thought. And that I could not bear...' Later, Christina says: 'I have a terrible need, a compelling need, to bring ease and comfort to her [Audra's] life. I want to give her the kind of luxuries she's never known...'

This was not, however, the case with Barbara, at least at this stage of her life. 'Of course I was very good to her, financially and in other ways, but I never felt there was a huge debt to repay. I wanted to succeed because I knew it would please her and that it would be wrong somehow if I didn't succeed ... even at Northcote Private School, for instance, I always knew that I had to, that I couldn't waste time or dawdle or not pay attention to my school work, because I knew that that would be terrible. She expected the very best from me.'

Barbara has also said that she wasn't conscious until some time later of the sacrifices her mother had made for her. Nevertheless, she felt a need 'to prove that I was the best, and that all my parents' love and devotion had come to fruition.' This in no way restricted her or repressed a desire to do otherwise: 'I *wanted* to please her,' Barbara stressed.

It would have been completely out of character for Freda to burden Barbara with thoughts of the debt she owed her, or what it meant to slip quietly into the background when it was time for Barbara to be parted from her. 'My mother never said anything to me at the time, but later I found out that the day I left for London she took a doll I was fond of and put it in her bedroom. She kept it there until she died in 1981. I think she was trying to hang on to a part of me. When she died I found her handbag and my childhood library cards were in it – the handbag in current use! – and I found her diary, all her diaries, and read an entry that said: "Barbara has gone to London today – all the sunshine has gone out of my life." It was all it said on the page. It made me feel incredibly sad.'

Earlier, Barbara and her mother had traipsed around London looking for a suitable place to rent. Had they come by car they would have had little difficulty parking, for, as Billie Figg recalls, many of the Second World War bomb sites were being used as car parks, 'and it was easy to park anywhere. Bombed-out London also became a rich bed for wild flowers.' Billie Figg, born in North London to Londoners who then moved to suburban Woodford Green, close to where she lives today, became Barbara's lifeline: 'She immediately treated Jack and me as friends. She would often ring, we would go out together, and she'd come down here, wouldn't she, first of all.' Jack remembered helping out at her little flat, putting up a curtain and rail to hang her clothes on. 'It was, as far as I remember, a living room, a bedroom, kitchen and bath,' he said. 'She was certainly living on her own. Looking back, I think we were just slightly stable anchorages in London, a place that was strange to her. She used to telephone us a lot, and so without complimenting ourselves there must have been some sort of comfort in that, whereas maybe quite a few of the other people she got to know, well ... perhaps ... they weren't married?'

Back in 1953, what *Woman's Own* meant to Alan Bennett's mum was columnist Beverley Nichols 'writing about his gardens and chronicling the doings of his several cats', Nichols' life seeming to her one of 'dizzying sophistication'. What it meant to broadcaster Sue Lawley was 'lots and lots of romantic fiction ... all those soppy love stories. Did you never want to write one of those?' she asked Barbara on *Desert Island Discs* fifty years later. Listening to the radio programme miles away I could feel Barbara bristling before she answered, 'No, and I never read them actually, to tell you the honest truth.' Lawley stemmed the flow from her lancing cut rather unconvincingly with, 'They were very good.'

Her snipe was in fact off target because it would be quite wrong to suggest that Barbara's lifestyle in London between 1953, when she became fashion editor of *Woman's Own*, and 1963, when she married film producer Robert Bradford and left for New York, bore even the remotest resemblance to that recommended by either Beverley Nichols or those romantic story writers. It came far closer to the one described in Barbara's novel, *Voice of the Heart*, which speaks to us of destructive relationships in a glitzy but ruthless world of showbiz, which it took Barbara but a short time to inhabit.

When she arrived at *Woman's Own*, Barbara discovered that she was in fact one of several fashion editors, and at once did what was required to adapt to their style, the young novice showing just how apprehensive and keen to swim with the stream she was: 'When I got there these women in the Fashion Department all wore hats, they came to work in them! So I went out and I bought a green hat, a pill-box we would call it today, but I always felt rather foolish because I'd worked on a newspaper before in a dirty old trench coat.'

A certain Patricia ('Triss') Lewis was the beauty editor. Brunette, sultry, sophisticated, Triss was extraordinarily attractive and far more experienced than Barbara. Straightaway Triss recognised the special spark in the twenty-year-old and took Barbara under her wing, introducing her to the fast-track world in which she operated from her Kensington flat.

'There were all these good-looking *men*!' remembers Barbara. 'We were a group. There was me and Triss, and because they were all show-business writers they dragged us to the nightclubs and to cocktail parties and that sort of thing.'

The men in the group, somewhat rakish and all of them much older than Barbara, included Roderick Mann, the then show-business columnist of the

Sunday Express, ex-Fleet Street political columnist Frederic Mullally (*Tribune*, *Sunday Pictorial*), who now ran a Mayfair showbiz PR company – both eleven years Barbara's senior – and their two compatriots, Logan ('Jack') Gourlay (*Express*) and Matt White (*News Chronicle*), also showbiz columnists (both now dead). 'The dashing men about Fleet Street,' as Barbara referred to them. An A&R man from Decca Records, Bunny Lewis, also tagged along.

Partly on account of the preoccupations of the members of this gang, what Barbara landed up in was not the traditional journalistic scene she supposed would envelop her in Fleet Street, but pure showbiz. 'My friends were mostly in the theatre or movies. I was in a much more writing/movie/showbiz world than I was in any other world when I lived in London.'

Before long, the celebrity culture swallowed up Triss, who was plucked from the Beauty department of *Woman's Own* to become a high-profile personality columnist for the *Daily Express*. 'They called her the Champagne Girl,' recalls Mullally. 'She was given a column of her own by Harold Keeble, who was the great assistant editor of the *Express*, the man who boosted all the great women journalists of his time. He invented page three of the *Daily Express* when it was at its peak. In terms of production, illustration, choice of pictures, choice of columnist, he was more than just Arthur Christianson [the famous editor]'s assistant, he was a dominating influence, the fresh wind that blew through the paper. And he *created* Patricia Lewis. Now, she and Barbara were very close.

They were the two "glamour girls" of Fleet Street. Fantastic! Beautiful! They went around the West End together.'

Said Barbara: 'It was a particularly glamorous period, the Fifties and the early Sixties, lots of Holly-wood stars around, and parties, openings, premières. When I look back, I feel very nostalgic for London as it was then ... so different from today.' Small sur-prise, then, that eventually Triss would marry classical actor/screen star Christopher Plummer, and Barbara would wed film producer Robert Bradford.

Mullally seems to have been something of a mover and shaker in the scene. He teamed up with (and married) Suzanne Warner, legendary film-maker Howard Hughes's representative in Europe. 'I left the *Sunday Pictorial* under Hugh Cudlipp, where for three or four years I'd had a column called "Candid Com-mentary", Suzanne left Howard Hughes and we formed this PR operation together in Mayfair. It was at that time that I first became aware of Barbara Taylor. The two girls, Barbara and Triss, were riding high, you see? There was an inevitable gravitation between my position and their interests. You have to remember that I was a more senior figure to these two girls in those days. I'd done my Fleet Street stint. I'd done my column. I'd written two books, political non-fiction. To them I was an attraction to be with, and I had my entrée to all the clubs of London. So there was no problem about calling them, they would call me. You know, "What are you doing today?" And I would invite them. I had a great situation in Hay

Hill, Mayfair, two floors of a building. Everything happened around those two floors. On one floor I had my PR office, a staff of maybe twelve people, and above that I had my personal apartment. I would give parties there. And round the corner were all the places . . . I would go out every evening, and it would be cocktails . . . All the glamour was in that square mile. A little overlapped occasionally into Soho and into Pimlico, but basically it was Mayfair.

'There were not clubs as we talk about clubs today. These were places where you did not show your face before seven o'clock unless you were perfectly groomed and perfectly dressed. You did not show your face if you were a man unless you were superbly groomed and suited. There was a cocktail hour in Mayfair then, as it has never existed since and will probably never exist again. Full of style and grace. This hour was seven till dinner, seven till eight. Mayfair buzzed in about six or eight venues within that square mile, where the crème de la crème suddenly appeared, the actors, the cinema people that wanted to be seen. Most of these restaurants in those days, like the Caprice, had a bar, a tiny bar. You crowded in at about seven o'clock. You didn't even get where you were to sit. You were there in what was a kind of party atmosphere. And gradually the people drifted into the restaurant and the bar would go empty. But for that one moment between seven and eight you were shoulder to shoulder, cheek by jowl with the most glamorous models, the great Barbara Goalens of that time, who were not like the models of today.

That was the scene; it was a very glamorous scene. Celebrities were celebrities. Today if you appear on television for five minutes you're a celebrity. In those days they were major, major stars. Actors, models . . . They got that much publicity, now it's flooded. There were only three, four, five magazines in those days.

'It's the forgotten era. As you came out of the war years into the Fifties, and rationing began to ease up, we were aware of Hollywood and were aware of Hollywood stars, trickle by trickle coming into London, into Les Ambassadeurs, into Ziggi's club . . . and we treated them as kind of nice pieces we were cultivating and would like to shake hands with, but we were not influenced by them at all. There was a British film industry that was appreciated around the world at this time – the Ealing comedies, and Sidney Box and one or two other greats. It was alive, and I was one of those involved with it. My company had clients like Sinatra, we had from top to bottom, we handled everybody, films by people like the Carrerases, you know, father and son, down to the lower end of it, which was the Hammer Horrors. We made the singer David Whitfield, managed him, got a deal with the A&R man in Decca to get the right songs. But it was tough, it was only just beginning, papers were fewer and smaller, and for a while the major Fleet Street newspapers were totally anti-PR. Express Newspapers had a ban on PR altogether – you were not allowed to mention the name of a club at which someone had appeared last night. Puffs were out, it was very tough. So we had to be more ingenious.

'In the Mayfair bars and clubs it wasn't principally a Hollywood scene, it was an elegant *English* scene, though Hollywood actors came. What happened was that there was an infusion from America. Any Hollywood stars that came to London were attracted by that particular London scene, that very elegant London scene. So they would be there, they would be in and out of these various little places where we met, and I would meet Errol Flynn for the first time in my life. I would meet Douglas Fairbanks. They swanned in and out of our London scene, to which they were attracted by its elegance.

'The great clubs of the day were the Casanova, run by Rico Dajou, the Don Juan (Rico had the two clubs, they were in Grosvenor Street), Les Ambassadeurs – downstairs restaurant and upstairs nightclub (called the Milroy and run by big John Mills – not the actor), and Ziggi Sessler's at 46 Charles Street, now Mark's Club. The Caprice of course, a restaurant, but a top restaurant for the other people, not even really journalists, the Mayfair crowd. They had a wonderful head waiter. I wrote about him in one of my novels – *Danse Macabre*. If he hadn't chosen to be the greatest maître d'hôtel in London he would have been an archbishop of the Catholic Church. He was that wonderful a person. Annabel's came later.'

I recognised names out of Barbara's novels immediately. Early on in *Voice of the Heart*, Francesca Cunningham, Katharine Tempest and others meet for dinner at Les Ambassadeurs in Hamilton Place, between Piccadilly and Park Lane. It's also a favourite lunch-time haunt of stylish film star Victor Mason, who is a model of what Katharine, Francesca, and, of course, Barbara consider a man should be: handsome, rough-hewn, suntanned, 'massive across the chest and back', clothes of the finest quality, chosen with panache, slacks with knife-edge creases, a man who cares about appearance. Francesca's family, the Cunninghams, whose aristocratic seat is Langley Castle in Yorkshire, also have a house in Mayfair's Chesterfield Street, which runs between Curzon Street and Charles Street, where Ziggi Sessler's 21 Club was. Maximilian West first walks onto the pages of *The Women in His Life* from his 'imposing house on the corner of Chesterfield Hill and Charles Street', and I knew that in the 1980s and '90s, when Bob Bradford was filming in England, he and Barbara themselves had an apartment in Charles Street. Annabel's, in Berkeley Square, which Barbara describes in the same novel as 'the chic-est of watering holes for the rich and famous, where the international jet-set rub shoulders with movie stars and magnates and members of the British Royal Family', actually opened during the summer before she decamped with Bob to New York in 1963. They are still members today. Berkeley Square was, and is, also home to bespoke yacht builder of distinction, Camper & Nicholson, where, in *The Women in His Life*, Maxim commissions the 213.9-foot *Beautiful Dreamer* for his wife Anastasia. And, as fate would have it, Barbara's English publisher (HarperCollins) was sited within the square mile at No. 8 Grafton Street where they first published her.

When she first came to the area at such a tender age in the early 1950s, Barbara could have had no idea that this was to become known worldwide as multi-million-selling author *Barbara Taylor Bradford's Mayfair*. Today it is, in every sense, her village:

Maxim came out of the imposing house on the corner of Chesterfield Hill and Charles Street and stood for a moment poised on the front step . . . Pushing his hands in his pockets, he forced himself to stride out, heading in the direction of Berkeley Square. He walked at a rapid pace along Charles Street, his step determined, his back straight, his head held erect. He was dark-haired with dark-brown eyes, tall, lean, trimly built . . .

He circled Berkeley Square, dodging the traffic as he made for the far side, wondering why Alan needed to see him, what this was all about . . . Oh what the hell, he thought, as he reached the corner of Bruton Street. Alan's been so special to me most of my life. I owe him . . . we go back so far, he knows so much – and he's my best friend. Crossing the street, his eyes focused on the Jack Barclay showroom on the opposite corner, and when he reached the plate-glass windows he paused to admire the sleek Rolls-Royces and Bentleys gleaming under the brilliant spotlights . . . He walked on past the Henley car showroom

and Lloyds bank, and pushed through the doors
of Berkeley Square House, the best commer-
cial address in town and a powerhouse of a
building. Here, floor upon floor, were housed the
great international corporations and the multi-
nationals, companies that had more financial
clout than the governments of the world. Maxim
thought of it as a mighty treasury of trade, for
it did hundreds of billions of dollars' worth of
business a year. And yet the buff-coloured edifice
had no visible face, had long since blended into
the landscape of this lovely, leafy square in the
very heart of Mayfair, and most Londoners who
walked past it daily were hardly aware of its
existence. . . . Maxim crossed the richly carpeted,
white-marble hall, and nodded to the security
guard, who touched his cap in recognition.

The Women in His Life

I asked Barbara which her favourite haunts were in the early days. 'I went to the Mirabelle a lot in the 1950s, when it was in its heyday. The maître d' was Louis Emanuelli – Welsh, of Italian descent. Louis was later the man at Annabel's. He was a great pal and would do anything for me. Les Ambassadeurs night-club, the Milroy, was always full of Hollywood stars, producers, etc. The famous bandleader there was Paul Adams. I particularly liked the Arlington Club on Arlington Street, a tiny club in Mayfair, but an "in" kind of place with a bartender called Joe who was a character. And yes, we went to Ziggi Sessler's.

And there was an actors' club somewhere off the Haymarket called the Buckstone, a minor club, but I used to go there and so did a whole group of actors – Richard Burton, Christopher Plummer, Peter O'Toole and Jason Robards – Richard Harris as well, all dedicated drinkers. I used to love that club . . . I believe it's still there . . .

'At this time I became a friend of Jeannie Gilbert, an American woman who was press officer for the Savoy, Claridges and the Berkeley. She was from Kentucky and not to be confused with another Jean, who was press officer at one point, before my Jeannie, I think.

'Jeannie had a little house in Minerva Mews in Chelsea and gave lots of parties with guests, sometimes authors – famous writers, like James Baldwin, the black writer. He was around at that time. Unfortunately she had a habit of introducing them sometimes by nickname. One occasion I remember in particular, I was talking to this man whom Jeannie had introduced to me as Snips, or something like that, and he was chatting away about writing. I said I wanted to be a novelist and he started talking about books. Finally he said, "You're a journalist, you're very young." – He was a rather portly man, middle-aged. – "You're rather young and pretty." I said, "You know a lot about books, what did you say your name was? Jeannie introduced you as Snips." And he said, "Oh, I'm Thornton Wilder." He wrote *Our Town*! Famous American writer! I was terribly embarrassed when I heard his real name.'

During the Jeannie years Thornton Wilder might well have been in London promoting his play, *The Matchmaker*, first out in America in 1954, to be adapted nine years later as the musical comedy *Hello, Dolly!* Mention of the literary novelist James Baldwin reminds us that Jeannie was dealing with a variety of 'product', their common denominator simply that they were staying in one or other of her hotels. Baldwin was born in Harlem, his fiction exposed taboos in courageous and disarming fashion and concerns both homosexuality and the plight of his disaffected people. His first novel, *Go Tell It on the Mountain*, was published in 1953, and caused a tremendous stir.

'There were also always famous movie stars floating around,' Barbara continued, 'people such as Victor Mature, Eddie O'Brien and other name stars of the day, also high-powered movie producers at her parties, such as Ilya Lopert (he made *The Red Shoes* among other films), Gregory Ratoff (also an actor), Arthur Krim of United Artists, and screenwriters Jack Davies and Michael Pertwee, who were partners ... Other actors around at the time were Tyrone Power, and Sean Connery, as well as Lyndon Brooke (son of Clive Brooke) and Terry Longdon – both English. Lois Maxwell was another friend through Jeannie; she was the first and most famous Miss Moneypenny in the James Bond movies. Jeannie had a way of gathering all kinds of people, from the UK and the US. Eventually she married the Broadway producer David Merrick, after returning to New York in the early 1960s.'

Mullally remembers Jeannie as 'the best press officer the Savoy ever had, and she did what most PR
people never succeeded in doing, she became friends
with every columnist in Fleet Street. At any time you
could drop in to her little suite of offices on the ground
floor of the Savoy – two rooms – have a drink, ask
questions and she would answer them. She cultivated
and seduced our columnists. I was one of them. She
was a great PR, wonderful; her model was a girl called
Jean Nichols, a PR of the Savoy who came before.
Jean married the author Derek Tangye, who went to
live in Mousehole in Cornwall. They grew daffodils
together and he wrote all those books, *A Gull on the
Roof* and all that. Jean was another beauty; tragically
she died of cancer.'

Jeannie Gilbert never had anything to do with
Barbara's work, but became her friend and another
means by which she came out into this glittering
world. 'Because Jeannie did PR for those hotels, she'd
always be having cocktail parties. If there were six
actors in town and she wanted a pretty girl around,
she'd call me up. I *could* ring her up and say, "Could I
do an interview with . . . ?" But I was never a celebrity
journalist. I did a couple, Dominguin, the bullfighter,
for the *Evening News*, and a few movie stars, and the
odd writer, but I was really doing the women's page.
Celebrity journalists weren't quite "in" in those days,
I don't think anybody ever got called a celebrity journalist.' Nevertheless, quite clearly, the Fifties opened
the door for them.

What so astonished Billie Figg, and will have

appealed to Jeannie, when Barbara stepped into a room full of her clients, was the way this twenty-year-old girl from the North 'felt very at home with all these famous people, as if it was only a matter of time when she'd be one of them.' Said Billie's husband, Jack: 'I noticed that she'd get into a room and suddenly you'd find that everybody was looking her way. It was the laughter in the eyes, they had enormous magnetism, they were *full* of laughter.'

'Her style is such,' continued Billie, 'that the feeling I always had was that Barbara, from her school days, had wanted to be famous and wanted to be successful and without thinking about it just had an inborn acceptance that she could, and that whatever she turned her hand to she would be good at. She had enormously high expectations of herself and a lot of assurance. It didn't cross her mind that anything she did would be second rate and she knew that she would work hard to ensure that it wasn't. I don't think she ever thought, I'm not very good at anything. I think it was built in. She says that her mother built that in to her, doesn't she. It was very obvious to me what a fuel it is to have that kind of confidence. It never struck her that she would in any way be boring to any of these people or that they would feel that, established though they were and up-and-coming though she still was. It didn't cross her mind that they wouldn't be entirely dazzled by her, and indeed they were, because Barbara had, without knowing it, a very good repartee, and she had the kind of huge sense of humour and comeback that makes very good conversation for men as well as for women. Certainly there was an immediate rapport in any conversation with men, and not just because she was sexually attractive.'

Soon Barbara's diary was studded with appointments at the smart places of the day, as some of those whom she met at Minerva Mews became part of her life. For example, she got to know Jack and Dorothy Davies particularly well, and from the mid-Fifties would live in a flat next door to them. Jack was the father of child star John Howard Davies, who played in *Oliver Twist* when he was nine, and was in *Tom Brown's Schooldays* at eleven, later directing *Fawlty Towers*, *Mr Bean*, *Reginald Perrin* and *The Vicar of Dibley*, among other comic masterpieces. Jack Davies had worked as a staff writer on the Will Hay films of the 1930s, before making his name on the semi-satirical *Doctor in the House* movies, hugely successful in Britain, the first of which was released as Barbara arrived in London, in 1953. It starred Dirk Bogarde as medical student Simon Sparrow, who runs foul of consultant Sir Lancelot Sprat, played by the robust figure of James Robertson Justice.

Mention of Justice jogged Mullally's memory of occasions when the actor joined him and Jack Gourlay at the Colony Club in Berkeley Square for an extended session, reminding us what a significant, often devastating, role alcohol played in the fast lane in the 1950s. 'In those days it was bottle parties after 11 p.m. You had to have your own bottle, due to licensing laws. Whichever club you went to, you bought a bottle of whisky the night before and they marked it up as to how much you'd drunk and put it in a cupboard with your name on it. In the Fifties that was it! You would go back to your club at eleven o'clock and they'd send for your bottle and put it on your table. You couldn't order another bottle that night because it was past the hour. That was the crazy licensing laws in those days. So, there I am with Jack in the Colony Club, we're with the owner – we only ever drank with the owners. And Jack and I were both after birds all the time. The owner would summon a girl from the show . . . Then, about 3 a.m., Jack would stagger off and I'd be left with Justice, and I'm living in South Audley Street, having split with my wife. I've got rooms. All I can do is offer him a couch. Biggest mistake of my life. I offer him a couch before he got the mail train to wherever the next day. Mistake, because when this giant of a man started to snore, the whole place shook . . .'

Of those she met at Jeannie's, Barbara also got to know Victor Mature well. I knew this because Billie Figg had mentioned an occasion when she joined them for dinner. Then, on a separate occasion, I happened to ask Barbara what the derivation was of the phrase 'the whole enchilada', which readers of Voice of the Heart will know movie star Victor Mason uses repeatedly when he wants to say that something is 'the complete works', an enchilada being a tortilla stuffed with a variety of things. Barbara replied: 'That was a saying used constantly by Victor Mature. He always said, "the whole enchilada". I really didn't know what it meant until I came to live in America.' A coincidence not only of initials, VM, and first name of Victor, made me wonder how far I was expected to stretch similitude between movie star Victor Mature and movie star Victor Mason in the novel. Victor Mason falls in love with Katharine Tempest's best friend Francesca, whereupon Katharine hurts Francesca terribly by suggesting falsely that he is the father of her baby. Francesca, being Yorkshire born, a writer and something of an ingénue in the fast, showbiz scene in which she found herself, had always struck me as drawing on the vulnerable side of Barbara, fresh from the North and less experienced than her new showbiz friends. Katharine was altogether the more complete operator, generous and loyal on the surface, but, as Barbara described her to me, 'a woman of great calculation, ambition, a degree of ruthlessness, and self-justification to a certain degree ... Always doing things for her friends, but somehow they all seem to serve her own ends.' Katharine dominates the book even when she's not on-scene, just as, quite clearly, the experienced Jeannie Gilbert was an important part of Barbara's life at this time. I knew that there had been a falling out between Barbara and Jeannie in later years. Did Francesca and Katharine represent the young Barbara and Jeannie respectively? Had there been something between them and Victor Mature? Had I stumbled on a real triangle of passion?

Barbara confirmed only that Victor Mature had met her via Jeannie – 'He actually was a boyfriend of Jeannie's, that's how I knew him.' But she denied that she had an affair with him or that, like Victor Mason in the novel, Mature had been the cause of bad blood between her and Jeannie: 'I had quite a number of male friends who were not my boyfriends, if you know what I mean. Most people would think that if you knew a man that you were sleeping with him, but that wasn't the case.'

In an extended interview with Allison Pearson in 1999, Barbara was quoted as saying, 'I interviewed all sorts of men – movie stars – and they tended to chase me.' Pearson told us: 'The PR at the Savoy introduced her to Omar Sharif and Sean Connery. There is a photograph of Barbara and Sharif taken at this time and you suddenly realise that all those ridiculous clichés about beautiful people on which her novels rely were, for the gorgeous young girl about town, the height of realism. I congratulate Barbara on the heroic restraint clearly required to not sleep with Omar Sharif and I get a wry, knowing look. "I wasn't prim, Allison." "Weren't you?" "Not at all, but I was cautious. I wasn't a big sleeper-arounder. I was scared of getting pregnant. Mind you, I'm not saying I didn't sleep with anyone before Bob, but I worried what people would think, mostly my parents."'

This is so telling a comment, too apparently unlikely a claim (given the distance that now separated Barbara from her parents) not to be true. There was an affair with the photographer Terry O'Neill, who would later, after his marriage to Faye Dunaway, become involved in Hollywood and movie producing. 'But mostly I seemed to go out with actors. In fact,

Mummy often teased me, said I always fell for the pretty face. My father would ask, "And what's this man's intentions?" like some Victorian, and I'd laugh and answer, "I don't know, Daddy, but my intentions are to have a career". The parental involvement reminds us how young and inexperienced Barbara was, and, however independent she seemed, how tied to her roots she remained at this early stage. Freda's strategy for her daughter's rise in the world had left little to chance in matters appertaining to her mother Edith's fall.

Sex is often bound up with ambition, however. It is itself a Hollywood cliché – 'All the little girls were scalp hunters,' said Frederic Mullally – and Barbara's youth, beauty and laughing eyes might have been in danger of steering her into the path of trouble of a sexual nature, if trouble it would have been deemed. The first oral contraceptive – the Pill – would not become available until 1961, but that doesn't seem to have reined in the expectations of Mullally and the other male members of the gang, for whom, if they are to be believed, sex was always available, if often in rather seedy fashion: 'It was Mount Royal or White House (Regent's Park),' said Mullally. 'Those were the two places where you didn't have to bring your luggage with you.'

It may be significant that overt sex is a relatively unimportant aspect of Barbara's novels. She was once asked about this in interview, and replied: 'Well I do labour over the sex scenes, yes, a lot. I do a lot of rewriting. I try really to work from the point of view of the emotions of the people involved in the scene, rather than describing parts of the anatomy or using dirty words or being that explicit. It was shocking at the time of Harold Robbins when Harold started writing very, very explicit and rather dirty sexual scenes. It's really feelings that I'm writing about.'

Billie Figg recalled Barbara seeking security in the group culture. 'There was no shortage of boyfriends,' she told me, 'but they weren't a terribly important element. She was something of a loner herself, in a way, in that she was "*getting on*", she was fashioning herself, and she was a great crowd person. She would go round in a crowd, she loved collecting people and creating groups.'

Lois Maxwell, who went to many of the parties at Minerva Mews, remembered this in particular about Barbara – her gang mentality at that time: 'Barbara was always beautiful and vivacious and full of mischief, and I am sure she has forgotten, but one day I was walking along the Kings Road with the man I thought I was falling in love with, and all of a sudden there was a dreadful whistle and who was on the other side of the road but Barbara and the two Jeannies and various other pals of ours, and they all looked at me, and she started to sing in high dulcet tones, "Love and marriage . . ." – and "Love and marriage . . ." followed poor Peter and me all the way down the Kings Road. I was blushing and he was a little bit put out about it. But I don't think this incident ruined anything because he did ask me to marry him and I did . . .'

. There was safety in numbers, and Barbara preferred relationships that kept her ambition the commanding focus, rather than any sort of instant satisfaction, although that didn't mean that sex was off the agenda. Memorable relationships were those that were chummy and kept her career centre-stage, as had always been the case at home. Later, she would date film director John Berry, who was, like so many other of Barbara's male friends, significantly older than her. Born in 1917 of a Polish Jewish father and a Romanian mother, Berry had been a member of Orson Welles's legendary Mercury Theatre from 1937, and in charge of it until 1943 when he followed Welles to Hollywood, directing a number of films including *He Ran All the Way*, a thriller but also something of a statement on American life, starring John Garfield. 'It was a film noir,' Barbara recalls, 'and the last movie Garfield ever made. He died just after it was completed, at the age of thirty-nine.'

At the House Un-American Activities hearings into Communist Party influence within the film industry, Berry had been blacklisted and couldn't work in the States. In 1951 he had directed the documentary that supported those accused of communist ties, *The Hollywood Ten*, and had gone to live and work in Paris before arriving in London, where Barbara met him. 'He came to live in London in order to write a script with his great pal Ted Allan, the Canadian playwright/screenwriter, author of *Lies My Father Told Me*, among other plays and films. These two were hilarious together, and played lots of pranks on me, but we were great chums.' She went out with Berry, 'but ultimately we became just great pals. He and Ted loved having me around, probably because I fell for all their jokes and pranks, and cooked dinner for them ... although they insisted they were the better cooks! ... The two of them had sort of taken me under their wing.'

Again it is the group culture, safe, fun, and *useful*: 'What a lot I learned from those two men! They were both in their forties ... and I was by then, what, about twenty-seven? It was like going to a theatrical movie school. I remember many of the discussions about *Oh, What A Lovely War*, which Joan Littlewood produced.' The famous stage musical about the First World War later became a film, but is known far and wide as having been composed by Joan Littlewood with her fellow artists in her Theatre Workshop at Stratford in East London. Ted Allan is generally only credited with coming up with the title, but apparently he was more completely involved with its genesis. 'Ted had written the original treatment,' Barbara told me, 'and there seemed to be quite a lot of dissension between him and Joan about the credits.'

In pursuit of her ambition to become a novelist, Barbara took every opportunity she could to talk to writers and to seek their advice. Jack Berry and Ted Allan encouraged her. 'I was writing a novel called *Florabelle* at the time ... they pushed me to finish it. Although neither of them liked the title, they did select one from a list – *The Things We Did Last Summer*.'

She told everyone she met that she intended to become a novelist, and no doubt many of them gazed into her laughing eyes and, like Thornton Wilder, gave her all the encouragement she needed.

She was far from being alone in this ambition. In the gang, Roderick Mann published novels from the early 1960s; one, *The Account*, was actually published by Barbara's own UK publisher and involves a PR lady for a hotel who is not unlike Jeannie. Meanwhile, Mullally was in print even earlier with his fiction – 1959 – and has a dozen novels to his credit.

Barbara also became good friends with the writer Cornelius Ryan, whom she thinks she met at a film screening and who Mullally remembers as 'a movie photographer for one of the studios, a very sociable guy'. In fact, from 1941 to 1945, Ryan worked as a reporter for Reuters and the *Daily Telegraph* covering World War Two battles in Europe and the final months of the Pacific campaign. His first book, *The Longest Day*, was published in 1959 and sold four million copies in 27 editions, before being made into a film by Darryl Zanuck in 1962. His second book, *The Last Battle*, was published in 1966, and he finished a third, *A Bridge Too Far*, in 1974 while terminally ill with cancer.

With O'Neill and Ryan both being photographers, we should not be surprised to see the profession figuring in an important capacity in Barbara's novels. I asked her if Clee in *Remember* had been based on O'Neill, but no: 'Not really, although Clee was awfully good-looking too . . . I made him out of whole cloth with a little bit of Robert Capa thrown in. And like Capa, he was a war photographer. In fact, so were the two male leads in *Where You Belong*. I enjoy writing about newspapermen and women, and photographers, because I know them well.'

The great thing about Ryan's books is his painstaking research and attention to detail. He built up a 7000-book library, and kept 'four or five hundred of the absolute best at my fingertips – a synthesis of the perfect World War Two library', as he told Barbara in an interview in 1968 for an article that appeared in a syndicated column she then wrote called 'Designing Woman'. She and 'Connie', as friends knew Ryan, became very close.

Barbara's own research is a strength already noted – be it the divisional labour-system of the Leeds clothing industry in *A Woman of Substance*, or a highly detailed salad and omelette-making scene in *Where You Belong*, or the procedure of an English coroner's court in *Hold the Dream*, or her meticulously drawn real-life environments: her Manhattan interiors, Yorkshire millworkers' cottages, French châteaux, or the dark waterways of Venice which inspired *A Secret Affair*.

She said to Billie Figg after publication of *Voice of the Heart* in 1984 that she suffered terrible embarrassment after she'd given the manuscript in to her American publisher, Doubleday. Her editor had criticised it for being too minutely descriptive. But her English editor, Patricia Parkin, who was with Barbara from the start and still edits her today, said: 'Don't you dare change that! That's what people want.' Time has proved it. 'I think that being a journalist has helped me greatly in many areas – not just the observation of people, but also in research,' says Barbara today, but she is happy, too, to acknowledge a debt long ago to Cornelius Ryan in this.

'We became good friends, before I knew Bob,' she told me. 'He taught me a lot about research. There was something of the teacher in him. He was always lecturing me – if you really want to write books you've really got to be serious about it and you've got to write so many pages a day and so on . . .' There may be something of Ryan in Nick Latimer in *Voice of the Heart*, who gives Francesca five Ds of which every writer should be aware:

> *Dedication, discipline, determination and drive.*
> *You've got to be obsessed with a book . . . And*
> *there's another D. D for desire. You've got to*
> *want to write more than you want to do anything*
> *else . . . [And] there's a sixth D, and this one is*
> *vital. D for distraction, the enemy of every writer.*
> *You've got to build an imaginary wall around*
> *yourself so that nothing, no-one intrudes. Under-*
> *stand me, kid?*

'We liked each other a lot and he was a bit of a mentor,' Barbara remembers of Connie Ryan. 'He was very Irish. He actually introduced me to the agent Paul Gitlin who represented me when I sold *A Woman of Substance*. We stayed friends off and on, and he and Bob became good friends, and then Connie got very sick with cancer, as you know . . .

'Dick Condon also became a good friend of mine. He wrote *The Manchurian Candidate*, and I met him through Jeannie Gilbert when Dick was Head of Public Relations for United Artists. He wanted to be a novelist, and he and Cornelius Ryan encouraged me, said that I really had to stick at it. They both were singing the same song.'

Condon's *The Manchurian Candidate*, a political assassination thriller set in North Korea and America, prophetic and of great social and political significance, came out in 1959 and was a storm of a hit as book and film. Earlier Condon had written a play (*Men of Distinction*, 1953) and a novel (*The Oldest Confession*, 1958) and went on to write many more of both. Back in the Fifties, at least until *The Manchurian Candidate* met with such success, he was one of the wider group of Jeannie's people.

'That was the Wardour Street PR guy,' recalled Mullally, 'drinks for journalists and so on. That's how he would have met Barbara and myself and everybody else. Now, Richard went on, to everyone's surprise, to become a very good novelist. And I followed him and we met in Mexico. I went to live in Mexico in the late 1950s, rented a villa. Richard had just done two big things with two novels. And on my way up through Mexico City I had a little party . . . Wonderful character, big, expansive character, dominating the communications, and we're sitting in a little circle in my sitting room and he's telling one of his stories, or we were telling a story against him, and there comes a point when in the middle of his story he falls over from his chair and there's a very slim little barrier between him and eight floors to Mexico City. I promise you I leapt across the table and caught him, stopped him from going through. Now everybody starts roaring with laughter, but Condon, who did not find it funny, got up on his feet, went into the bathroom and stayed there for about a quarter of an hour. I knew what was happening. He had lost it.'

Every occasion in the Fifties seems to have been attended by drink and cigarettes. There were none of the health scares, they were the essential accoutrements of style, and alcohol in particular became reason for deep unhappiness and the kind of tragedy that Condon narrowly avoided. Barbara didn't start to smoke until she was twenty-nine, and with her *Yorkshire Evening Post* strategy well in mind, alcohol never lured her into serious problems. But it did for both Jeannie and Triss in the end. Their respective marriages, to David Merrick and Christopher Plummer, both ended not only in divorce but in tragedy on account of it.

In Jeannie's case there was a legal tussle over her child. Merrick got custody after Barbara and other friends were subpoenaed to appear in a court of law on his behalf. As a result, she and Jeannie didn't speak for years until, as Barbara recalls, a mutual friend 'asked me if I would see her because she was actually dying and I said OK. We had, the three of us – this other woman and me and Jeannie – a very nice dinner and then she said, "Can I come back and talk to you?" and the minute we were alone she said, "Why did you testify against me in a court of law?" I said, "I didn't testify against you, I testified for your child."'

There is a section at the beginning of *Voice of the Heart* inspired by this moment when two some-time very close friends – Francesca and Katharine – who haven't spoken for years come back together, Katharine returning to seek forgiveness from all the friends she has hurt. 'Jeannie wasn't the model for Katharine,' says Barbara, 'nor did she do anything to hurt anybody like Katharine did, who actually ruined Francesca's life by lying. But that section was the whole thing with Jeannie Merrick, as she had become, and it was the idea of a friend trying to become . . . it was two friends *becoming* friends again.'

In Triss's case, her very marriage to Christopher Plummer was cast in tragic circumstances, as Mullally recalled: 'One night they were driving back to London and opposite Buckingham Palace there was a terrible crash. She went through the window and her whole face was taken apart. She had to go to the top plastic surgeon who did the job in those days for the Airforce in one of the great hospitals for reconstructive surgery. They literally put her face back together again. I saw her after months of surgery and she had wires coming out of her head and scars all over her face. She nearly died. They were not married at that point. He then said, would you marry me. So, in between surgeries, they married. It was a bad way to get married and their marriage was never a success. I knew them

both at that time ... She followed him wherever
Christopher was making movies: Madrid – they
stayed in the next apartment to me there – New York.
Then they divorced. He had bought a house in Park
Street, Mayfair. She gave a New Year's Eve party
at Park Street where she invited ... Barbara wasn't
involved at this stage, must have been in America ...
Triss invited two or three big Hollywood stars, there
was haggis and whisky ... It was a disaster. I was
invited with my then girlfriend. The butler was drunk.
The Hollywood stars did not like the haggis, didn't
know what it was all about. And dear Triss kept
boozing and trying to forget what was happening.
That was a typical post-Christopher event. But that
house, a big townhouse in Park Street, was left to her
as part of the divorce proceedings, which she flogged
and has probably sustained her.' Triss retreated to
Brighton and died in October 2003.

Barbara, Mullally and Mann are the three survivors
of the gang today, and it is interesting to look at what
it was in Barbara's make-up which may have ensured
her survival. First, she didn't lose sight of home. Her
mother would come and stay at regular intervals, and
Barbara made a habit of going back to Leeds whenever she could. It was important to her to keep the
two worlds in some way co-existing. Subconsciously
she attached truth to Freda and Winston, to her upbringing, to what they had done for her. The glitzy
world in which she was moving she knew to be all
about appearance, and she was not ready to agree
wholeheartedly with Oscar Wilde that 'Truth is

entirely and absolutely a matter of style,' even if the next few decades would be a push-pull matter of indecision on that score.

Whenever Freda came to stay, Barbara made a point of taking her out with her. 'What was very nice, I always found in Barbara,' said Billie, 'was that every so often she'd have her mother come up and stay in London with her and she took her to all the places she frequented. You hear what I'm saying? All those places, whether her mother appeared to fit or not she was going to take her and she came.'

In *Act Of Will*, when Christina goes to London, her mother Audra lives for the times when she returns to Yorkshire or Audra goes to London to see her. When Barbara returned to Armley it was always a tremendous occasion, but one that also emphasised the difference between their two worlds, as Barbara's Ripon-based childhood friend Margery Clarke remembers: 'Barbara always brought her parents presents, like hampers from Fortnum and Mason . . . Her father, being a Yorkshireman, found out how much they cost and shook his head and said, "Now then, our Barbara, they've seen you coming!"' A Fortnum and Mason hamper comes to Francesca's rescue in the making of a meal in *Voice of the Heart*. There is caviar, pâtè de foie gras Strasbourg, aged Stilton cheese with port, and three tins of turtle soup – goodies not exactly compatible with Freda and Winston's simple diet, one suspects. Billie remembers having Freda and Barbara for dinner one evening and serving a vegetarian meal, quite daringly radical even in suburban London in the 1950s: 'I suppose it was a bit ingenuous of us. Freda ploughed through this meal and was saying, "Yes, it is very interesting this," but at the end of the meal she really couldn't contain herself and she said that she was not one hundred per cent for it. She said, "Daddy likes meat!"'

These were little markers, a few of many that showed that however much Barbara might want to keep her past, present and future as one, it was going to be difficult. It is a difficulty to which she admits even today, although she couldn't survive if she didn't return at regular intervals. 'It's just that when I go there I am a totally different person than I am in Manhattan, than I have become. I have to go back into the Barbara people knew, and it is difficult sometimes.' On another occasion she brought Freda home a squirrel coat, something she had always told Barbara she wanted, a kind of symbol of what her life had been sacrificed for. When Barbara gave it to her, Freda said, 'Where will I ever wear *that*?' The story seems to resonate with the differences between Armley and Mayfair, and Barbara made a point of telling me, 'You must remember, I became a completely different person when I went to London. I lived there for ten years . . . I'm very far removed from Leeds now.'

In some ways, however, Barbara did not change. She never became trendy, for example. In fact, it is interesting to see just how inured to outside influences was this traditional, stylish Mayfair scene into which Barbara had fallen with as much relish as if she had been coming home – which, in a sense, she had: home to the fantasy world of Edith Walker, which she was fast making real. Only just across Regent Street from Mayfair, into Soho, things were happening that would change the world, and yet Mayfair remained almost disdainfully oblivious. 'All the glamour was in that Mayfair square mile,' said Mullally. 'A little over-lapped occasionally into Soho and into Pimlico, but basically it was Mayfair. Soho was crumby. Nothing was happening in Soho. It was just crumby.'

'What about the French Pub and all that?' I pro-tested.

'Soho wasn't dressed up for cocktail Mayfair,' he replied. 'You'd go slumming in Soho.'

Soho was London's Bohemia. During the war, artists, the military on leave, intellectuals, black-marketeers, prostitutes, pimps and local working people made merry together in its pubs every even-ing, the painter Nina Hamnett occupying a central role and acquiring almost mythical status. 'After the fall of France, the York Minster, already a popu-lar watering-hole with the Bohemians,' wrote Judith Summers in her book entitled *Soho*, 'became the unofficial London headquarters of the exiled Free French.' It became known as The French Pub, its host Victorienne Berlemont, whose name, since the First War, meant something to squaddies all over the world.

Then there was Dylan Thomas's famous watering-hole at the Café Royal on Soho's western border, and drinking clubs beating the tight licensing laws – the Horseshoe in Wardour Street, the Byron in Greek

Street and the Mandrake in Meard Street. 'Since the turn of the twentieth century London's so-called Bohemians had been associated with Soho and [on the other side of Oxford Street] Bloomsbury and Fitzrovia.'

In Barbara's day, during the 1950s, Soho was once more a magnet for the eccentric, the creative, the unconventional and the rebellious. 'To the young especially, Soho is irresistible, for it offers a sort of freedom,' wrote Daniel Farson in *Soho in the Fifties*. 'When I arrived there in 1951 [to take up a job with *Picture Post*], London was suffering from post-war depression and it was a revelation to discover people who behaved outrageously without a twinge of guilt and drank so recklessly that when they met the next morning they had to ask if they needed to apologise for the day before.' Soho was a place for characters and conversation, for ideas and revolution. It no more mattered whether you had wealth here than it did at La Coupole, or on the left bank of the Seine where poets, painters, intellectuals and revolutionaries gathered in similar fashion in Paris.'

Names like Augustus John and the by then alcoholic Nina Hamnett gave Soho media currency, along with journalists such as *The Spectator*'s Jeffrey Bernard, painters Francis Bacon, Robert Colquhoun and Lucien Freud, the writer Colin MacInnes (*Absolute Beginners*, 1957), playwright Frank Norman (*Fings Ain't Wot They Used T'Be*, 1959), and jazz musician and writer George Melly. Gaston Berlemont now had the York Minster, and the famed drinking club the

Colony Room in Dean Street had opened in 1948; its soon-to-become-legendary owner was the eccentric, warm but ruthlessly selective Muriel Belcher, for, as in the key meeting-places on the other side of the tracks in Mayfair, you had to be a member.

A defining mark of 'Fifties Soho', however, was the coffee-bar scene, where, as Summers writes, 'for the price of a cup of frothy coffee, Teddy-boys, Rockers and skiffle fans could sit for hours behind a steamed-up window listening to the latest Elvis or Chuck Berry hit on the jukebox, accompanied by the loud hiss of an espresso machine.' Soho coffee bars were the music Mecca for the young, and youth was, for the public at large, what the Fifties was all about.

As it happened, Billie Figg wrote the first article about Britain's first home-grown rocker, Tommy Steele. It appeared in *Picturegoer* in 1956 and was headlined, '*The* Coffee-Bar Sensation'. Steele, the piece tells us, was discovered by John Kennedy in the *Two I*'s bar in Soho. When Kennedy, who ran a picture agency and happened to be in there drinking coffee, heard him sing, he immediately arranged for a Decca A&R man to come and listen to him. Kennedy became Steele's manager, and Steele took the charts by storm. After that, Soho, and the *Two I*'s in particular, was the place to be discovered. Tommy Steele, Terry Dene, Adam Faith and Cliff Richard could be seen performing here in their earliest days. As Bruce Welch of The Shadows recalled: 'If it was good enough for Tommy Steele it was good enough for us . . . we almost lived there . . . If we were lucky we'd play downstairs four nights a week, from seven till eleven – mostly Buddy Holly and Everly Brothers numbers. It was a small place, very hot and very sweaty, with a tiny eighteen-inch-high stage at one end, a microphone and a few old speakers up on the wall ... always packed.'

When Kennedy flipped through a sheaf of photos of Tommy Steele during Figg's interview, he stopped at one showing his charge playing a gig at London's swanky Stork Room, and said: 'But Tommy's not interested in Mayfair Society. He wants a girl just like his mum.'

The comment showed agent Kennedy's nose for a good photo caption, but it also pointed up precisely the breakaway nature of the scene Tommy Steele was setting. Glamour was no longer the dream. Hitherto, Mayfair Society had been the thing. It, royalty, Hollywood and couture fashion were all the news on the society and women's pages. But now a music scene was about to erupt onto the pages of newspapers and magazines which would change all that. Hollywood kept producing stars like Ava Gardner, Elizabeth Taylor, Rock Hudson, Grace Kelly and Stewart Granger in the old glamorous tradition, but the male iconography of the period belonged to the late Marlon Brando dressed in leather and sat astride a motorbike in *The Wild One* (1953), or, in mid-decade, to the smouldering, challenging youthful features of James Dean in *East of Eden* and *Rebel Without a Cause*.

Barbara left London on the cusp of a change that dealt a killer blow to Mayfair glamour as the dream of the young. Brian Epstein first heard The Beatles at the Cavern Club in Liverpool in October 1961, the year that Barbara met her future husband. In 1963, the year that she married and left England for America, they topped the charts for the first time with 'Please Please Me'. Beatlemania was upon us. The world would never be the same again. Yet, for Barbara, despite being a decade younger than Billie, change was never on the cards. She continued to wear conservative, classic, smart clothes, and her taste in music was still her father's – Eartha Kitt, Lena Horne, Frank Sinatra and Tony Bennett. 'Just as she was conservative with clothes, there's a parallel with her taste in music,' observed Billie. 'At that period the other music that was square dancing, which had come over from America, bop and bee bop and all those sort of things . . . they were nothing to do with Barbara.'

Far away from all this, and yet so close to its centre geographically, was the glamorous Mayfair tradition to which Barbara belonged, and for which it now seemed Freda's educational programme had prepared her. On the face of it, as far as Barbara was concerned, what was established in Leeds was built on in London, not discarded, and contrary to her insistence that she was a completely different person when she went to London, there was no great change. 'But,' said Billie, 'the person *did* change. So, the appearance and the person were not the same.'

'On the outside,' Barbara says, 'people see a part of me and that's the part I allow to be seen. I think I'm a very shy person in many ways. I think the profession I've chosen should tell people that. It's private, it's an interaction between the author herself and characters. My typewriter is my psychiatrist ... the Barbara Taylor Bradford complexities I save for my work.'

We have seen that identity is her constant theme, and this matter of truth and appearance is always worked out in the context of identity in the novels. From the moment she left the world that she identified with truth – the world of her childhood, her mother and father – up until the moment she rediscovered it in writing *A Woman of Substance* and *Act of Will*, Barbara has, so it seems to me, been on a pilgrim's progress of challenges, many of them self-imposed but without which her life would have been, for her, unbearably ordinary. In the process, her style has not changed, but over the years the person on the inside has been transformed, and the whole gamut of experience has allowed her to view what she started out with and where the trail has led her in a telling new light – the light in which her fictional characters glow. So, she can give us characters who are forgers, like Camilla Galland in *The Women in His Life*, who believes we can only ever have an unnatural identity, that we create a life out of more or less conscious choices, adaptations, imitations and plain theft of styles, names, social and sexual roles, that we write our own scripts and live by them. And she can give us others alongside them who are deeply centred on their natural, 'real' selves, like Anastasia in the same novel, or like Francesca in *Voice of the Heart*, and still others who, bereft of their own identity by dint of fate, create themselves whole new natures, like Maxim West, only to find there is something missing, there is a vacuum where his real self should be.

Barbara was, however, still a long way from this level of perception. At this stage of her life, in the 1950s and early 1960s, she was writing a script of her own to live by, while still drawing on the values of her youth for that script, which gave her a resilience that others around her – Jeannie, Triss – didn't have, and which inured her from the danger of becoming sick with celebrity narcissism, which did for so many in that showbiz world, even though one might think that Freda had inadvertently prepared her for it. Barbara used the self-assurance Freda gave her; she found security in Freda's conviction of her perfection, her superiority over others, her extraordinary qualities, but always knew it was something she needed to prove to be true for herself.

'One of the charming things about her,' remembered Jack Figg of Barbara in the 1950s, 'is that she never took all of that glamour very seriously. She did appear to, she was involved, but there was always a twinkle in her eye, as if to say, isn't this fun, all these people, who are not really part of us, but we are joining them.'

Now, the impression Jack has of this could conceivably have been one that Barbara intended him to have – another example of a persistent desire for psychological unity in the diverse scenes (Armley, suburban London, glamorous Mayfair) in which she moved.

For, as Jack is the first to admit, he did not fall into the Jeannie-person category. On the few occasions he did find himself 'standing about with a wine glass in hand and chatting at one of Jeannie's bigger receptions', he made 'quite a lot of booboos. I remember once I was speaking to a chap about Norman Wisdom [the slapstick comedian] and I said that I thought Norman Wisdom was very, very clever, very funny, but his material was absolutely appalling and I felt that he needed better writers, one thing and another. And then Billie took me aside and said, "You are talking to Jack Davies, he IS Norman Wisdom's scriptwriter."'

An ability to rumble the celebrity culture was the best protection any girl in it could hope for. A sense of humour, an ability to laugh at herself, and to find genuine friends beyond her circle, would give the necessary objectivity – and in this the Figgs were so important. They regarded themselves as definitely off the celeb circuit: 'Sure I was a journalist,' Billie said, 'but I was a journalist who was coming home every night to a suburb. She'd obviously got these several circles of chums, which is healthy.

'I remember, Barbara often used to come down in a pale-blue Ford Zephyr that she had rather early on, a lovely pale-blue Zephyr, very stylish, and she'd come down to our other house, which was even more suburban than this. She stayed for a few days and I was away working, and Jack had just taken a new job – a travelling job . . .'

Jack seized the opportunity to develop what was,

after all, his story. 'Yes, Barbara was staying, and Billie I think had gone to Paris, to the Collections. So this chap, who was showing me the ropes, said, "Can we go somewhere quiet and go over some paper-work?" So I said, "Let's go home." He said, "Will your wife be there?" I said, "No, she's in Paris at the moment." So that was all right. So, we were sitting in this bay window we had, going over this paperwork, and Barbara roars up the drive in this pale-blue Zephyr with a mink stole that she used to trail around, and she had her own key and she came in, and I said, "Oh, Barbara, this is Maurice Brown," and Maurice Brown's eyes were popping out of his head. Barbara, who was a great prankster, her eyes twinkled and she said, "I'm going upstairs, darling, I'll be up there if you want me." Maurice was waiting for an expla-nation as to who this other woman was. Nothing was ever said. I just left it. But I'd arranged to meet Maurice Brown the next morning somewhere, at some station, and Barbara said that she would take me and drop me off, which she did. There he was waiting as we roared up in this pale-blue Zephyr, and she got out and put her arms round me and drew my head down and kissed me full on the mouth, and put her leg back as people do, and said, "Bye darling, see you later!" Well, I just sat in the car with Maurice and said, "Good morning, Maurice," and off we drove.

'That was typically Barbara really. It was the way she twigged immediately that there was a very funny situation to be made out of this.'

Although Jack is wont to describe himself and his

wife as 'loose-end people . . . someone for Barbara to lean back on', it is quite clear that they were as close then as they are today. They were close enough then for Barbara and Billie to go on holiday together to Paris, and indeed to indulge, on a few unlikely occasions, in the Figgs' sport of camping.

'We were campers,' said Billie, 'and we went away every weekend at that time, with a tent and our car. If Barbara was at a loose end, as happened on some of these weekends, she came with us and we brought a little tent for her, a separate tent. I can tell you, she didn't stay under canvas. When we got there the first time, she looked at this thing we erected . . . Well, it was all right during the day, but then when we decided to prepare for retirement (it was quite early when we made the beds) there was this sudden scream and she shot out saying there were beetles in there. We said, "Oh yes, that's part of it, you often get beetles, you just brush them out." But no: "Oh, I'm not staying there!" So we had to go and find her a pub to stay in. On another occasion she came to a little piece of land my father had down on the River Crouch in Essex and we all camped on there. She was very tickled because my father had said, "It will be very nice to see you on our little estate!" When we got there, there was this tiny bit of land that we pitched our tent on. They were fun times. We roamed over half of Essex with Barbara.'

Typically, Barbara turned the Paris holiday with Billie into something of a journalistic coup. There never was a distinction between the worlds of work and play. As far as Barbara was and still is concerned, they are a seamless whole. 'We agreed that we'd like a holiday, a week in Paris,' Billie recalled. 'We just thought that would be nice to do. We took a hotel, which was a pretty run-down sort of Left Bank hotel. It had a bed in the wall, you had to press a button and the bed comes down. Somehow it worked out that Barbara was going to be on the side near the window. There was a fire escape outside which went right past the window, and I remember Barbara saying, "Oh, Billie . . . what if somebody comes down that fire escape? What if some man breaks in?" She paused and looked across at me and said: "I'm first!" And then she said, "I don't mean I want him first!" I shall never forget that. Did we laugh! Anyway, it was a pretty run-down kind of place, but Barbara had fixed with a man she knew, called Escarti – he worked for a film company – to get an interview with Ingrid Bergman. This was an incredible coup because she'd only just come in out of the cold, as it were, after the seven years' banishment that Hollywood had treated her to. She'd run away with Rossellini seven years previously and America had shunned her. [She had left her husband Peter for director Roberto Rossellini and ignored the moralistic machinations of the Motion Picture Association of America to bring her to heel. Incredibly, Senator Edwin Johnson declared she should never again set foot on American soil.] No American film company would deal with her. But now, only that year [1956], they had starred her in *Anastasia*, and the British Press – us, if we got it –

would be the first to interview her. It was a scoop! We did get it! Amazingly, it was agreed to! We fixed up that *Woman* magazine would take the article.

'Bergman was at the Théâtre de Paris playing in *Tea and Sympathy*, and we turned up about ten minutes before she did. She came in looking very ordinary with her hair in pin curls and a scarf over them, frightfully mumsy really. The story we wanted – the sort of thing that everyone wanted at that time – was Bergman's philosophy of life. Barbara and I each had some questions ready. We sat in a place full of sofas, so many we had one each, I remember, and we just fired questions at her as we went. She answered them all.'

The article begins with a comment about Bergman's characteristic lack of affectation, that she was a complete natural, not into the appearance culture – 'it is impossible to imagine that what she says is part of a pose,' and knowing that 'is important when you are talking to an actress,' wrote our two reporters. Then Bergman tells them about the early childhood loss of her mother – she died when Ingrid was two – and of her father, who died when she was twelve. Truth, appearance, loss, loneliness, the very themes that would, years later, dominate Barbara's novels, and already dominated her life now. The positive theme of the interview is about courage . . . the courage to do something with your life and not be 'put off by other people's advice or opinion . . . the courage it takes to stand on your own feet and do what you think is right . . . It is a duty,' says Bergman, 'each of us owes to the rest of the community as well as to ourselves . . . You have only to look about you to see a world full of people with chips on their shoulders. They wanted to do something with their lives but were put off by other people's advice or opinion. And so they feel cheated. They are impossible to live with because they have built up resentment within themselves. If I had not gone ahead and studied for the stage in Stockholm, my disappointment would have poisoned my whole life.'

Barbara and Billie hung on her every word. Thinking 'of the people who felt they could have been artists or writers but were afraid of the insecurity,' as they wrote, 'this aspect of Ingrid Bergman's philosophy of life became clearer.' For Barbara in particular, this was completely on song. She must have left the theatre walking on air, more determined than ever to move her own plans along.

By the time she interviewed Ingrid Bergman, Barbara had been out of *Woman's Own* for two years. In 1955, at twenty-two, she had been hired as columnist and celebrity profiler by Reg Willis when he became editor of the *London Evening News*. At that time it was the capital's largest circulation paper. 'I was working with a woman called Gwen Robyns, who you must have heard of because she wrote many books about Grace Kelly. She was married to a Dane or a Swede and she was this plumpish, jolly, nice woman. She was our boss and it was a room full of women. We did all sorts of features, and I used to be sent out to do stuff for the diary page, too.'

As usual with Barbara, the move forward was ser-
endipity; she got the job in the course of what today
might be termed networking, but was for Barbara
simply an evening out. 'I met Reg Willis when he was
features editor. It was probably a movie thing. Roddy
Mann was probably there and Jack Gourlay and Matt
White, and my little group of people that we all went
around in. I noticed there were mostly men there with
me, and I remember I had a blue hat, a knitted beret;
it was a sort of bluish purple, but it had sequins that
were like long tails; it was a glittery beret and very
pretty. And that's how I met Reg. He came over and
he said, "I love that hat, who are you?" And I said,
"I'm Barbara Taylor." We chatted and he asked me
who I worked with, and I said, "I'm with *Woman's
Own*, but I really want to get back on a newspaper,
I'm beginning to hate this." And that is how Barry
Horniblow's name came up. I told him about *YEP*
and my great editor Barry Horniblow, and we spoke
about how Barry had gone out to South Africa, and
eventually he said, "I'll see you around and if you ever
– you know my number, it's the *London Evening
News*, give me a call some time." Then, of course, I
kept running into him and finally one day I did call
him and said I really would like to come and have an
interview for a job on his newspaper. So I went down
to see him. I remember Reg interviewing me about my
experiences in Leeds and what have you, and then he
took me in to see the editor and when we left the
editor's office, Reg said, "How long notice do you
have to give, how many weeks?" So I said I'd have to

find out, and he said, "Well, better give your notice anyway." Now nobody had offered me the job, the editor didn't say he was giving me a job. Reg just said, "Don't worry about it, Barbara." Then I found out I had to give two weeks' notice to *Woman's Own*, and when I told Reg, I don't remember how I said this, but I was nervously saying to him, "Are you sure I've got this job because the editor didn't tell me that I had the job." I wanted to hear it from the boss man, not the features editor. He said, "Barbara, I promise you, it's really all right." So, I gave my notice in with trepidation, and then I got a letter from the *News* and it was signed, "Reg Willis, Editor". He knew that the other chap was on the way out. So that's how I moved to the *London Evening News*.

'Then one night, after I'd been there maybe a couple of years – I often stayed late because I liked to get my desk totally cleaned up and do all the things that get neglected if you've been out doing stories, and Reg often used to look in – on this day he came in and said, "I see you're still here, Barbara, come on, I'll buy you a drink." And I do remember him standing in the doorway with a funny look on his face. He had some papers in his hand and I don't know what the words were – it's too long ago – but I must have said something like, "Is something wrong?" I knew . . . I always could read people. And he said, "I've just got something on the wire service, Barbara." He looked at me and said, "There's only one way to say it – Barry Horniblow just died." Well, of course, tears . . . I got sort of choked up. I didn't start sobbing or anything.

I'd got tears in my eyes and I started to cry and he said, "Come on, I'll take you out for a drink." And I don't recall going for that drink, but maybe we did – El Vinos, somewhere like that. Horniblow ... of course I worshipped him ... Although then he was white-haired, he must have been a man in his fifties when I was fifteen, or maybe in his forties, I don't know.'

How far the death of Horniblow widened Barbara's perspective on what was going on in her life I cannot say, but he had started her off professionally, had been the first impetus, and his passing may well have encouraged her to look hard at where she had taken herself since. She had built up a great deal of journalistic experience, and contacts, too – perhaps now was the time to make a play for something more her own, or to buckle down and realise her ambition to write novels. Had she done so, it would have been no surprise to her friend, Billie: 'I always knew she was fiddling about with plots [for novels of her own] and trying them. She was very up on all the new books coming out. She had a knack, the books she chose – I remember Bud Schulberg's *What Made Sammy Run* in the early Fifties, things like that. They were the big bestsellers.'

However, instead of pursuing her ambition to write novels, as Keith Waterhouse, Roderic Mann, Frederic Mullally and Richard Condon were doing, and as Ingrid Bergman would certainly have advised her to do, Barbara looked for independence in what she already knew. She went the journalistic route with a new newspaper, which turned out not to be a good idea.

The paper was a weekly, geared to appeal to Americans living in London (there were some 80,000 at the time), and to American troops stationed in the UK. No doubt the thrill of the start-up appealed. As Barbara recalls: 'The staff was small and we all had to pitch in,' she as woman's page editor. An American, Bill Caldwell, was the first Editor. He had the distinction of appointing a youthful Bob Guccione, an artist and cartoonist before he launched *Penthouse* magazine.

Embellishing a story she had recently given to Anthony Haden-Guest (*New York Magazine* and the *Observer*), Barbara recalled the day Guccione first stepped into the office: 'I saw this man in reception when I went to lunch,' she told me. 'He was still there when I returned.' When she asked the receptionist who the visitor was and what he wanted, she replied 'Robert Sabatini Guccione. He's waiting to see the editor, but he doesn't have an appointment.'

Barbara, yielding to courtesy – 'It's so impolite to leave someone waiting for two hours' – conceded that she had 'better have a word with him'. The receptionist grinned, 'Oh yes, he just said he'd like to talk to the beautiful strawberry blonde,' and delivered the Sicilian to her door.

They became friends. After Guccione had made *Penthouse* a success, Barbara would attend dinner parties at his New York mansion, the walls hung with his collection of Van Gogh, Matisse, Renoir, Chagall, Degas, Modigliani, Picasso . . .

Meanwhile, on their first meeting he showed her his 'rather clever cartoons, with a feeling of Jules Feiffer about them', and she set up an appointment for him to meet Bill Caldwell. 'Bob told me he could also write, and that he had an idea for a political column called "Foggy Bottom",' she recalls. Caldwell hired him on the spot the next day. 'Everyone on the paper liked Bob Guccione,' Barbara remembers, 'and his column became very popular with the Americans.' His work routine was rather singular, however: 'He wouldn't come in until one or two, but he would stay there very late. He often worked all night.'

It was while Guccione was so doing that *Penthouse* began to take shape in his mind. Caldwell had by this time been replaced as editor by Derek Jameson. 'After he had been there a few months, Guccione tried to press sexy material on him,' Barbara said. 'Derek, a real dyed-in-the-wool newspaperman, declined. He told Guccione: "Look, we can't put tits and arse on our front page. We'll all end up in the nick!"' Given that Jameson would later become editor of the tabloid *News of the World*, and editor-in-chief of the *Daily Star*, his protestations must surely have been influenced by the prevailing, rather different market perception of *The London American*, though one can't help wondering if a move, however tentative, in Guccione's direction might have enhanced the newspaper's appeal to Americans, who were already being well prepared for it by Hugh Hefner. 'Later, Bob brought in a dummy of a magazine he wanted to start. It was beautiful. He was very professional in everything he did. I said, "Bob, it looks great, but isn't it a total copy of *Playboy*?" He said, "If there's one, there's always room for two." And he was right.' *Penthouse* went on to sell five million copies a month at its peak.

The London American fared less well. It ran for sixty-six issues between March 1960 and June 1961. '*The London American* lacked advertising revenue,' Barbara states today, 'and this in the end was the cause of the paper's failure. It couldn't justify its existence. The owners had other business commitments. So they finally lost interest. The paper closed down . . . I felt sorry for some of the people who were without work, and we were all sad to see it disappear. We'd all enjoyed being together, there had been a lot of camaraderie.'

Barbara returned to freelance work, moving in behind a desk in Billie Figg's 'funny little office on the fifth floor in Covent Garden, overlooking the *My Fair Lady* show in Drury Lane', as Billie herself described it: 'At that time I had a PR company with Shirley Harrison, the author. Barbara used to come and use a desk, not as part of Shirley's and my business but as a friend.' This was, without doubt, a low point for Barbara, the demise of *The London American* a terrific blow. 'By the end of the Fifties I think she was feeling disappointed that she'd not brought off anything very big,' recalls Billie. 'I remember, and Barbara agrees with me, she had an uneasy period. What she was up to was not meeting her aspirations.'

'I did feel out of sorts,' Barbara admits. 'I was rather irritated with myself, disappointed that I hadn't written a novel. That was my dream.'

Initially, she had begun to freelance for a Belgian magazine, specialising in celebrity-type interviews, while at the same time working on *Florabelle*. Soon, however, another reason not to pursue her declared ambition to be a writer of fiction would present itself and she would grab it. She was offered a job with a magazine called *Today*, a title from the IPC stable for whom Billie had once worked. 'I was a big admirer of the editor of *Today*, an energetic and talented American called Larry Solon, so I took the job immediately . . . I enjoyed it there, and perhaps that's why *Florabelle* never got finished. I was back in journalism full-time again.'

Then, not long afterwards, fate played Barbara a winning hand. Jeannie Gilbert, who by this time had made New York her home, was staying with her fiancé, the Broadway producer David Merrick, at the Beverly Hills Hotel in Los Angeles, where she ran into an old friend, a movie producer by name of Robert Bradford, who was waiting to meet a colleague for lunch at the pool where, famously, the Hollywood glitterati met. As he was about to go to London, Jeannie told him he must call on her best friend, Barbara Taylor. But she didn't have her telephone number, so she scribbled on a piece of paper the number of Barbara's then neighbour.

Barbara had recently moved to a swish address in Bryanston Square, Marylebone. 'Jack Davies and

Dorothy, his wife, had a duplex apartment there,' she told me, 'what you would call a maisonette in London. You went in on the street level and then they also had the downstairs that opened on to a garden. I had the garden apartment next door to them, and next door to me was Sean Connery with a garden apartment . . . Dorothy was an interior designer, and we sort of did it up together. It was warm, cosy, with a living room, kitchen, bathroom and bedroom, just right for a single girl.'

Bob Bradford takes up the story: 'When I got to London I was inundated with work on a movie called *The Golden Touch*, a costume picture about the Louisiana Purchase [the transaction in 1803 which saw the sale of the French-speaking Mississippi state by Napoleon I to the US for $15 million].' There couldn't have been a more apt title for the project that would bring Bob and Barbara together, though it was a couple of weeks before he came across that bit of paper with Jack Davies' number on it: 'I phoned it and they invited me over. It was a Saturday night. They had promised to get Barbara in for a drink, but when I arrived there was no sign of her.'

Many miles away in Gloucestershire, Barbara was attending a friend's birthday party, unaware of what had been cooked up. Jack and Dorothy had failed to make contact. But they and Bob got on well and that night they asked him to join them for dinner in Soho. 'I did, and then when the bill came Jack discovered he'd forgotten his chequebook. So I lent him some money. Dorothy then insisted I come to lunch the next day, so they could repay the loan, and she promised to have Barbara for lunch as well.'

Barbara drove back from the country early that Sunday morning. No sooner had she parked outside her flat when she heard the phone ringing. 'It was Jack asking me to come to Sunday lunch. I explained I had a deadline to meet [but] he brushed it aside, said a friend of Jeannie's was in town, that he was a handsome man with lots of charm. I just laughed, explained I couldn't miss the deadline . . . Then Dorothy called and explained what had happened the night before. They would be embarrassed if I didn't show up . . . So I said, "Oh all right, but I can't stay long. *I have a deadline*!"'

When she made her way next door she was told to expect three people, one of whom would be this Bob Bradford. When the three arrived, there was an attractive red-head in a green suit, a smaller man, somewhat nondescript, and another man. It was quite obvious to her that the taller of the two men just had to be with the red-head, and that Bob – the one for her – was this smaller nondescript fella. As it turned out, she was wrong and not to be disappointed. The woman was Pat Lasky, the smaller man screenwriter Jesse Lasky Jnr, who was working on the script of *The Golden Touch*, and 'Bob just came across the room with Dorothy and was introduced. He sat down next to me, started to talk about Jeannie, and how he had run into her in the Beverly Hills Hotel. We got on immediately: he was so warm and friendly, and he had the loveliest brown eyes, they were kind. I can remember thinking what a nice man he was, and also how attractive he was as well. I'd been led to understand that we were having lunch at the maisonette, but Jack announced that we were going to a restaurant. And so, half an hour later, we went to a nearby Indian restaurant. I'll never forget Bob leaning into me, whispering in my ear that he wasn't too fond of Indian food. Neither was I.'

What had been Bob's immediate reaction to Barbara? 'She was twenty-seven, twenty-eight. What did I see in her? I can't really say. She was very pretty, an attractive young woman. She was bright, and I put a lot of value on intellect, intelligence. She was *outcoming*, and I guess that really caught my attention. After lunch I asked her what she was doing. And she said, "Nothing."'

'That's true,' said Barbara. 'I'll never forget Dorothy's face. It was a picture, as silently she mouthed, "*What about the deadline?*" Of course, the deadline was forgotten. I went with Bob to the movies, and we've been going to the movies ever since.'

CHAPTER FOUR

Change of Identity

'*Most nights he lay awake, prowling the dark
labyrinths of his soul, seeking meanings for his
life and all that had happened to him.*'
Maxim West in *The Women in His Life*

In *Voice of the Heart*, people are not who they appear
to be. Immaculate, wealthy superstar Victor Mason
started life as 'Victor Massonetti, construction worker,
the simple Italian-American kid from Cincinnati,
Ohio', and tempestuous leading lady Katharine
Tempest has also changed her name. She was born
Katie Mary O'Rourke in Chicago. They have both
become something else by their own efforts; they have
risen in the meritocracy, which the western world is
in the process of becoming, and – so it seems – have
changed their names to signal their new identities.

For Katharine in particular this becomes quite an
issue in the novel, her lover Kim reading her conceal-
ment of her true identity as deception, a sign that she
is incapable of true love. Then we learn that indeed
her decision to change her name signals something

dangerously repressive, a desire to blot out her past. In Katharine we get to understand the effect that dire childhood experience can have on a girl. This is surely what Barbara sensed, however subconsciously, about Freda when she said of her, 'I believe that my mother always had a great sense of loss, in fact I know that she did,' although Barbara did not at the time know the details of that loss.

The particular childhood problems Katharine suffered were quite different from Freda's, although childhood loss is the common denominator. The reason the fictional Katharine changes her name is that as a child she was exiled from home by her father, sent to boarding school in England because of her influence over her brother Ryan, an influence which is benign, but at odds with their father's plan to turn Ryan into a politician. She isn't even allowed home for the school holidays. Then, she is abused by her father's business partner. 'In the ensuing days she began to realise how much that horrifying child-hood experience had scarred her, what a devasta-ting effect it had on her adult life.' In effect, Katharine has been cut off from love, cut off at her roots, and she changes her name in an effort to make a fresh start.

But it isn't possible to wipe the slate clean by chang-ing your name, whatever cosmetically salutary effect it may have on self-image, and we see the results of that in the novel. There is more to identity than appearance. A name change will not suffice; this is very much the thematic material on which the author is sharpening her claws in *Voice of the Heart* and in *The Women in His Life*. Identity is again the theme, her message to her readers being, in her own words, 'to know who you are and what you are'.

If Barbara came to this theme subconsciously on account of her mother Freda's sense of loss, it was also brought home to her when she met Robert Bradford, her future husband. Like Barbara an only child, Robert Bradford was born in 1930 of a German Jewish family living in Berlin. He was three years of age when the Nazis seized power and at five he was taken out of Germany with a cousin and placed with a French family in Paris. 'His father was dead. He never saw his mother again,' Barbara told me. 'He prefers not to talk about it.' The final tragedy was that after the end of the war, Bob's mother, who did survive, went to America to find him, only to die shortly before they could be reunited. 'His mother took him out of Germany in 1939 and subsequently she herself got out but she couldn't get to him because the Germans had occupied France. Eventually when she got to America, because of the confusion she still could not find him. When he finally made it to America in 1946 she had died a few weeks before. I cried quite a lot when I wrote *The Women in His Life*. I suppose I thought of Bob as a child. I think he found the book very haunting, very moving.'

Exiled, cut off from his root culture, Bob changed his name, just as in *Voice of the Heart*, Nick's great-grandfather, also a German Jew, changed his when he emigrated to America. If we need confirmation that

Barbara's preoccupation with identity owes something to her relationship with the man she loves (as
well as to the mother she loved), this is surely it.

Fellow Jew Bobby Caplin makes the point that
name change is common among this generation. 'Well,
I've got a friend, his real name is Gerald Goldstein.
At school he changed it to Jerome, then when he left
school he changed it to Goddard. Who knows, having
come through the holocaust maybe you don't want to
be reminded . . . I mean it's not just a name, there's a
whole lot of other baggage that comes with that. It's
all very well saying, well I wouldn't do it, but we
haven't been through those circumstances, where you
do not want to be acknowledged as a Jew, which I
can thoroughly understand.'

I was not surprised to learn from Barbara that Bob
was always very tender with Freda. They cannot have
had a great deal in common, but I could imagine
an unspoken, subliminal acknowledgement of their
shared sense of loss, similar because it had to do with
identity, aloneness, being dispossessed. Just as Freda
was drawn back to Ripon time and again in search of
her lost world – the shadowy figure of her father
and the environment in which her whole incredible
childhood had been played out – so, in *The Women
in His Life*, the character who comes closest to Bob
in all the novels, Maximilian West, is drawn back to
the places of his childhood loss, too:

*The lure of childhood, he thought, how strong it
is with me . . . is it because I lost so much when I*

was a child ... had such irretrievable losses? Do
I come back to Paris and Berlin in the hopes of
finding something which escaped me long, long
ago?

Maxim's eternal quest is successfully completed in
the novel. He comes to articulate the nature of his
childhood loss and finds the something he did not
know about himself, about his parents, about the love
he thought he'd lost.

Another thing that Freda and Bob had in common,
of course, was their love for Barbara, and, coming as
they did from this similar ground of childhood loss,
one is bound to speculate whether they drew something similar from her in recompense. Barbara, of
course, was Freda's saviour. She will not stint in heap-
ing praise on her mother for her encouragement and
love, but it is also true that Barbara gave Freda a
reason for living. Most significantly, she was, in her
very character, an impressive expression of the very
identity lost to her mother – her style, as I see it,
an amalgam of the sparkle of Edith and the sheer
persistence of a Ripon.

Is it also true to say that Barbara compensated
Bob's childhood loss? Certainly she came to root his
work in her own strong Yorkshire culture (nine films
would be shot based on Barbara's novels). It is not
chance that many of Barbara's heroes and heroines
call upon her Yorkshire-rooted values in order to
make their decisions and to make their judgements.
Bob, bereft of family and alienated from his home

culture, will surely have benefited from the stability of so certain a cultural influence.

In the fact of their meeting in Bryanston Square lies an eerie coincidence, which pulls Freda and her mother Edith's story into the picture of Bob and Barbara's relationship from day one. For Bryanston Square is the very place where Edith's Studley Royal contemporary – her rival in Frederick's affections, the Most Honourable Constance Gladys Marchioness of Ripon – died less than half a century earlier. She was occupying No. 13 at the time. Barbara lived at No. 5.

Of course, loss was the last thing that Barbara read in Bob's brown eyes on the day they first met; nor did he need any help in the direction in which he saw himself going. He was already successful in the film industry, he was a sophisticated, cosmopolitan figure, and plainly, in that sense, he knew where he was coming from. He was the epitome of the suave Hollywood producer, with all the outward accoutrements that she had always deemed essential in a man. He had style, he dressed well and he gave the impression of being able, like a fine batsman, to deal with the swiftest of balls at his own pace, a master of timing with no small amount of wit.

Friends of Barbara could see immediately that they shared something in their personal style, something of the glamorous tradition, but then one also commented, 'I think my feeling, when I very first met him, was that he was someone I couldn't access, if you know what I mean.' This was, I think, the key comment. There was an emotional detachment. At one and the same time one can see this as an alienating factor (perfectly consistent as a response to the sadness of his own childhood loss) and as a key element in his success as a modern man. There is no way you can be successful in the high-powered world of movie finance, where tens of millions of dollars are at stake, without a certain detachment, inscrutability even. 'And he was a major player,' said Bobby Caplin. 'He is certainly very shrewd, and I think in the part of the film business he was involved with, you have to be.'

Jack Figg had a taste both of Bob's inaccessibility and of what he presumed to be the tacitly structured nature of the film business when once Barbara was away and suggested Bob take him and Billie to dinner. 'Barbara wasn't with us,' said Jack. 'I was flattered. We went to a place – I think it was in Charles Street – more or less opposite the flat they had there. It wasn't a restaurant, it was just a big black door.'

'Mark's Club?'

'That's it. The door was opened by a chap with white gloves and we were shown in. We sat at a table and I was making small conversation, "Nice place this, etc." Billie and I suddenly felt very uncomfortable and nothing happened, and I was saying, "Do you want us to order, Bob?" "No, no, no," he said. And we sat there and the atmosphere was charged with some sort of tenseness and after a while I just said, "What's happening?" He said, "Well we're in the wrong place, we're down in the B Room. We've got to go into the other room." And there was a little flight of stairs leading up into it. He said, "That's the

A Room." So we said, "What does it matter we're in the wrong room, aren't we all right here?" "No," he said, "And I can't be seen here. If I'm seen here everybody will start talking about Bob Bradford, did you see him there, etc."'

There is a prerequisite in business to get behind the face that is presented, to be accepted somehow into the inner sanctum, and personal style may be as important as the product you are selling in order to achieve that. Also, there is no way you can carry off the big deals, or handle the prima-donna personalities, unless you are utterly straightforward. You can be brutal, so long as when it comes to the crunch you are straightforward. Otherwise, no one will ever deal with you again. If, at the same time, you are able to disarm your interlocutor with a sense of humour, you are in, and Bob has this very nice, quiet, dry sense of humour, which Barbara loves and made a point of stressing to me: 'No day goes by when he doesn't make me laugh.' That is something for a wife to say of her husband after more than forty years of marriage. In 1961, others were soon shown this side of him, as one close friend recalls: 'I discovered, as we would see him more and more personally, that he's very easy to get on with and rather warm – and I thought, how odd!'

The period of Barbara's first meeting with Bob was one in which she couldn't have failed to be aware of the nature of his childhood loss, for their meeting occurred at precisely the moment that the world was examining the dispossession of German Jewry at the hands of Adolf Eichmann. 'I was stupendously aware of what had happened to the Jews of Europe under the Nazis,' Barbara said. 'I suppose because it was the persecution of innocent people. Though I was always into history ... I couldn't bear the thought of it.' There could have been no more powerful a delineation of the loss that Bob had suffered (to be so tenderly described in Barbara's novel *The Women in His Life*) than the real-life re-enactment of the horrors of the Holocaust daily in the English newspapers as Barbara first met her future husband.

SS-Obersturmbannfuhrer Karl Adolf Eichmann, head of the Department for Jewish Affairs in the Gestapo from 1941 to 1945, chief of operations in the deportation of millions of Jews to extermination camps, was brought to a controversial and highly publicised trial in 1961. It lasted from 2nd April to 14th August. Eichmann was pronounced guilty, sentenced to death and, on 31st May 1962, hanged in Ramleh Prison.

> *Stepping over to the table, she grabbed the paper, stood staring at the headlines and the photographs, her eyes widening with shock, her face freezing into rigid lines of horror.*
>
> *Names of places leapt off the page at her. Ohrdruf ... Belsen ... Buchenwald. The most fearful words stabbed at her eyes. Death camps ... atrocities ... inhumanity ... extermination ... Jews ... millions murdered ... genocide.*
>
> *She lowered her eyes to the pictures. They*

stunned and horrified her, so graphic were they
in the foul, inhuman story they told of the most
unspeakable brutality and cruelty, a terrible testa-
ment to the pitiless torture and mass murder of
innocent people.

Teddy (Theodora Stein) in
The Women in His Life

Barbara was drawn deeply into the reportage. It had
a marked effect on many, especially those involved
with Germans. Bob Bradford told Barbara little about
his own history, but the Holocaust recurs frequently
in her novels. 'I do have strong feelings about it
because I'm a child of Europe,' she explains. 'I grew
up in England during the war, and my husband Bob
was born in Berlin and taken out of Germany to Paris
when he was five, because he was Jewish. Unlike many
German Jews who didn't ever believe they would be
hurt or touched, this family did. His mother got out,
but all the aunts and uncles disappeared.'

Just how deeply Barbara mined the emotional
strata of Bob's early life in her book was shown years
later: 'I was somewhere in Ohio to give a little talk,
most likely Dayton. Seats had been set out in a book-
shop, you know the kind of thing, you could have a
coffee, a soft drink. And this woman came and sat
down and put her copy of *A Woman of Substance* on
the table. She said: "I'd like you to sign it, but I haven't
read it."

' "Don't worry," I said (as I do). "Millions have."

'She then pulled the book from her bag and said

that she had been going to Switzerland by plane when *The Women in His Life* had just come out. She tried to read it on the plane, but figured from the opening that it was another business story like *A Woman of Substance*. She'd got to Zurich and her husband had become involved in a lot of business meetings so she had picked the book up again. "I picked it up in desperation!" she said (which was good to know!). "When I got into the part in Germany when Maxim is a small boy I became enthralled . . . the part when his mother and Teddy got on the train and said good-bye [to his family] . . . when she worried about the Germans on the train" – it was full of uniforms – "and Maxim was saying all sorts of Jewish things about what he had been eating. When I read this," she said, "I had cold chills, and when they got to Paris I felt tremendous relief . . . I started to cry and I cried and cried for hours and I didn't stop. You see, I was taken out of Germany like that and I had my mother's jewellery stitched into my clothes too. And you, your book, was a catalyst for me. I had not been able to cry since I was taken out of Germany in the 1930s. You're not Jewish, are you?"

' "No," I said.

' "How can you understand?"

' "Because I am a human being," I said.'

The women in the title are those behind her hero, Maximilian West – his mother, his grandmother, the woman that subsequently brings him up (Teddy), his first wife, his daughter, various women who have helped to form the man or are important to the man.

As he grows up, he wonders whether his dear parents are still alive. After the war, Teddy goes to Berlin literally to unearth Maxim's identity in the bombed-out rubble of the city, searching among the *Trummer-frauen*, the rubble women, who play their laborious part in the rebuilding of the city, counting out the bricks they retrieve at the storage depot every Saturday afternoon, to be paid accordingly. It is among the rubble that Teddy finds the Russian princess, Irina Troubetzkoy, a friend of Maxim's parents. She takes Teddy into her squalid cellar room below ground and informs her that Maxim's parents have gone to their death, his father in Buchenwald, his mother in Ravensbruck. When, finally, his worst nightmare of their murder is realised, 'Maxim suddenly understood that the sadness inside him would never go away. It would always be there. For the rest of his life.' His loss becomes the driving force in his life. He makes a pact with himself that he will become a dollar millionaire by the time he is thirty, and does so with time to spare.

Exiled from country and family at so impressionable an age, brought up by another family in Paris, his relations themselves victims of the death camps and his mother lost to him even after she had passed over to freedom, Bob, too, was deeply alone, bereft of loving parents, but also of the value-system that's part of the baggage of a national or religious culture. Like many other German Jews, he felt dispossessed as much of his German as of his Jewish heritage by the Nazi onslaught. Likewise, in *The Women in His Life*,

Maxim's father, Sigmund, and mother, Ursula, are from 'great and ancient families', real Germans, as well as being Jews. Bob would need courage to attain the inner sense of unity on which a personality can normally count when rising out of the culture of his birth to make his way in the world.

Somehow he found it, and worked his way into the movie business. He was a protégé of Jesse Lasky Sr, founder of Paramount, and was employed at one stage by the Hal Roach Studios in California, famous for stars such as Charley Chase, Will Rogers, Harold Lloyd and Laurel and Hardy, and for seeding the careers of the likes of Jean Harlow, Janet Gaynor, Fay Wray, and Boris Karloff, before their post-war TV production of classics like *The Lone Ranger*, Groucho Marx, Abbott and Costello, *The Life of Riley*, and *The George Raft Show*.

The late 1950s found Bob in Spain as Executive Producer for Samuel Bronston Productions. Among his film credits from this era are *John Paul Jones*, *King of Kings*, *El Cid*, *Fifty-five Days at Peking* and *The Fall of the Roman Empire*. From this time, producer Samuel Bronston, a sometime official Vatican photographer, developed Spain into a European capital of movie-making out of massive studios near Madrid. But when, in 1964, the big-screen epic *The Fall of the Roman Empire* failed to meet audience targets demanded by its enormous budget, Bronston went bust, was sued in court and forced out of production, still owing $4 million as late as 1975.

The Sixties saw Bob as Executive Vice President

and CEO to Franco London Films S.A. in Paris, making among other films *Impossible Object* with Alan Bates and *To Die of Love* with Annie Giradot. By then Barbara and Bob were married, and there was a period in the late 1960s to early 1970s when they lived together in the French capital at the Plaza Athenée, an elegant hotel off the Champs Elysée that appears in *Voice of the Heart* and *The Women in His Life*, and where she and Bob stay regularly even today. 'I'm a creature of habit,' says Barbara, 'I always stay at the Plaza Athenée because for months we lived there when Bob was running a film company in the Sixties.' It is where Maxim, his mother and Teddy stay when first they flee Berlin to Paris. *The Women in His Life* is redolent of those days, Bob's childhood in exile, places which he came to share with Barbara from the early years of their marriage:

The lights changed to green and Maxim crossed the Place Saint-Michel and headed towards the Rue de la Huchette. Within seconds he was sauntering down that narrow old street, experiencing a sense of nostalgia as he glanced around. Here on his left was the hotel Mont Blanc, where he had stayed on a couple of occasions, and immediately opposite was the El Djazier, the North African nightclub which they still frequented sometimes, going there to drink mint tea, ogle the exotic belly dancers, and eat couscous with harissa, the hot piquant sauce which blew his head off, but which he nevertheless enjoyed. And a few yards further along were the famous jazz joints, where some of the American jazz greats came to play and musicians of all nationalities to listen, as did he from time to time.

He paused when he saw the Rue du Chat Qui Peche. It was only a little alleyway, but he had never forgotten this street because the name had so delighted him when he was a child. 'It means the Street of the Cat Who Fishes,' Mutti had said, translating the French for him. Filled with glee, he had laughed out loud, tickled at the idea of a cat who fished. They had been on one of their outings, he and Mutti and Teddy. 'Investigating the quaint bits of Paris,' Mutti had called their wondrous excursions, and ever since those days this picturesque area had remained a favourite, and he often returned to walk around these narrow cobbled streets, to browse in the bookstores and galleries.

Barbara enjoys and nurtures her association with France in her books, most recently in 2002, of course, in *Three Weeks in Paris*. In 1994 she attributed her success as an author there to being one of the few foreign writers who paints an accurate picture of the country 'and actually gets the Eiffel Tower in the right place'. In *The Women in His Life*, Paris is a magnet to Maxim West, because he is the fictional persona of Bob Bradford as a child, and Monte Carlo is where later he moors his magnificent yacht, *Beautiful Dreamer*.

In *To Be the Best*, Paula and Emily go to Monte Carlo to meet their cousin Sarah, who has been living up the coast, near Cannes, for five years. Barbara used to holiday in Cannes before she even met Bob. In *Her Own Rules*, Meredith Stratton's quest for her mother takes in parts of France within Barbara's best-remembered experience. Havens Incorporated – the American-English-French group of upmarket inns, hotels and châteaux, which Meredith inherits – has its Paris office in rue de Rivoli, which is where eligible architect Luc de Moutboucher lures her to his château Clos-Talcy between Talcy and Menars in the Loire.

A Sudden Change of Heart is set in Connecticut, New York and Paris. In *Angel*, the heroine, Rosalind Madigan, returns us to the Loire Valley, to a band of country running 'from Orléans to Tours . . . through a verdant landscape known as the Valley of Kings', and gives us Montfleurie, 'the most magical of all the Loire châteaux'. Rosie looks into the dust of history for the spirit of the place, 'where once violent battles had raged when Fulk Nerra, war lord, predator and ruler of the area, had stalked this valley'.

In *Hold The Dream*, Emma Harte's will includes her Avenue Foch apartment in Paris and a villa at Cap Martin in the South. Both Paris and Cannes were of course part of Barbara's life before she met Bob, and in *Act Of Will*, her young alter ego, Christina, spends three days with her friend Jane in 'the lovely little town of Grasse . . . situated in the Alpes Maritimes high above Cannes,' where the painter, Fragonard, was born, famous for its gardens and Gothic cathedral. They go to the perfumery there when they're developing two fragrances, Blue Gardenia and Christina.

Was it here, too, that Barbara began seriously to paint? 'I remember we called in one night to have dinner with her,' Jack Figg told me, 'and she greeted us with absolute excitement – "I've learned I can paint!" She had just returned from a holiday in the South of France, where she'd met a Portuguese man called José, and she painted him at home. Suddenly she realised she could paint! She had these pictures expensively framed and they looked absolutely ter-rific.' Such is the power of France for this writer.

Bob Bradford's childhood experience may have been less happy there, at least to begin with, but together they have enjoyed many happy times in Paris since. In any case, in 1961 his life was set on an upward trajectory. If being cut off at the roots from his family had amounted to an existential challenge, he had by this time met it with success in his film projects. If you had asked him, he might have said that his idea of 'roots' wasn't Berlin or Paris, but the things that led up to the work he was doing now, things which, like tributaries of a river, flowed together to make his life what it was. It is a significant conceptual difference to the traditional roots meta-phor, which carries with it the burdensome possibility that precepts of your birth culture can tie you down. Bob's past had ceased to exist for him, he had only a future – a feeling perfectly in tune with his new girlfriend's own ambitious nature and drive for autonomy – particularly welcome following the failure of *The London American*, which had temporarily sapped that drive.

If there was a feeling of disappointment that she hadn't measured up to her own demanding aspirations in the late Fifties, by the early Sixties, with Bob, 'there was an infusion of new excitement,' as Billie recalls, 'and then she went off to live in New York, which had got far more "go". Although London had got a lot of "go" in the Sixties it wasn't Barbara's scene. But New York was, and they loved her.'

Bob was the tonic she needed. Life for such men is all about flow, change, movement *to* somewhere – the future. The modernist concept challenges the old idea of rootedness and static identity and, indeed, the whole notion of loss (which is why it appealed to him). In place of roots and family and community, there is freedom – man constantly on the hoof, constantly *in change*, man whose environment of airports and hotel rooms delivers the extraordinary *emotional detachment* that Barbara's friends had noted about Bob, while in his future-orientated projects he sought to deliver the sense of unity within that we all require – his autonomy, his values, his identity.

Maximilian West, the hero of *The Women in His Life* and the character whom Barbara has said, 'I truly love as if he exists,' and who, unusually for her, she brought back in another novel, *A Sudden Change of Heart*, is just such a man. His personal style is immutable, cast out of the materials of loss that his genetic and historical background has engineered, but he, like Emma Harte before him, makes it an uncompromising philosophy of life, which women in particular find irresistible.

At the start, Maxim *is* his projects. He has become identified with them. We are not sure what, if anything, he is beyond the performance of them.

> *His work comes first. It always has and it always will. It consumes him entirely. I know that now. He's not normal, you know, not when it comes to work. Maxim is beyond a workaholic, Mother. They haven't invented a name for a person who works the way he does. Around the clock.*
>
> *He has the stamina of a bull, and the most extraordinary concentration.*

He is managing director of Westrent and Westinvest at twenty-five, with a goal to make his first million by thirty. Business is Maxim's discipline and only real pleasure. He has the accoutrements of success and the women to go with it, but considers them to be 'so much folderol'. Personal autonomy and cool self-sufficiency characterise his power over others, which is specifically contrasted with the boot-in-the-face power of the Nazis: 'strutting, arrogant, vulgar and bloated with self-importance'.

Maxim's brand of power is 'dangerously attractive' to women and at the start of the book excites his PA, Graeme Longdon. What turns Graeme on is something to do with the clinical, undemonstrative effici-

ency with which he attends to his projects – 'the
intellect, the brains, the drive, the energy, the ambition
and the success'. This may be the author telling us
what she found exciting about Bob's lifestyle. What's
for sure is that, at the start of their relationship,
she didn't bring him to Yorkshire; rather, she let him
take her further away from her roots, to New York.
Barbara couldn't have been more ready for it at that
time.

New York is an environment which fairly crackles
with the belief that anything is possible. Bob Bradford
took Barbara physically out of England, where
making money and having ideas above your station
were still frowned upon (particularly in the case of
young women), into an environment where these
things are a patriotic duty. A journalist once put it to
Barbara that her personal claim never to have felt
inadequate is rare in England. She replied: 'Don't you
think that's why I live where I live today?'

At that stage in their lives, when Barbara had been
left feeling dissatisfied and unfulfilled after the demise
of *The London American*, and irritated with herself,
disappointed that she hadn't yet written a novel, she
would have found Bob's altogether pragmatic
approach attractive. One can sense in her response
to it the ambitious daughter Christina's need for a
pragmatic set of values at a similar stage in her life in
Act of Will. Christina's mother, Audra, has a perception of a *moral hierarchy* against which she deems her
daughter, who has given up her art and become
a commercial dress designer, a failure. But in *The*

Women in His Life, in Maxim's modernist 'project-culture', there is no such moral hierarchy. Instead, project-goals achieved are used to elaborate a value system to replace the deep-truth culture in which Audra lives in *Act of Will*. There are no absolute values, no ultimate rights or wrongs, there is only project and the value of action, which is defined in terms of where action will lead. The Ten Commandments are justified on the altar not of Judaism or even on that of Yorkshire working-class culture, but on the altar of pragmatism – you abide by them for no other reason than that if you don't, no one will deal with you again.

In Maxim's world, morality has a *cash value*, which doesn't mean that you do whatever makes the most money in the short term, any more than his project-orientation suggests that he is mad for making money (which he is not – he is at ease with money but not overly impressed by it). Cash value in the moral context means, simply, pragmatism – what a decision will flow on to. The point in being morally pure is that no one will trust you if you are not.

Once the heart is taken out of morality and replaced with the head, art and commerce are on a level pegging. There's a particularly pertinent moment in *Voice of the Heart* when Victor Mason gives Francesca (the character who appears most like Barbara) an antique copy of *Wuthering Heights*. Because Emily Brontë's work was always central to Barbara's aspirations as a novelist, the idea reminds us that in this high-powered milieu, art is a collector's item, a thing's cash value is not considered to be at odds with its artistic value, nor less intrinsic to it.

It is no longer 'better' to write a great novel or paint a beautiful picture than it is to put together an elegant deal. In the world of film (art at its most commercial), Maxim's flair as a financier is likened to that of an inspired artist. His father-in-law Alexander Derevenko observes, 'I can no more explain to you the creative impulse, what it is inside a painter that makes him capable of producing a breathtaking work of art . . . than I can explain to you what it is inside Maxim that enables him to put together an incredibly successful company or a stunning deal.'

It may seem amazing that such a man as Maximilian West should consider marriage at all, let alone to sensitive Anastasia Derevenko, whose life is centred on the deep-truth-culture that his modernist approach is set on replacing. But then, as we later discover, Maxim is not so secure in his new project-identity as his outward display suggests, and it is the play between his philosophy (modernist) and Anastasia's more meaningful deep-truth philosophy, with which the book ultimately deals.

As for Bob, he seems to have been a similarly unlikely candidate for marriage in 1961. At thirty-three he had already been married before, and was well suited for all the reasons I have given to an autonomous, self-sufficient, single lifestyle. I remember Barbara telling me that her friend, the writer Cornelius Ryan, had said to him: 'If you don't get on and marry Barbara, *I will*!' It had been a joke, but the point is made that Robert Bradford had not been looking for marriage when he was swept off his feet by Barbara Taylor. That, however, is precisely what they did. Bob and Barbara were married in London on Christmas Eve 1963.

CHAPTER FIVE

Coming Home

*'The city of his birth and childhood. It had forever
pulled him back, and he had always believed it
held a secret for him. It had. The secret had been
revealed to him today.'*

Maxim West in *The Women in His Life*

Having a man behind her is what Edith Walker had
lacked in her intended rise in the world, and 'a man
behind her' is what Emma Harte in *A Woman of
Substance* is given by her creator to get her project
going.

The man Emma Harte selects to expedite her
business is Joe Lowther. 'Quite by accident, when she
had been shopping she had seen *it*. The shop. *Her
shop . . .*' The shop, the first in her empire, is in Town
Street, Armley, and it is to let. Joe Lowther is the
name of the landlord she should contact. Emma goes
to his home and offers him a deal. Against his better
judgement – Lowther doubts that she has enough
experience to make a go of it – he accepts her offer,
partly because Emma has the temerity to put hard

cash down on the table, and partly because 'he was drawn to her. Dangerously attracted to her.'

Lowther's considerable portfolio of property, which 'included eight shops in Town Street, a row of cottages in Armley, several terrace houses in nearby Wortley and . . . two large plots of land near St Paul's Street in Leeds itself,' was built up by his mother and her mother before her. When 'his ancient great-aunt' dies he inherits an additional £150,000, a large house in Old Farnley and 'four commercial properties in the centre of Leeds.'

Pursued by Lowther, Emma agrees to marry him, even though she doesn't love him. She is honest enough with herself to see that in marrying Lowther she is 'cheating him' of love, but that doesn't stop her. It is a bad match. Even the physical side of the marriage is unsatisfactory. The marriage is simply part of Emma's wider business strategy, although she tells herself that she needs him to 'protect her and Edwina' (her illegitimate daughter, you will recall, by Edwin Fairley). We have to conclude that she is using Lowther and that her action is completely unethical, but Emma then exercises her extraordinary business skills to turn the Lowther properties into an enterprise beyond his wildest dreams. Hers is an intricate and powerful strategy, which she executes with ruthless precision. We can only marvel at her performance.

There are some aggressive, apparently feminist traits in Emma Harte, particularly in her treatment of Joe Lowther, and one is tempted to hail her as something of a heroine of the feminist movement, which was gathering pace during Barbara's own rise, peaking as she wrote the novel. In 1953, the year that Barbara uprooted from home for London, Simone de Beauvoir first coined the phrase 'women's liberation' in her book, *The Second Sex*. In 1963, the year she uprooted from London for New York, Betty Friedan set the feminist fuse alight in *The Feminine Mystique*. Seven years later came *The Female Eunuch*, Germaine Greer's bitter landmark examination of women's oppression. Then, leading up to publication of *A Woman of Substance* in 1979, came associated bestselling novelists like Judith Rossner (*Looking for Mister Goodbar*, 1975), and upfront commercial ones like Erica Jong (*Fear of Flying*, 1973) and Judith Krantz (*Scruples*, 1978), their all-woman themes leaving Jacqueline Susann standing, and characterising 1970s New York women as forceful, funny and free – figures epitomised by Diane Keaton in movies such as *Annie Hall* and *Looking for Mister Goodbar*.

None of this was quite *Woman of Substance* territory, however. When Barbara picked up her pen in 1976 to write her first novel, she did not pick up the feminist gauntlet as well. Emma, like many of her other heroines, is ambitious, disciplined and self-possessed. She can be ruthless, and is when crossed; she wants to win, and is not averse to using her feminine wiles, but she always needs a man behind her. In the novel, she says: 'Being underestimated by men is one of the biggest crosses I have had to bear ... [but] it was also an advantage and one I learned to make great use of ... When men believe they are dealing with a foolish or stupid woman they lower their guard, become negligent and sometimes even downright reckless. Unwittingly they often hand you the advantage on a plate.' She uses men, but she does not get her kicks out of crushing them or castrating her male lovers. I was reminded of what a commentator once wrote about Margaret Thatcher: 'Her femininity added a frisson of sexuality to one's engagement with her and disturbed the public-school code of conduct and decorum formerly operating within the all-male preserve of the party's higher echelons.' Henry Rossiter, Emma Harte's financial manager in *A Woman of Substance*, is a paid-up member of just such a code of conduct and his loyalty to it is clearly disturbed by the allure of a woman whose 'mind was logical and direct. She did not think in that convoluted female way ...'

A Woman of Substance showed Barbara's female readers how to go out and take up the opportunities that the feminist revolutionaries had opened up for them, but Barbara was not arguing the politics of feminism or any other movement. She already had her vehicle – the style to which she was born. She believes we all have this, if only we can find it, as Freda found it in her. The novels do not tell women what to believe, only to know themselves, thereby to put themselves in control of their own destinies. Movements are out. Feminism neither appeals nor appals. Barbara advocates not feminism but a brand of existentialism in which the feminine principle is preserved: 'I think that you have to *do it yourself*. I did it myself and Emma Harte did it herself . . . and it can be done without being abrasive.'

When Barbara married Bob in 1963 she was nowhere near ready to pen the character that would make her her fortune, however. It would be thirteen years before she did. So, what happened in the intervening years to bring Barbara to Emma Harte?

Marrying Bob meant weighing anchor altogether – on her family, on England, on the whole culture of her birth. A picture on the author's website captioned 'The Bradfords in Morocco on the set of *Impossible Object*' suggests that she slipped effortlessly into Bob's world, travelling with him on location. The film, made in the early years of their marriage by the company Bob ran, Franco-London Films, was based on a novel by Nicholas Mosley about a writer who finds it difficult to distinguish fact from fiction. When a journalist asked Barbara whether she had had difficulty in adjusting to life in the Manhattan glamour world, she was able to reply, quite truthfully, 'No, I'd been in it in London.'

But there were real differences in her life, which cannot have been effected without some measure of emotional insecurity. Contact with Yorkshire and friends like the Figgs was necessarily now limited. 'We lived in New York in Manhattan and in California in Beverly Hills. Bob had the apartment in Beverly Hills before we were married, so we went backwards and forwards, and then he gave it up because he ran a film company in France, so I commuted from New York to Paris and stayed three months in Paris then went back to New York for a month.'

Also, the irony was that, through marriage to Bob, she no longer needed the ambitious drive that defined her personal style and set her apart. She needn't have bothered with a career at all. She was able for the first time in her life to buy antiques of her own, and began to design and decorate their homes, capitalising on all those childhood trips with Freda to the country houses of Yorkshire. Bob saw to it that she wanted for nothing. Right from the beginning of their marriage he took a practical interest in the clothes that Barbara wore. In Paris, she was introduced to Ginette Spanier, the *directrice* of Pierre Balmain, who became a friend. 'I was very much into *haute couture*, but only a couple of pieces a year. Later, many of my clothes were by Pauline Trigère, the great American designer who was French born. Pauline and I were great friends until the day she died. She made the kind of clothes I love. Very sleek, very tailored, no frills and flounces . . . I also get clothes from Place Vendôme in London. Most of the things I choose there are by Italian designers. The owner, Seymour Druion, buys his collections in Rome and Milan, and picks out things for me which he knows I'll like and which Bob will like as well – dark colours for winter, no patterns; pastels, especially blue and pink, for summer.'

So, back in 1963 she had already made it. Becoming a multi-millionaire in her own right nearly two decades later apparently required little adjustment: 'I have always had quite a good standard of living and it hasn't made all that much difference,' she was able to say when asked what she was doing with her royalties from *A Woman of Substance*. 'I bought some English antiques and paid too much for them in New York, but the rest is simply invested carefully. I already had two fur coats and I didn't want any more. How many fur coats can you wear at one time?'

But, of course, the difference was that back in 1963 Bob was sourcing the finances of 'the whole enchilada'. He was strong, with definite ideas about the way he liked things to be. How far did he exercise control? How did the balance of power work then?

In 1994, the *Orlando Sentinel* quizzed Barbara as to how she and Bob had got on during their thirty years of marriage. She replied, 'We're both very bossy, so we lock horns a lot. So he calls me Napoleon, and I call him Bismarck. At Christmas in Palm Beach I saw an embroidered cushion that carried the words: "Napoleon lives here, I married him". And I bought it and crossed out "him" and put "her". And I gave it to Bob. Well, I've resigned my generalship now, I've come down to a lieutenant-colonel.'

This story is retold in numerous interviews, and it happened so long ago that no one is quite sure whether Barbara bought the cushion and crossed out 'him' or Bob bought it and crossed out 'her'. But on one occasion she did speak plainly: 'I always think Bob's controlling and I know that I like to control.' But it is usually she who gives in: 'I say: "Oh, to hell with this, it's not worth arguing about."'

It was in these pre-*Substance* years, too, that

Barbara wrote the trio of books to which I have already alluded and which seem to suggest an uncharacteristic compliance: *How to be the Perfect Wife: Etiquette to Please Him, Entertaining to Please Him* and *Fashions That Please Him*.

'Yes, I laugh about that these days,' Barbara told Sue Lawley on BBC Radio Four. 'They sold like crazy and, having written *A Woman of Substance* about this warrior woman who goes out to conquer the world, people have teased me about it, especially the press who have managed to dig up these books and say, but Barbara this is terribly opposite, and I say, well I meant it when I wrote them . . . now my attitudes have changed.'

She meant it when she wrote them, so what does this tell us about Barbara as young wife? Was it a period in which she luxuriated in pleasures of which most women dream, or one in which she was fighting to retain her self-respect and autonomy? Was it one in which she learned to play Lettice Keswick in *Everything to Gain*, 'a woman a lot like me . . . a homemaker, a cook, a gardener, a painter, a woman interested in furniture and furnishings and all those things which made a home beautiful'? Or was it Emma Harte to the rescue in the mid-1970s when marriage threatened to cast Barbara forever in the role of second fiddle? One novel in particular plays over the whole range of possibilities for just such a woman in her situation.

The two really interesting wives of Maxim West in *The Women in His Life* are Anastasia Derevenko and actress Camilla Galland. After Anastasia's chance meeting with Maxim in Paris they fall deeply in love. Maxim gives her everything she could possibly want materially, but in time it is not enough. 'Maxim could not give all of himself to her.' We are not talking impotence here on a sexual level, rather on an emotional level. A dam holds back Maxim's emotions, and the block is to do with his childhood loss, to do with his being cut off from his roots by the war. For all his commercial genius, his successful projects, there is, deep down, a vacuum where his real self should be.

He cannot give Anastasia what she truly wants, for what she wants is *him*, and he is out of touch with himself. One night on their luxury yacht, after a spectacular party at which she has worn his gift of a diamond necklace, she felt 'something cracking and splintering inside her . . . "That's all I am to you these days, isn't it? The giver of your parties, the decorator of your homes, the wearer of your diamonds," she exclaimed coldly.'

This is a crucial point in the novel. Two sides of a coin are made to face one another. On the one side is Anastasia, whose nature encompasses a deep sense of truth and beauty and love; on the other is Maxim's project-obsessed psyche, which provides their riches but denies her access to his true self.

Maxim reels at her onslaught. Anastasia accuses him of infidelity, even though she knows he is a faithful husband, and she leaves him in the early morning. She attacks him because her womanly intuition tells her that what's missing is the crucial element of life: love. Maxim's script is not rooted in his true nature, he is still running away from who he is, which is why he is afraid to let anyone in, even the woman he could truly love.

In his second wife, Maxim finds someone who is able to meet him on his own terms. He and Camilla Galland live a kind of parallel existence, each engrossed in their own projects and deriving a shared exultation in their mutual success. 'If you marry me,' says Maxim to Camilla, 'I wouldn't want you to give up your career ... I need plenty of space. In fact I must have it in order to do my work properly. I don't want you clinging to me, making me the core of your existence. I have to travel a great deal, and I hope you understand this. Of course you can come with me on the extended trips. I'd love it, love to have you with me. But not on the short, quick trips. They're too hectic, and I'm always locked up in meetings. I don't want distractions. Or to be deflected from what I have to do – because I am worrying about my wife. I've always had great direction, concentration. I can't change.'

Theirs is to be a project-marriage. There are to be 'ground rules', and we are conscious that the rules are set by Maxim not by Camilla, his very name a synonym for a rule of conduct. Nevertheless, Camilla is happy at the prospect: 'I have to work, Maxim, just as you have to ... they'd take me away in a straitjacket if I didn't.' She feels like 'the luckiest woman in the world', and then fate steps in to end it – Camilla breaks her neck by falling down a steeply pitched basement staircase.

Maxim replaces her with Adriana Macklin, who, like him, is consumed with business projects. He becomes unhappy, in fact he becomes impotent, though not with beautiful blonde Blair Martin, who wears pale-green silk pyjamas by Trigère, and lives in Sutton Place, Barbara's own apartment, overlooking 'the East River and a portion of the 59th Street Bridge'.

We shouldn't get too sidelined by matching up the biographical elements, which have been scattered across the canvas so that no real-life colours attach to any one character in particular. What we are dealing with here is a theme which does have relevance to real players, indeed to us all, and has to do with life in the modern world in which, too often, truth is deemed merely to be the opposite of a lie.

Camilla and Adriana share Maxim's thoroughly modernist outlook. For all three, project – making things happen – is all. There is no great depth to their relationships, or if there is, as might have been possible in the case of Maxim and Camilla, both parties agree that it is not the priority. Emotional complications have been eradicated by ground rules, or, in the case of Adriana, by the fact that she is a similar operator to Maxim. But, as Anastasia knows, they cannot be so easily dealt with. Anastasia haunts Maxim, and Adriana attacks him for always 'flinging that ex-wife of yours in my face'.

The rest of the novel leads up to Maxim's moment

of truth. He is softened up for it by an accident, which delivers the crucial volte-face that 'there are more things in life than big deals.' He returns to his roots, finds his birthplace in the post-war rubble of Berlin, 'the city of his birth and childhood, [which] he had always believed held a secret for him'. Finally, he learns the secret, and 'the sadness inside him slipped away'.

Appropriately, when he discovers his true identity (a complete surprise, in which Barbara cleverly discovers the absolute value of love at the core of the concept of identity) he becomes whole again in Anastasia's arms just as the Berlin wall comes crashing down and his homeland is made whole again too.

Barbara and Bob had themselves crossed into the Eastern sector of the city in 1986. The trip had sparked the idea for the novel. 'I had always had this compulsion to go to the East zone,' she said at the time. 'So we went through Checkpoint Charlie and when we were there I had this flash in my mind's eye of a woman in a white satin evening gown in the style of the Thirties, blonde and very ethereal. Somehow I knew that her name was Ursula [the name of the woman we believe to be Maxim's mother], and I asked Bob if he had ever mentioned anyone of that name. But he just kept telling me it was my writer's imagination!'

The dam against emotion had been holed, the message was once again about identity – to remember where you came from, because 'it defines who you are.' By the time Barbara wrote *The Women in His*

Life it had been revealed as the lesson of her own life, for it was Barbara's imaginative return to her very deepest roots in the landscape of Yorkshire in the mid-1970s that had enabled her to write the novel that would define her. Her return brought her back to the values of the landscape of Yorkshire to which her mother had introduced her as a child, 'a sense of honour, duty and purpose', the need for 'integrity in the face of incredible pressure and opposition' and 'not only an honesty with those people who occupied her life, but with herself'. It is for this reason that her woman of substance is not quite the model of modernism, which at face value she seems.

So what led Barbara back?

For her part, soon after marriage to Bob, Barbara decided that she must have a project of her own and said, like Camilla Galland: 'Bob was busy being a movie producer – so if I didn't work, where would all my boundless energy go? I couldn't just sit at home and do nothing, I've never been one of those ladies who lunch and I loathe shopping.'

But she did not immediately buckle down to writing a novel, her true ambition, the one that would define her, which now for the first time she might have embarked upon unimpeded by want. Instead, she pursued a freelance journalistic career, writing about the homes of the famous in a syndicated interior-design column called 'Designing Woman' – first for *Newsday*, then, moving with editor Tom Dorsey, for the *New York Daily News*, and finally the *Los Angeles Times*. Her column went across America to

185 newspapers and she wrote it for twelve years. She also wrote a number of interior design books. I have seen them in her drawing room, now beautifully bound in leather, including the bestselling *Complete Encyclopaedia of Homemaking Ideas.*

Appearance, design, beauty – an arena in which the aesthetic and the commercial are indistinguishable – all absolutely in tune with the world in which she was now moving, and all the time she was learning, building up her knowledge base in an area that would, as it happened, prove useful for the novels, for she realised how compellingly she could write about the most exquisite artefacts of European origin – her favourite Biedermeier and Art Deco furniture and Impressionist paintings. America was looking to Europe in this arena, in which indigenously it could not of course compete. Barbara was unmistakably English, and brought up to the task. As she said: 'Mummy gave me this eye for antiques. She taught me to look.'

The design column and books became her project, which ran parallel to Bob's in the film world, and so began a pattern of life that in time would bring Bob and Barbara project-bound together in the marketing and filming of her novels, something Maxim and his wives never quite achieve in the novel. Today, this is the pattern of their lives. Bobby Caplin summed up the position well: 'I don't think either of them would have been as successful without the other.' Bob tends to get what he wants, he is a tough negotiator, but what he wants is now what Barbara wants.

One of Barbara's favourite shots of her husband, Robert Bradford, with the book that realised a dream. Between 1984 and 1999 Bob set up no fewer than nine TV mini series based on Barbara's books, producing them himself (*Hold The Dream, Voice of the Heart, Act Of Will, To Be The Best, Remember, Everything To Gain, Love In Another Town, Her Own Rules* and *A Secret Affair*). The impact of such television exposure – six hours in the case of *A Woman Of Substance*, starring Jenny Seagrove and Deborah Kerr – was astronomical in terms of book sales.

Left and above: Jenny Seagrove as Emma Harte, the woman of substance shown here with Liam Neeson, who played Blackie O'Neill.

Right: Deborah Kerr takes over as the older Emma, with Sir John Mills as Henry Rossiter, Emma's financial adviser.

With Lindsay Wagner as Paula O'Neill, Emma Harte's granddaughter in *To Be The Best* is Sir Anthony Hopkins, who played Jack Figg, named in the novel after Barbara's great friend since the '50s: 'When they came to write the screenplay they decided to turn him into a much bigger character, cast Sir Anthony to play him, and made him the hero of the film!' recalls Barbara with delight.

Barbara with the stars of *To Be The Best*, based on the third book in the *Woman of Substance* sequence. Fiona Fullerton and Lindsay Wagner flank their creator. Standing are Christopher Cazenove and Sir Anthony Hopkins

Victoria Tenant as Audra and Kevin McNally as Vincent in *Act Of Will*. Barbara loved Victoria Tennant's portrayal and the fact that she made a point of sitting down and discussing the character with Barbara in New York.

Barbara's beloved Bichon Frises, Beaji and Chammi (above), lay claim to being part of the family.

Alan Bennett and Barbara receiving the degree of Doctor of Letters from Leeds University in 1990, thereby going some way to satisfying Freda's wish for her daughter to attend university.

Barbara with Reg Carr, the then Keeper of the Collection of the scholarly Brotherton Library in Leeds. In 1988 the library became the Keeper of the Barbara Taylor Bradford archive. Her manuscripts sit next to ones by Charlotte Brontë.

Barbara Taylor Bradford by Lord Lichfield. Her name now synonymous with the character she created: when she stands up in public she is the woman of substance.

They are a formidable team, now that their project is a shared one. Bob has engineered some unbelievably good deals for Barbara in America, involving many millions of dollars. Her personal wealth was quoted this year in the Rich List as £95 million (currently around $170 million), which puts her at 419th position in the world.

But this was only one side of the coin, the other was the fulfilment of those contracts. Her first English publisher, Mark Barty-King, became seriously concerned in the early days that she was working so hard, never seemed to go out because she did little *but* work. 'She was riding high on a worldwide reputation and there was always such big pressure to produce something,' he said.

The picture that came to mind was of the miller's daughter confined by the king to her room and spinning gold thread out of straw, the beautiful girl working away, working away, spinning a golden yarn according to magical directions from Rumpelstiltskin. But Bob would have none of it.

'*A Woman of Substance* was her first book. She sweated the book for two years, twenty-four hours a day. I used to go to Hollywood to work and she worked twenty-four hours a day on that book. It's unbelievable and thank God she's not doing that any more. She doesn't have to . . .' But Barty-King remembers that the second book, *Voice of the Heart* (the finished edition, 928 pages in length), was another draining experience. Certainly it was not published until 1983, and yet Barbara had a contract and started writing it more than six months before *Woman of Substance* was published in 1979.

In an interview with Richard Whiteley, she once set out the regime that her life had become by this time: 'It's the salt mines. I do ten or twelve hours a day, seven days a week. I get in here [her study] at six o'clock in the morning. I'm wearing a pair of cotton trousers and a tee shirt, winter and summer, in winter I put a cardigan on, no make-up, no jewellery, just my glasses, very underdressed. And I edit what I finished yesterday, and at about seven thirty to eight o'clock I take Gemmy [the dog] out. So I've already done about two hours' work. I start at six a.m. in here, and then I work till noon, and then she [the dog] has her lunch and I have a salad and I take her round the block, bring her back, and go back to work till 6 p.m.'

I asked Bob how Barbara would relax. 'She doesn't like cocktail parties because you stand around and talk nonsense, totally idiotic stuff, and she'd rather sit at home and read a good book. She loves to read and to think and to work, and she likes to go out to dinner and she likes to be with close friends and relax. Particularly when she's working on a book, she doesn't want to sit around with people who talk nonsense. They have nothing to say but blow hot air and for her it's a total waste because her head is in the book, thinking, thinking out the plot.

'Although what we do keeps us apart we are not shut out of each other's lives. When Barbara is shut up in a room writing for days, I am her window on the world, telling her what I've seen, who I've met.

She tells me about her next chapter and uses me as a sounding board. I am very proud of her and what she has done. I'm a very secure individual, unworried by her fame and fortune. I had mine before her. She was my back-up and now I'm hers. My greatest relaxation is long weekends. I leave our New York apartment, take a plane and fly to Miami or Puerto Rico. I swim, I read and be away from people. You can't be a happy couple if you are always in each other's way. Barbara doesn't like the sun; I do. When she is "off the book" she travels with me.'

From the start of their marriage, Bob was himself project-bound in a difficult and highly commercial industry, and it was ever a two-career household with no idea of working nine-to-five. In the early 1970s, still some years before she started work on the novels, Barbara made a move to escape from the relentless urban vortex into the country, and one is minded how much she must have been missing her regular trips home to Yorkshire that she had always made from London. In 1971 she persuaded Bob to look for a country retreat in northwest Connecticut. She told *Architectural Digest*: 'Our search began when my husband, Bob, and I were guests of conductor-composer Skitch Henderson and his wife Ruth, at their house in New Milford. We were instantly entranced by the region, seeing elements of England and Europe in its scenic, sweeping beauty composed of rolling, tree-covered hills and shining lakes.'

Readers may recognise the connection in four of her novels. *Everything to Gain* (1994) began a series of books with narrative set in Connecticut, continuing with *Dangerous to Know* (1995), *Her Own Rules* (1996), and *A Sudden Change of Heart* (1999). She accords it great significance in the novels. In *Hold the Dream* it is the place selected for the long-awaited coming together of the Hartes and the O'Neills. Emma Harte's granddaughter Paula first realises she loves Shane O'Neill, grandson of Blackie O'Neill (Emma's dear friend from the start of *A Woman of Substance*), when she is visiting Shane's converted barn in the country town of New Milford, near where Bob and Barbara's new home would be sited. In *Everything to Gain* it is where Mallory Keswick retreats to consider her future before she yields to the pull of the Yorkshire moors, where her late husband grew up and where she gets her idea about what to do.

'I fell in love with it the moment I saw it,' says Barbara of the house they finally bought, 'a wonderful old Connecticut colonial, classically elegant in its design, surrounded by ancient maples and smooth green lawns flowing down to a large pond. Dominating that pond, and adding to the decidedly pastoral feeling of the property, were two regal white swans floating on its surface against profuse pink water lilies.

'The first thing we did was hire Litchfield architect Paul Hinkel, whose work we had seen and admired. Paul is an authority on colonial architecture, and since he was nearby he could supervise the construction daily. He was quick to understand our requirements, agreed with us about the restoration and remodelling,

and made other good suggestions. After much consul-
tation and endless refining, Paul presented plans that
turned a thirteen-room house into one with eighteen
rooms, plus a wine cellar and storage space. He also
redesigned the guest cottage.'

They could not have settled for less. However, this
weekend retreat did not come as a release valve during
the early years of their marriage. Though the search
began in 1971, it would be twenty-one years before
Barbara and Bob made the purchase. 'He bought it
for me in May 1992, for my birthday,' said Barbara.
It followed a spectacular deal Bob made with her
American publishers, at the time the biggest author
contract in history.

So, in the meantime, there was still no weekend
escape. And even after they did buy it, 'We didn't go
there much,' said Barbara.

'It wasn't Bob,' as Bobby Caplin pointed out, 'that
home in Connecticut – magnificent, quite unbelievable, but that certainly wasn't Bob. That was one
hundred per cent Barbara. Bob is a city man. This was
maybe one of Barbara's dreams, with the lake and the
swan. They were in the middle of nowhere!'

The Connecticut episode delineated once more
Bob's pragmatism on the one hand, and Barbara's
unfulfilled emotional needs on the other. 'Ten thousand square feet, enormous house,' Bob said when I
asked him about it. 'It was wonderful! Paradise! But
it was too big for us and we were never there, it was
just draining us of money. The pool men, the tree
doctor, the gardeners, every day there was something

else. And it was two hours' travelling, over two hours to get there.'

'I think Barbara loved it,' I began. 'I remember . . .'

'She loved the country, she is a country girl, she is English, but I mean she is also a very practical lady and she works best at her home in New York.'

That may be so, but the novels give an impression that Connecticut meant something important to Barbara in a creative, imaginative sense. When she writes about the countryside around the Litchfield hills, the brilliant skies of the region are described in a manner not dissimilar to that in which she refers to Yorkshire. When I took this up with her she agreed: 'Connecticut has that very special kind of light, a clarity of light that I talk about in *A Woman of Substance*, *Hold the Dream* and *Voice of the Heart* – the part set in Yorkshire – because it's like Northern light and it seems to emanate from some hidden source like the light in some of Turner's paintings. It's also rather an undulating countryside – I like moors and hills, though it's not, of course, the moors.'

That light of Yorkshire is a symbol of creativity – Barbara says as much when she finally returns to it in imagination to write *A Woman of Substance*. It is 'quite extraordinary. It's almost as if it comes from another source. A writer must turn inward in order to write – everything comes out of me and this is what I remember, that extraordinary clarity . . . that love of the light.'

Their work was indeed their life and vice versa, and Barbara would never have wanted it any other way. Bob knew that and in that sense Bob knew best. But there was this emotional side that did need an avenue if Barbara was ever to achieve her expression. Was part of her being denied? It was an unlikely bedding ground for a traditional family, of course, and there would be no children.

I detect a sadness that she and Bob didn't have children, but also no shadow of regret at the lifestyle they chose, which they are both so good at. 'I don't have any regrets at all,' said Barbara twenty years ago, and she says the same today. 'I don't think you miss a person that you haven't known. Bob and I got married in 1963 and I was then thirty years old. We didn't want to have children immediately. We said, "Well, maybe in a few years." Then somehow it was suddenly too late. It's the luck of the draw. I'd have loved children but I didn't have them. I've got a wonderful marriage, I've got Bob, who is a great supporter of mine in every way, as I hope I am of him, and we've got to be content.'

There is a touching moment in the old nursery at Pennistone Royal, towards the end of *Hold the Dream*, where Paula, Emma Harte's granddaughter, sings her twin children, Tessa and Lorne Fairley, to sleep with 'The Sandman' song, for which Barbara proudly claims authorship. 'I wrote that! That's my creation!' she says excitedly. 'I also wrote a children's book and edited a couple for a publishing house. They had bought the most beautifully illustrated book I've ever seen for children. It was in Czech – each page had an illustration and a poem in Czech, and they asked me to write a little poem for each of these wonderful illustrations, and I thought, well, why not? I drove Bob crazy! I'd ring him up at the office and say, "Just listen to this for a minute." And he thought something wonderful was coming –'

> *The sandman has the swiftest wings and shoes that are made of gold;*
> *And he comes to you when the first star sings and the night is not very old . . .*

'– Bob would say, "Do you mind, I'm in a meeting!" It was a lovely children's book, I enjoyed doing it; it was a challenge. It wasn't that we set out not to have children, you know. And I didn't say, "Oh I'm going to have a big career." I had a miscarriage and I never got pregnant again.'

I talk to Bob about Barbara's relationship with her own mother, the love she gave her, and he says, 'That's why Barbara is so keenly interested in working with children today and with literacy problems. She works with Literacy Partners in New York, a charity that raises money and opens centres to teach people to read. She is on the Madison Council of the Library of Congress in Washington, and has worked with the president's mother Barbara Bush and First Lady Laura Bush on literacy and the National Book Festival. Over eighty million Americans can barely read, or can't read at all . . .'

She is also on the committee of PAL, a children's charity (the letters standing for Police Athletic League) which has, at different times, attracted Barbara Bush and Hillary Clinton to fundraising luncheons. 'PAL is a charity devoted to underprivileged children in the New York area,' Barbara told me. 'It was started in the 1920s to get poor kids off the street, but it is run more by business people today. Recently we opened one centre in the Bronx, a tough area of New York, and I sat in on a session and listened as fifteen-year-old girls talked about wanting to get their boyfriends out of the Latin Kings, a gang. "The only way you can get out," one girl said, "is to commit suicide or they will kill you because they don't want you to leave – they won't let you leave."'

It's a world Barbara drew on in *Everything to Gain*, where Mallory Keswick's husband and children are fatally shot in a tough area of New York. Their killer had been smoking crack cocaine.

Again, in her charitable work in the UK, children are the focus. She is on the board and is a trustee of PACT – Parents and Abducted Children Together. Again it is her fundraising capability that is to the fore. The charity was started by Lady Meyer, wife of the former British Ambassador to Washington. Catherine Meyer is a good friend of Barbara, and it was she who asked her to become involved. 'Catherine's children were abducted by her first husband,' Barbara told me, 'and I can't imagine how she lived through it. It must have been harrowing.'

In this context, suggestions, much proffered, especially by female journalists, that Barbara's dogs are substitutes for her unborn children seem almost pathetic, although it is perfectly true that she has, perforce, made her beloved bichons frises part of the family, and she explores the entire history of the breed in *Voice of the Heart*. If you ever get to meet pretty, fluffy Beaji and Chammi, do not refer to them as poodles or they'll have you. Barbara finds it mean of reporters to question her affection for her dogs, given that most pet owners shower affection on their animals. It is, after all, the point, isn't it? Beaji and Chammi have a very good lifestyle and they know all Barbara's secrets, for they sit under her desk when she is writing and thinking and working out characters and stories aloud.

When her first bichon frise, the late Gemmy Bradford, fell ill in 1987, Barbara flew home on Concorde straightaway. 'I went immediately to the vet, where the housekeeper had taken her. She was operated on, and miraculously lived. She died when she was twelve. She wrote a lot of books with me. Gemmy was short for Gemini, even though she was a Scorpio. My parents were both Gemini and so is Bob, and my agent. So I'm surrounded by Geminis.' Astrologers may be interested that Barbara herself is Taurus, and Taurus and Gemini are the two most likely signs for members of the Rich List, followed by Aries.

Beaji and Chammi undoubtedly enable Barbara to express a side of her that otherwise gets scant exercise, but it is of course the writing that provides the real fulfilment. Why then did it take so long after marriage to Bob, which had, after all, removed the need to earn money by other means, to start the novel that would make her name?

It was not for want of trying. She worked on four novels during the period up to 1975–6 – four false starts. 'I didn't like them, I'd get halfway and be bored with it, and I thought, if I'm bored then obviously the reader is going to be bored, and I'd put it away and start another one. I did this four times, four different novels before I got the idea for *A Woman of Substance*. I had been trying to write romantic suspense like Helen MacInnis.'

Helen MacInnis wrote espionage thrillers with romantic sub-plots, which benefited from her extensive research skills into political events of the regions in which the novels are set. After her husband was assigned to intelligence work in the British army during the Second War, there was even suspicion that she had inside information. Once again, Barbara would not have been blind to the fact that research was a key element in the bestselling mix. By the time of MacInnis's death in 1985, more than twenty-three million copies of her novels had been sold in America alone, and they had been translated into twenty-two languages.

However, the reason why Barbara Taylor Bradford came to write the eighth most popular novel in the history of the world had nothing to do with an editorial analysis of what was currently selling well, and everything to do with leaving that side of her thinking alone.

With the distance of time, her own development

away from the person she had once been, and the geographical distance from home that marriage to Bob entailed, and with a growing sense of frustration, as I have outlined, Barbara began thinking about her past and her family more.

'I only really began to understand my mother's life when I was in my forties,' she told me. Barbara turned forty in 1973, three years before she put pen to paper on her first published novel. She had begun to talk to her father about his relationship with Freda. 'I know that she rejected him constantly. No, she didn't talk about it, but I knew about it somehow when I was in my teens and the only person I discussed it with was my father. When she used to come and stay with me in London, when she first arrived she'd be saying, "Your father is terrible" and he is this and that, and she'd be sort of running him down – and after about a week, when she was supposed to stay for ten days, she said, "Oh, I really have to go home, your daddy can't manage without me and I miss him," and I looked at her in amazement. I never actually said to her, "Why did you stop sleeping with him?" but once, when I was in my twenties, I did say, "Why are you like that with Daddy? Sometimes you seem so cold with him."'

This was the occasion Freda told Barbara that she had wanted only her, that if she had had other children she would not have been able to give her everything, and that she was glad that Barbara had not been a boy because then she would have gone off more with her father. It must have begun to come clear to Barbara, now that she was thinking about these things with the benefit of some distance and objectivity, that there was more to all of this than met the eye.

So, in her forties, Barbara was going back into her roots more, and recognising that Freda was a person in her own right, not simply a mother with whom she was joined at the hip, and she was set on the road to realising that Freda's extraordinary mothering was a response to some deep loss of her own. Although she did not talk to Freda about this, maybe pieces of the mosaic – the 'bits and bats that I picked up over the years' – began to fall into place. Her subconscious will have set to work, and because her childhood, her parents and the landscape of her beloved Yorkshire were so far distant, these things would soon begin to occupy her imagination as well as her thoughts.

'There is something about Yorkshire which is deeply ingrained in me and I am moved by the beauty. It stirs me inside. I had this joy in it as a child, but I didn't know I had it. Being away from it, on this side of the Atlantic, and looking across the Atlantic in my mind's eye, I see it with great perception . . . There's also a lot of nostalgia in it, that yearning, the memories of my childhood are bound up in it, so to me it's very emotional . . . A writer draws on memories.'

The objective frame of mind that enabled these perceptions was made available by more than the physical distance that now stood between Barbara and home. She was looking out from the window of a completely different culture and her emotional side was beginning to understand that she had left something important behind.

Then, at some time in the mid-1970s, Barbara read an interview with Graham Greene in *Time* magazine, which suggested a bridge between her writing and what that something might be. 'Greene said, "Character is plot."' One sentence, which marked a turning point in her approach to writing fiction. 'It made me understand what writing fiction is all about. I realised why I'd gone wrong in those four books that I'd started and never finished. It was because I'd come up with a plot and then tried to fit people in. Character is destiny. Develop character, *then* the story comes.' It fits, of course, the message of the novels: once you know where you are coming from, the 'narrative' way forward is clear.

As in life, so in fiction. 'We are what we are, character is what he or she is; that is what creates their lives. We live our characters, don't we? One lives one's basic character. If you're a weak person then you're going to have a quite different life from someone who is strong. Then, also, adversity can develop your character or shatter you. So many of the strong characters grow from adversity. I'm fascinated by the indomitability [of people]. Life is hard, it's always been hard, it doesn't get any easier and it's not important that life is hard, what is important is how we overcome that adversity, or the adversities we have in our lives. I think I'm writing often about courage, conflict, inside oneself and between people.' As in fiction, so in life, for Barbara herself grew from Freda's adversity, because Freda would not have mothered her in the way that she did, had Freda not suffered her own and Edith's loss.

So, marriage to Bob, which took her away from her roots, ironically served also to refocus her on them. Yorkshire was the bit of deep-truth reality and it produced Barbara's first offspring together in Emma Harte, her unique character forged in the landscape of Barbara's youth.

Marriage to Bob also served to internationalise the arena in which the woman of substance would operate, which is why, unlike Catherine Cookson, Barbara is able to write about people and places beyond her homeland, and appeal to readers beyond the country that formed her. By the time she came to write her first novel, Barbara was able to call up the spirit of place that imbued character not only among the crags of Ramsden Ghyll, where she ran as a teenager 'on her beloved moors high above Fairley village', but also among Manhattan's skyscrapers, 'a living painting of enormous power and wealth and the heartbeat of American industry'. Cut off in her Manhattan eyrie, free from the cultural baggage of either Yorkshire or America, she was in touch with the spirit of both. So it was that when she came to write *A Woman of Substance* it featured a woman in tune with Manhattan, but with her roots in the gritstone hills of the Yorkshire moors.

Barbara's imaginative homecoming – her writing of novels which mine the two cultures in this way – was an emotional experience of rediscovery, and

THE WOMAN OF SUBSTANCE

determined that the books would themselves have strong emotional and psychological dimensions. It meant that she would put her characters in touch with their true selves, as she had done herself, releasing them from the value-vacuum of their modernist world by returning them to their roots, often to Yorkshire, her own home culture, but in Maxim West's case first to Berlin, where he discovers that his real parents are not even the German Jews he had supposed to have been lost to him by the war. Then, finally, Barbara returns him to the love of the one woman, Teddy, who has been a true mother to him but is not even a blood-relation, thereby returning to us the notion of absolute love at the root of identity, the value which will henceforth organise rich and powerful Maxim's life along other than pragmatic lines, and to which he will refer for his values. This was the point of the homecoming.

One morning in her early forties, Barbara called up her subconscious and provoked her imaginative homecoming with a series of questions: 'Well, you haven't liked these four books you started and you put them away. So, what do you want to write and where do you want to set it? And what kind of book would it be? And what is it about, basically? And who are the characters?

'I didn't ask the questions out loud, obviously, [although] I do that of myself today. Walk around muttering to myself. But my answers were: set it in England because I'm English and I know the English. No! Set it in Yorkshire, because you really know the

Yorkshire people. I want to write about a woman who makes it in a man's world ... when women weren't doing that, at the turn of the century maybe. I realised as I answered these questions and wrote them down on a yellow pad that what I was describing ... was a saga. I was really talking to myself about writing a traditional, old-fashioned saga.

'That's what I did write. And when I realised I was going to write about a woman who makes it in a man's world when women weren't doing that, and that she'd be a businesswoman, I thought I wanted to write about a woman who becomes a woman of substance. And I looked at that and I knew at once that I had my title, and I also knew that this would be the novel I would finish. I thought it was a damn good title, especially since it can have two meanings, substance: money, and the development of her character. You know, certain people didn't like this title! And I said: "Well, I'm not changing it. I love this title. And I didn't ask your opinion."' Barbara laughs. 'I mean, Bob loved it, but people are funny, you know? They think they know better than you if they're in the business. I said: "I will never change this title."'

'A week later I had written a twelve-page outline and I was on my way. For the next three months I sat at my desk in our Manhattan apartment creating Emma Harte in my imagination ... and I dug back into my memory for the countless details about Upper Armley and other parts of Yorkshire where the story is set. After I had written 190 pages I went back into the past in the novel. I was suddenly at the turn of the century, when Emma was a little girl. I swiftly realised that I had to make a trip to Yorkshire to discover more. I telephoned my father and asked him to look for old books on Armley and Leeds in the local library, which he did. It was rather fortuitous for me that my mother had been clipping out a series on old Leeds, which the *Yorkshire Evening Post* was running at the time. I talked at length to my parents, relatives and older friends and spent hours in Leeds Public Library studying old copies of Leeds newspapers, histories of Leeds and Yorkshire, interviews with local people who had worked in the mills, and visited old mills in Armley and Stanningley, drove into the Dales, and tramped around Ripon, Middleham and Studley Royal.'

Bobby Caplin remembers this period well. 'I remember Barbara came back to Leeds doing research into the old mills for *A Woman of Substance*. She had gone away a provincial girl and come back a very, very smart and intelligent person. It was great to see. But basically she was still Barbara. This friend of mine had a birthday party during the time she was here. This was Ronnie Sumrie, her old boyfriend, and Barbara contacted Ronnie as an old friend (he was well married at the time) to come and explain to her about manufacturers and to introduce her to the top mill-owners.'

There's a story attached to Barbara's meeting with her old boyfriend after so long. 'I ran into Ronnie on a Saturday, on a Pullman train from Kings Cross. I was coming up to Leeds to see my parents, and to do more research for *Woman of Substance*. It must have been about 1976. Ronnie and I found ourselves sitting in the same carriage; it was the restaurant car. I was further down but facing him, though I didn't immediately recognise him, and then this most enormous girl sits down with him. And it's a totally empty carriage. And I see this flick of horror enter these eyes and he looked across at me, those blue eyes full of horror. I thought, My God it's Ronnie Sumrie! And I stood up and sort of edged towards him and said, "Aren't you Ronnie Sumrie?" And he leapt to his feet and said, "It's Barbara, isn't it?" And as the train was pulling out I answered, "Yes," and so we sort of embraced in this rolling carriage, and I asked, "Do you want to come and join me?" "Oh yes, I do!" he exclaimed. And he was sort of polite enough and gentlemanly enough to say to this woman, "Oh would you excuse me. I've met an old school-friend." We have often laughed about that.'

It was a homecoming that determined her future as a novelist and would in years to come be reciprocated by the city of her birth. In 1990, two years after the scholarly Brotherton Library in Leeds had been granted their request to become the Keeper of the Barbara Taylor Bradford archive (her manuscripts sit next to ones by Charlotte Brontë), she was honoured by Leeds University with the degree of Doctor of Letters, presented by the Duchess of Kent. (Five years later, the city of Bradford would bestow on her an honorary DPhil.) The great coincidence was that Alan Bennett was similarly honoured at Leeds on the very same day – 12th May 1990. They hadn't set eyes on one another in more than half a century, and had no notion that they had attended the same school until broadcaster Richard Whiteley pointed it out backstage, 'and,' stressed Barbara, 'we are both the same sign – Taurus!'

Bennett at once slipped comfortably into character, his ear for dialogue, on which he had made his reputation, as deft as ever. 'Alan was so funny,' said Barbara. 'When we were getting robed, he suddenly looked down, looked at his feet, and he said disconsolately in this broad Yorkshire accent: "I wish I had known it was going to be this posh. I've got dirty suede shoes, Barbara." I followed his gaze and he did have on a rather mucky pair of stained suede shoes, and there we were being put in these velvet robes! Tremendous talent, and his father a butcher in Tong Road!'

The idea of *A Woman of Substance* had brought Barbara home. Suddenly, yesterday was now, the past was about to become a part of her. It was the psychological unity she needed to move forward. Acknowledging her anchor in Yorkshire had given Barbara back her centre.

CHAPTER SIX

An Author of Substance

'*No matter what the publishers do, they'll never stop this book. It'll go through the roof.*'

Inevitably, with a book about a character who had so many parallels with that of her creator, Barbara was an important element in its sale to publishers. 'When I came up with the idea for *A Woman of Substance* I wrote a twelve-page outline and showed it to Bob,' said Barbara. 'After he read it, he said it was a great idea, but that I was undertaking something quite enormous . . . the story of a woman's life from childhood to old age. I agreed, and he nodded and said, "You'll do it." He always had confidence in me.

'Although I had an American agent, Paul Gitlin, who had been introduced to me by Cornelius Ryan and had sold my design books, I decided to show the outline to my English agent, George Greenfield.' Greenfield was a leading literary agent in the rather traditional agency of John Farquharson, and had represented Barbara since she was a journalist in London. He liked the outline, but the first bite he got was

ironically from an American – editor-in-chief Betty
Prashker of Doubleday, when she was in London
scouting for new authors. They'd had lunch, she'd
told him she was looking for traditional sagas, and
he had given her Barbara's phone number in New
York. A week later Barbara received a phone call from
Carolyn Blakemore, senior editor of the firm, who
invited her to have drinks with her and Prashker.

'When we met, they were very cordial,' Barbara
remembers. 'They told me they wanted to see the outline as soon as possible; I agreed to messenger it down
to Doubleday the following morning. Within two
hours of receiving it, Carolyn was on the phone telling
me, "It's the best outline I've ever read, bar none!
When are you starting work on it? When can we see
pages?" I remember saying, "It's now early June, I'll
give you at least one hundred pages the first working
day after Labor Day Weekend."'

In early September Barbara kept to her promise,
actually delivering 192 pages, 'which was the whole
of Part One and the beginning of Part Two. Three
days later she called me and said she loved it . . . They
wanted it. I told her to get Paul Gitlin to make the
deal. That was in about 1975–6. I delivered the book
two and a half years later.'

In London, in the meantime, Greenfield had shown
the original outline to Mark Barty-King, the then
editorial director of Granada Publishing, part of
Lord Bernstein's media empire, which included the
Granada TV company. Then, by chance, Barty-King
bumped into Barbara on a street corner in New York

City. He already had the treatment and was intrigued, so, when he was in town on other business and caught sight of Greenfield walking along with a beautiful blonde companion, he was pleased to discover that she was none other than its author. 'I was so pleased to meet her,' recalls Mark, a handsome six-foot-four operator whose nickname in publishing circles at the time was Captain Marvel. 'She was an attractive woman of course, but what was palpable when she spoke about the manuscript of *A Woman of Substance* was her determination. Call it Yorkshire grit or what-ever. I had no picture in my mind of her until that day, but I went back to England determined to buy that book, which we did for what was then the highest advance ever paid for the right to publish a book in the UK – £55,000.

'What swayed me was her cold certainty that it would be a success – it was determination rather than enthusiasm. There's a subtle difference. You trusted her judgement. She did not for one moment doubt that it would be a success. The only question was whether one wanted to be a part of it, and there was no question as far as I was concerned.'

When I described the scene to Bob, he replied, 'That's the way she's always been. You cannot take her off the track; once she's on the track she's like a locomotive . . . I mean, she goes. She puffs away and it's very hard to move her or to stop her.'

In due course (1982–3), Bernstein sold the pub-lishing side of Granada to the old English firm of William Collins and it became known as Grafton

Publishing, with Mark still heading up the editorial side, Patricia Parkin as chief editor (fiction) and Ian Chapman, from the Collins side, its managing director. Before long (1989), they with the rest of Collins would be bought by Rupert Murdoch for £320 million, and renamed HarperCollins. 'We met Ian Chapman,' Bob recalls. 'Ian became a great fan, he was a great champion of Barbara's because he was running the company. So, everything seemed to be rolling along, everybody was with us. She has never had any real problems with the UK publishers, I must say. They are the same today as they were then, though the executives have changed, except Patricia Parkin. Patricia, she's unbelievable.'

When Bob saw the enthusiasm both in New York and London, he became involved in the book's marketing, but there was some delay before publication. 'I finished *A Woman of Substance* and delivered it to Doubleday, New York on May fifth, 1978,' remembers Barbara. 'I know it was May fifth because it was just before my birthday. It was very long, it was 1520 pages, the weight of a small child. Then they took a year to publish it, which was perfectly normal in those days. We had to cut three hundred pages without it showing,' she laughs. 'Try it! You've got to do a page here and a page there and five pages there and you usually do description and I actually did lose three minor characters whom we felt we could get rid of. That took them a few months. Then the Doubleday editor Carolyn Blakemore said to me: "We still haven't lost enough pages. There is one chapter where Emma's not in it." So, she took out a chapter in its entirety.'

The dropped chapter was about the First War. 'And I said, "My favourite chapter!" It wasn't really my favourite chapter, but I wanted her to feel bad because I really didn't want to cut any more pages. Anyway, she said: "It lifts out and you don't know it's gone." I read it and it was true: Emma waves goodbye to Joe Lowther and Blackie on the railway station, they go off to war and the next chapter is six months later, she's there with her children, she's going to work, she's doing everything she normally does. Then of course one of the reviewers said: "Bradford goes into great detail about" – whatever – "and yet hardly touches on the First World War!" But there is a funny story attached to this. When Bob was making the film of *Hold the Dream*, which was the second book in the *Woman of Substance* trilogy, some magazine in London asked me if I would write them a short story about the Emma Harte family and I said: "I can't. I'm in the middle of a novel . . ." They came back and said: "Are you sure you haven't got anything? It doesn't have to be about the Hartes. Anything at all will do. What about a short story?" And I told them I didn't write short stories any more. Only when I was a child. And they said: "Oh! We'll have one of those." "*No*," was my answer.

'But then Bob was at the studio in London and he called me and said: "Try and find them something. You must have something somewhere because they're driving me crazy and it's very important that we get this big spread about the miniseries." So as I'm talking to him, I said: "Oh, Bob. There's the lost chapter." I sent it. They ran it. And then the British publisher said: "Why have we never seen this chapter! We want this chapter. We're putting it in the book." And they had reason to bring out a new edition, which said: "For the first time, the missing chapter", with a big medallion on the jacket. Then they did the same in America, they put that chapter in the book. It is a good chapter, actually, and it was one that I liked because it was the war.

'So, they took a year with *Woman of Substance*, it was delivered May '78 and within a few weeks I had also sold them the idea of *Voice of the Heart*, so I actually embarked on that book without knowing that *A Woman of Substance* was going to be successful. The first novel came out in May '79 in the US, and by that time I'd worked since the previous September on *Voice of the Heart*.

'In England it [*Woman of Substance*] was published in 1980. This delay had something to do with Mark holding it back because he wanted to get a deal with the book club.'

Mark remembers serious problems in getting the jacket right. The jacket of a book is of course crucial marketing territory, and the marketing on a first-time author is key. If the publisher goes light on that aspect you don't stand a chance. Bob didn't think twice about pitching in on Barbara's behalf. 'She really put everything she had into that book and when it was finished I'd already taken over a great part of her promotion, supervising the marketing of it, working with the American publisher. I was always concerned, right from the beginning, that I didn't want her to be buried. When you are a new author coming in they don't want to spend the money unless the book takes off right away. If you're not careful, they can put you on the list and let the book ride by itself – good luck! So, I was very attentive to that, and she was on the road for the book. She did ten cities promoting the book, and I made sure that when I wasn't there, there was always somebody with her. I mean, it was the first time round, you know?'

I asked how Doubleday took to that. As a mass-market-paperback publisher myself at that time I knew that with no track record in Barbara's career it would have been deemed interference on Bob's part. Most husbands of new authors would have been shown the door.

'The publishers,' he began. 'They get a little nervous. They don't always like me.'

'I haven't heard that,' I said encouragingly.

'I don't know,' he said, flicking his eyes up at me, wondering just where I was coming from. 'I think that they are a little nervous of me.'

'How did you handle it?' I asked, cutting to the chase.

'I am always very polite and have no case against them. The point is that I do push. I was up in Doubleday and I met with the marketing people, advertising people, and if I saw this wasn't moving I came in there every day, made my phone calls till I got what I wanted. Barbara and I, we had a good relationship with Doubleday, a friendly and good relationship once she got going. In the meantime I had to ask to see advertising and marketing. You know, the guy working on *A Woman of Substance* and the next one, *Voice of the Heart* . . . I saw them failing in terms of marketing. I didn't see the energy there, so I was up to see the Vice President of the marketing and advertising. I'm afraid I used to drive the guy nuts. "What's happening? Show me what you're doing." I couldn't understand what they were doing. He was telling me, "Well, we're going to do publicity [as opposed to advertising]. That was nothing. So I finally had to go down the hall to see Nelson and get him on board and get him to give them more money.

'So I was with Nelson Doubleday. This was in 1979, when Nelson Doubleday owned the company, and I was sitting with Nelson in his office. Not too many people do that. I always remember he took off his jacket, I was off with my jacket and he said, "Let's talk." I said, "Listen, I treat a book like a motion picture, so let's start from that point of view. I know you don't have thirty million dollars to spend on a book, but let's start from that point of view: you are selling a motion picture, that's the way you tackle it. He was telling me that he'd allocated about fifty thousand dollars to promote the book and, you know, I said he had to do more. He didn't like it, but I think down the line he quite admired me for my persistence.

'We also – that's me and Barbara – took a big risk because I spent money. I believe my statement is correct when I say that I was the first person in the publishing business in the United States to take full-page ads in the *New York Times*. There was nobody before me who did that. I started it and I'm sure there were heads turning in the publishing industry thinking this publisher is spending a lot of money, because at the time we didn't tell anyone. I didn't want the publishers to be embarrassed, so we wouldn't tell and the publisher always got the credit, they got their name on the ad, but I paid for it. I did it on most of the books. Sometimes the publisher paid. Every book Barbara has ever written has had a full page in the *New York Times*.

'*Recognition* factor. It explodes on the scene, people see the name, they see the book, I don't know whether they buy the book or not, but the key point was the media in New York, the media in Washington. They saw. They saw that huge advertisement and you didn't have to call them and explain to them what you were talking about, they knew it, they had all seen it. I also bought spreads in the *Publishers Weekly* [the trade magazine of US publishing], so everybody in the business would know.

'My key market, target market, where work was needed, was always the United States, never England. I hired PR firms in England, but I never got into the advertising. I only did it in the United States because you've got three hundred million people to collar there.'

As Bob was only too aware, everything follows on from the American market. First publication happened in hardcover from Doubleday in 1979. There was so much noise that paperback publishers were alerted, and foreign publishers took *Publishers Weekly* and saw the spreads Bob had placed. He was doing the bedrock business, from which everything, even interest from the movie industry, would flow. And as one by one people picked up on this interest and made offers for rights in their territories and markets, the whole thing began to snowball. He knew what would happen and never doubted for one moment that the product could carry the interest that followed.

'I didn't know it was going to be a bestseller; in the US nobody knew. In fact, the hardback only sold 55,000 copies, but 55,000 copies in 1979 was a damn good shot for a hardback book when you are unknown. Like 250,000 today.'

Separately, I asked Barbara what she remembered about the book's first publication. 'In hardcover there was a rush for the book in some of the big cities like New York and Florida, and in Texas and California where I went to promote it. Surprisingly, for not a lot of money being spent by the publisher, it did get to the middle of the bestseller list, about number five or six, and did very well for a first novel with very little money spent either on advertising or promotion. They did do an ad, which was very clever. The person who did it actually ran all the Doubleday stores because in those days Doubleday had bookstores of their own, and he was so convinced it was going to be a huge bestseller that he did this ad saying that if you don't like this book we guarantee your money back. They had no returns on it. I remember going to one bookstore in Atlanta and the buyer said to me, "No matter what Doubleday do, they'll never stop this book, it'll go through the roof." It did well, and then it was bought for paperback by Avon.'

Avon was Bob and Barbara's prize for all the hard work. With the paperback publisher's interest came another Bob into Barbara's life. 'Bob Wyatt discovered the book; he was the one who bought it for Avon from Doubleday for quite a lot of money in those days,' she remembers. 'They paid about $400,000 for paperback rights. It's not a lot today, but in those days it was. He discovered the book; the book somehow came to his desk, they bought it and he did a very clever commercial for television where they had an actress dressed up as Emma, as a little maid, with a white apron and a frilly cap. I remember the commercial very well because first of all it was a very gloomy moorland setting and then it became a village street with cobblestones and the sound of horses, and a carriage and horse going down. Then suddenly it cut to this – well, actually to the inside of a grand room and a young girl carrying a tray piled up with a silver pot and all that. Then it flashed some other actors' faces and there was a voice-over which said: "A great family saga in the grand tradition. The story of the servant girl who became a world power . . ." or whatever it was. So, it was Bob Wyatt and whoever he worked with who made the book – he remained my friend for years. When the book came out it quickly went up to Number One on the paper-back list and it stayed on the list for more than a year. Everybody talked about it staying there so long, it just never went off the list. It sold three and a half million copies in that first year in paperback. That edition came out in the summer of 1980 and it came out in England in hardcover at that time, too.'

The ball was rolling. In 1985, with publication of *Hold the Dream*, Barbara's third novel, her English publishers were boasting that '*A Woman of Substance* has been in the top twenty listings since its publication.'

Wyatt remembers the Avon TV advertisement as 'a first for fiction at least', but he was wary of taking too much of the credit for spotting the book's potential. 'Page Cuddy was also important to *Woman of Substance*. She was maybe the first reader on it,' he said. 'And that whole women's fiction thing was Nancy Coffey's at Avon. She invented it.'

Avon, through the 1970s and early '80s, had been enacting a publishing revolution, putting out romantic historical novels with explicit sex scenes known in the trade as 'bodice-rippers'. Authors such as Kathleen Woodiwiss, whose first novel, *The Flame and the Flower*, they published in 1972, and Rosemary Rogers (*Sweet Savage Love*, 1974) were sweeping the market with sales in the millions.

These authors had a huge impact on the marketing of women's fiction in paperback form in both America and England, where they were marketed by a company called Futura. Hitherto, the big-selling fiction titles on a paperback publisher's list had been bought in rights deals from hardcover publishers. Paperback publication had relied on publicity generated by the hardcover a year earlier. But now paperbackers were publishing their own original lead titles and had learned how to market and promote them in far more bullish fashion than any hardbacker.

Particular attention was paid to the cover artwork. Wyatt remembers how Coffey gave the Woodiwiss bandwagon its initial momentum with a 'certain look, a very specific, hand-drawn typeface which became the standard for the industry. No one had done things like this until then. After the soft Woodiwiss books came Rosemary Rogers, and another entire look and feel was established for that writer.'

A Woman of Substance was no more akin to *The Flame and the Flower* or *Sweet Savage Love* than was Maeve Binchy's *Light a Penny Candle*, first published in England in 1982, but both Maeve Binchy and Barbara benefited from the powerful marketing techniques that had been honed in the publishing of these and other similar books. Maeve Binchy was actually marketed by the paperback publisher of Woodiwiss and Rogers in England, and Avon would not have had the sophisticated conceptual reach via cover artwork and TV advertising for *A Woman of Substance* had they not built up to it with these precedents.

So, everything was falling into place. What had seemed good from Doubleday, now seemed fantastic from Avon, but it was still only the start. Between 1984 and 1999, Bob set up no fewer than nine TV miniseries based on Barbara's books, producing them himself (*Hold the Dream*, *Voice of the Heart*, *Act of Will*, *To Be the Best*, *Remember*, *Everything to Gain*, *Love in Another Town*, *Her Own Rules* and *A Secret Affair*). The impact of such television exposure – six hours in the case of *A Woman of Substance*, starring Jenny Seagrove and Deborah Kerr – was astronomical in terms of book sales. But Bob was not simply building sales of books any more. He was creating a brand.

Very wisely he kept out of the first film, retaining only approvals of locations, stars and script on Barbara's behalf: 'I didn't want to be the one to produce *Woman of Substance* as it was her first book. Since it contained so much of her Yorkshire childhood and youth, she was very emotionally attached to it, so I backed off making the miniseries, believing we would have terrible arguments as she was so emotionally involved. I flew over six or seven times while the series was being made in England and watched at arm's length. There wasn't a great deal of financial experience on the part of the producer, and there was another company, a British company, involved. So when I stepped in they had somebody to talk to about business. We were able to pull it together. I gathered some money and we pulled it together and got out.

'And, yes, the film promoted the book. There was a line-up of about 165 independent stations in the United States who locked together as a network for two nights. Very unusual. The independent station in New York was WPX; in Chicago it was The Tribune.

165 stations, it was enormous. They were all independent programming, but they locked into CBS, ABC, whatever, to show *A Woman of Substance*! Very unusual. We were going against the networks!'

Both he and Barbara became more closely involved in *Hold the Dream*, which would be transmitted the following year (1985). It again starred Jenny Seagrove (this time as Paula Fairley, Emma's granddaughter), Stephen Collins as Shane O'Neill and Deborah Kerr as the ageing Emma Harte. 'Barbara had just finished the book, *Act of Will*, when I flew her into London and talked her into writing the script for *HTD*,' Bob said. 'Four writers had not been able to give me the screenplay I wanted. I was in trouble. Barbara had her mind still full of *Act of Will* and practically had to start writing *HTD* again. It was unbelievable. I've known a lot of writers, seen some of the great ones in Hollywood. She'd never set foot in a studio in her life, at least not to work in. She'd never written a script. I put her in a studio – Shepperton – locked up in a room with a script typist. Her routine was 6.30 a.m. to 9 p.m., seven days a week for six weeks. We were already in production. I had over one hundred people waiting to get a script, a proper script. The typist who I had for her, who was typing the script, waiting for dictation, she said, "I think, Barbara, we've got to start doing something here. You can't just sit there and think! We have to start somewhere, so what's the location, where are we, where do we start?" Barbara says, "We are in Yorkshire. Outside scene, country." The secretary says, "Who's talking to whom?" That's the way the script was written. It turned out to be a brilliant miniseries. And Barbara was amazing.

'She did it twice – she did it with *Hold the Dream* and *Voice of the Heart*.' The latter, starring Lindsay Wagner, James Brolin, Victoria Tennant and Honor Blackman, was produced by Bob in 1990. Later came the film of *Act of Will* (Liz Hurley, Victoria Tennant, Peter Coyote), which Barbara remembers as more madness: 'Bob had a line producer at that point called Aida Young, and together they got a script of *Act of Will* developed, but for some reason he suddenly found himself with two miniseries going – he was doing *To Be the Best* (with Lindsay Wagner, Anthony Hopkins, Stephanie Beacham, Christopher Cazenove and Fiona Fullerton) at that time, and had to go to Hong Kong to shoot it. Naturally, Yorkshire Television didn't want to do *Act of Will* – God knows why, I've never been lucky with Yorkshire Television – so he let it go to Tyne Tees Television.

'He is extraordinary. He not only makes the movies of my books but he manages my career. I do have a literary agent for the publishing, Mort Janklow, but Bob's the one who deals with the publishers on a day-to-day basis. My only sadness is that he's never been able to get a TV deal for *The Women in His Life*, which is my own favourite novel among those I have written. He's got a script that's fantastic, and they say "No", and so he doesn't even bother to show it any more. "Oh, but it's not going to work, it's a little boy and what actor wants only part of a role," etc., etc.'

Altogether, advances and royalties from Barbara's

novels total over £50 million, and she is reputed to be earning at the rate of £8 million a year still today. Following the original deal with Doubleday for *A Woman of Substance* and shortly afterwards for *Voice of the Heart*, and their subsidiary paperback deal with Avon, a contract was drawn up in April 1983 for $8 million with Barbara's three English-language publishers – Doubleday, Bantam and Collins – for three new books, which would be *Hold the Dream*, *Act of Will* and *To Be the Best*.

Three years later, with only *To Be the Best* not yet published under this contract, another three-book deal with leading US publisher Random House was signed for £6 million, which Bob recalls was a deal Mort Janklow (at that time the world's most successful agent) put together. This covered US rights for *The Women in His Life*, *Remember* and *Angel*.

Then, in 1989, Rupert Murdoch decided to take over Collins in London and publishers Harper & Row in New York, and turned the whole thing into Harper-Collins. An executive called George Craig, who had been Collins' chief accountant in London, went over to New York to run the new HarperCollins company there as Chairman of the Board. Three years later, in 1992, Barbara, who was already with HarperCollins in London of course, made a move from Random House to the US side of HarperCollins, the sister company of her London publisher. The idea was that she would have one English-language publisher with a massive, cohesive, worldwide marketing effort.

The move caused quite a stir for a number of

reasons. Ex-*Sunday Times* editor and husband of Tina Brown of *Vanity Fair*, Harold Evans, was head of Random House at that time, and he was not best pleased. Dialogue reported in the press showed that Evans was having to swallow the bitter pill that his old boss at the *Sunday Times*, Rupert Murdoch, was taking his author. The real story, as far as Barbara was concerned, was never told, however, and makes more fascinating reading. Naturally, Bob was in the middle of it.

'The new contract with George Craig. That was a historic event, that contract,' Bob told me.

I said I had a report to the effect that in 1992 a contract was drawn for £17 million between Barbara and HarperCollins.

'There was a contract. First of all it wasn't in pounds, it was in dollars, and I will tell you exactly the way this happened. That's a very interesting story. I had made a picture called *Voice of the Heart* and I showed the picture to George Craig. I said, "Look, I want you to see it. I want you to see all the things I'm doing." He'd seen *A Woman of Substance* and *Hold the Dream*. So George said, "Bob, this is a terrific series, really great, looks fabulous." I said, "Well, actually I have a favour to ask you," and he said, "Well, what's the favour?" I said, "The favour is I want to sell this series to Fox Studios [in Los Angeles]." And he said, "What do you want me to do? What exactly are you thinking?" I said, "I think this series is going to be terrific for Barbara's books and I want to sell the series to Fox Television because you are both part of News Corp, so it's a natural." He said, "What did you have in mind?"

'I said, "If I can be quite honest with you, I would like Rupert Murdoch to see this film . . ." And he said, "Look, the man is flying all over the world and he never looks at films."

'Anyway, here's what happened. I got a call two weeks later when we'd just finished editing the film (George had seen the rough cuts). It was just finished. I get a call from George. He says, "What are you doing today? You're not going out of town?" I said, "No, I'm here." He said, "You've got an appointment with Rupert Murdoch at 5 p.m. today. Hire a private studio and get the film over there. He wants to see the film at 5 p.m. sharp."

'I almost fell over. So, I was suddenly scrambling, getting a copy of the film, hiring the studios . . . At one minute to five, in walks Rupert Murdoch with his wife, Anna. I couldn't believe it. We sit in the theatre and I just explained to him a little bit about the history of how I made the film and he looked at me and said, "Where's Barbara?" I said, "Well, she's home writing, she's working." He said, "I'm not seeing the film unless Barbara comes here, I want her in this room." So I had to call Barbara at home. I spoke to her. I said to her, "I don't give a damn whether you are in blue jeans or a sweater, you must come, we are not running this film until you get here." So Barbara scrambled to get dressed in a hurry and came over. She arrived and we sat in that screening room for three hours. Three hours and thirty minutes – it's a four-hour miniseries

with the commercials. I'd made it in thirty-five millimetre. I wanted the quality of the best motion-picture
you can get. So I showed this in thirty-five millimetre
to Rupert Murdoch. It was just unbelievable in this
room on the big screen, and he sat there enthralled.

'After we'd finished, he just said, "*Amazing* piece
of film, fantastic, I love it." So then he said, "I am
taking you to dinner." It's a good thing Barbara had
changed. "I'm taking you to Le Cirque." It was unbelievable, we walked in. Champagne. He stayed there
till about eleven . . . eleven thirty with Anna.

'I didn't discuss the next move with him, I was
careful. The next day George called me and said, "We
are flying to the west coast, I'm flying with you. I've
arranged a meeting, I think you've got two or three
days to get it organised and I have the studio organised. A meeting with Fox, with the whole group at
Fox. Without Rupert, but with all the heads of departments. George had called the head guy and talked to
him and he said, "You want me to look at this film?
What do you think, I've got nothing else to do? I don't
look at my own films here in the studio. I give them
three minutes, ten minutes, and you want me to look
at the whole thing with you? You're crazy." George
said, "Well the big boss asked me to call and he wants
you to look at it because I think it's something we
want to talk you about – putting it on the Fox
network."

'George wouldn't let me go by myself,' Bob continued. 'We arrived at Fox and there are fifteen, twenty
guys in the conference room, every head of depart-

ment showed up. At the meeting there was a lot of conversation. Yes, we're going to like this, yes we're going to do this. But, to make a long story short, nothing happened. Later, much later, they turned down the film. Finally, they said, "Well, it's a woman's programme, our network is a new network [which it was at the time], and we are looking to attract a young male crowd. Anyway, they didn't turn it down that day and George and I flew back to New York together, and that is where history was made.

'We were sitting together having drinks. We were friends, we were talking publishing, pictures and publishing – what he was going to do with the company, all his plans. And then George said to me, "What's with our contract with Barbara? Since we're talking business, what's with the contract?" At the time our contract must have been very close to expiration. I said, "Well, George, frankly I haven't figured out all the things but I think Barbara is entitled to get more money." He asked me my opinion on a lot of things. I said, "Primarily I want to make a deal that equals her talent and what she's going to contribute to the company. You know, she wears the uniform of HarperCollins, she's totally HarperCollins, and I think it needs to be given consideration." So he said, "Look . . ." He took out his pen and started to write on a paper napkin, and said, "All right, let's work." So, we started doing the figures and he made all kinds of calculations – and George was a good calculator, he's an accountant by trade – we started working figures on a napkin, and we made our contract right there. It was for $24 million, the biggest contract ever written in the history of publishing at that time. The contract was initialled by me. I think Barbara has the napkin. That was our deal. England and America, English-language rights, but not foreign language. Right there on the plane, on the napkin. Mort knew nothing about it, and certainly he was startled when he heard about it.

'From then on there were all kinds of rumours, resentment and jealousy; nothing directed at Barbara, because they all loved Barbara. They said, "This guy Bradford, he's a killer," and the publishers were apprehensive with me. Marketing guys said, "If this guy comes up we are going to be in trouble." Which wasn't the point. My job is only to protect Barbara and to promote her career.'

CHAPTER SEVEN

Hold the Dream

'You will never die, Emma. We are both going to live for ever and ever, here at the Top of the World.'

Edwin Fairley in *A Woman of Substance*

Many to whom I have spoken during the research for this book come back to the question of what has made Barbara's career so incredibly successful. Clearly, good management and marketing have helped to make her books big bestsellers. Unusually, if not uniquely among novelists, her name is synonymous with the character she created, which suggests a certain iconic status. When she stands up in public she *is* the woman of substance.

Barbara's first novel was published at the right moment for reasons apparently outside the author's intent. 'It was looked on as a saga,' Barbara remembers. 'It was the first time anybody had written a matriarchal dynastic saga.'

It was a new twist on a highly respected genre that had been enjoying a resurgence of interest. The family saga had been popular since the 1920s. John Galsworthy's *The Forsyte Saga* was first published in 1922, the second part of the family chronicles, *A Modern Comedy*, followed in 1929, and, in 1931, a further collection appeared called *On Forsyte Change*. John Galsworthy established the Edwardian family saga as a genre of its own and had many imitators. In the 1960s an English television production, *The Forsyte Saga*, became such popular Sunday night viewing that vicars changed the time of Evensong to accommodate it. It also swept North America.

The Edwardian era was very much in vogue for another reason, too. *The Country Diary of an Edwardian Lady*, a naturalist's diary for the year 1906, found first publication in 1977. It remained at No. 1 on *The Sunday Times* bestseller list for an unprecedented sixty-four weeks, and, again, was similarly popular in America. Then, in 1978, *Dallas*, the family saga of the oil-rich Ewing family, started life as a five-part TV miniseries and ran for thirteen seasons. Small surprise, therefore, that the two biggest audience hooks in Avon's TV advertisement for *A Woman of Substance* were 'saga' and 'Edwardian'.

But the woman of substance herself is a woman of our times with universal significance. The opportunities of which Emma Harte avails herself are those later made available to many as working-class exploitation was eased by socialism and socialism gave way to meritocracy, with an emphasis on the individual, self-respect, self-belief, autonomy and self-sufficiency.

Emma Harte, woman of substance, was in the vanguard of this great change. She led the way in her fictional world, and in her we see clearly the character that will be required to survive and prosper in the modern world in which we all now live. That is what has made her so popular and inspiring. In an interview in the early 1980s, Barbara said: 'I hadn't realised how much people find Emma's story inspirational. I've had almost two thousand letters. Many of them said, "Emma Harte has been an inspiration to us – we lead this kind of life, very tragic, very difficult, and if Emma can get through it, we can." The strange thing is that they spoke of her as if she is a living person.'

Meanwhile, in the more modern novels, such as *Voice of the Heart* and *The Women in His Life*, there is a keener focus on the psychological trauma attached to having arrived, having uprooted and risen in the modern world. Weighing anchor altogether can leave modern man bereft of a sense that there is anything beyond the projects he works on so obsessively in his effort to get somewhere. Once again, Barbara could write about it because she had come this route: 'These characters couldn't have been created without my own development,' she has said. She can write about it because her project has become her.

She resolves her characters' trauma in a return to their roots, but this return is no retreat – Barbara doesn't see herself as Yorkshire, any more than she sees herself as American. Her life has taken her out of belonging to any one culture. Hers is the emotional circle we all need to make, to live and be loved, to break free and grow to a position of autonomy and independence, from which we can independently assess, use and not be used by the values on which we were bred and which formed us. Is there any better recipe for fulfilment in life?

There is, however, one other – I think central – reason for the novels' incredible success, which has to do with the work of the subconscious which generates unawares the ideas that claw at a writer's inner self and drive his or her best fiction.

When Barbara first read in the manuscript of this book that her own mother, Freda, and two of her siblings were illegitimate, and that Freda had been confined with them in Ripon Workhouse from the age of only six, she was deeply shocked. Bob had walked into the room at the crucial moment of her reading this and, seeing her turn white, he had asked what on earth was wrong. For a moment she had been speechless.

When I began researching Barbara's life and works with her full cooperation she told me that *Act of Will* in particular was very autobiographical, a lightly disguised story of her parents. Her mother Freda's fictional persona is Audra Kenton in the novel, a woman born into a middle-class family, who lives in a long, low, eighteenth-century manor house called High Cleugh. However, Audra's father is not who she thinks he is. Adrian Kenton, 'a shadowy figure in Audra's mind', had died in 1909, when she was only two years old. It is subsequently revealed that Adrian was not her father at all, that she is illegitimate and that her natural father is 'Uncle' Peter Lacey, who has been 'benefactor and protector' of Edith and her children – Audra and her two brothers, William and Frederick. When Lacey dies in 1920 after being gassed in a First World War action on the Somme, Edith follows soon after, dying of a broken heart. Orphans Audra and her brothers are then split up. Frederick and William are shipped to Australia. Audra goes to work at the Ripon Fever Hospital and later goes to Leeds to work as a nanny and meets Vincent Crowther, who is Barbara's father Winston Taylor's fictional persona. They marry. They have a son, Alfred, who dies in infancy from meningitis. They then have a daughter, Christina, on whom Audra focuses her not inconsiderable energies to the exclusion of everything else (including her relationship with her husband) to ensure that Christina lives the life that fate denied her.

Just how closely autobiographical this novel is should now be evident to readers of my book, and the question arises as to why Barbara should have been so stunned when my research made the match between fact and fiction more complete. Clearly, her mother Freda told her a lot about her background, enough to write the novel, but withheld the fact that Edith was not married when Freda was born, even though, in the novel, Edith is not married to Audra's father. So why did Barbara find herself inserting in this overtly biographical novel this true-to-life theme, which had been deliberately withheld from her and which she did not know to be true? The answer that suggests itself is that the story demanded it – in the context of the story it had to be so. Audra's abnormal ambition for her daughter needed a motivation. The tragic death of Alfie was not enough.

Oddly, however, Audra's illegitimacy is more or less immaterial to the story. It is there but little happens as a result of it. What motivates her extraordinary education of Christina is her loss of status – the fact that fate (the death of her parents) has robbed her of her true position in life. Audra's coming from a different world (being 'a lady born and bred') is the key factor in her relationship with her husband. It is what Vincent must overcome to make their marriage work. She goes regularly to gaze on High Cleugh, her 'memory place' in the novel, just as Freda went to the real High Cleugh (in reality a window onto Studley Royal) – but there is no suggestion that it is Audra's illegitimacy that has robbed her of her status.

In that sense, Audra's illegitimacy isn't even a very necessary ingredient of the story. So why *is* it there? The answer has to be that the issue of Freda's uncertain paternity lay buried deep in Barbara's subconscious and she couldn't help it rising to the surface when she began writing about Freda's father. Was it planted there perhaps by Freda when Barbara was small? Things stick in our minds as children, particularly when they represent a threat, as mention of the words 'fancy woman' in relation to Barbara's father did when she was a young child. Perhaps someone once said something about Freda's illegitimacy and she attached it in her mind to the sense of loss inherent in her mother's personality, which she admits always to have noted, blanking it out until she returned to her roots as writer, and then up it came.

This subconscious memory or feeling was evidently of significance to the writer right from the start. Seven years before *Act of Will* she had used the theme in *A Woman of Substance*, making it the principal motivation of her narrative. Emma Harte has an illegitimate child, Edwina, by aristocrat Edwin Fairley, who refuses to recognise her. It is this that motivates Emma's incredible story, and, I believe, Freda's too.

This is the grit in Barbara's oyster: her characters and plots are secreted in layers around the fundamental psychological problem of identity which Freda's childhood raises, so to produce the pearls of her success. The magic is that the conscious mind is not involved. The issue of Freda's identity at the root of the novels is a piece of the past – Freda and Edith's past, and now Barbara's past too – which rose up and appeared in present time, unbidden.

A Woman of Substance launched the whole theme of identity and loss that permeates so many other of her works, and which, to the benefit of their sales, mirrors a universal sense of loss and alienation that modernity engenders in those who cut themselves off from their roots, the values of home. There is this desire in almost all her main characters to find out or remind themselves where they are coming from, who and what they are, even in Maxim West, who comes closest to Bob, who as a German Jew was dispossessed of his identity as a child. It is *the* theme of Barbara's works and it is, too, *the* theme of her life, because her return to her Yorkshire roots in the novels is, as I have shown, an affirmation of her own identity. The process of its uprising from Barbara's subconscious (from the past unbidden) is akin to the process of the past rising up into the present to which she warms in places she visited in her childhood, like Middleham Castle and of course Studley Royal, which she characterises as déjà vu. This, again, is caught up in Freda's problem of identity, her need to belong, expressed in the intense way she – orphan child of the Yorkshire she so loved – held these places when she took Barbara to them as a child, determined that her daughter would inherit their mettle, which she felt was rightfully hers.

Ten days after Barbara first read my manuscript, and many transatlantic phone calls later, she accepted what I had discovered and concluded: 'I don't know what I write. You know, I don't. You have found out what I don't know. You have analysed why I do what I do, but I never knew I was doing it.'

Mother and daughter had been unusually close, their relationship exclusive. 'No one knows what went on in that house with my mother . . . not even Daddy,' she said to me. 'I don't think my father knew any of this because my father and I got very close after I married and moved to New York, and we had some very intimate talks, but he actually never said anything about her past, only that she had a heart the size of a paving stone.'

If it is really true that Freda kept so much secret

from her own husband, she must have been a troubled as well as a determined woman, unless of course Edith had told her that her father was the Marquess of Ripon and she had learned not to share the information because no one believed it. It is also possible that Freda did tell Winston, but he chose not to share it with his daughter because he didn't really believe it either, or didn't think Barbara would, or it had become an issue that upset the balance of his family (as it does in *Act of Will*).

All that we know from Barbara is that she did not know.

In the days before genetic fingerprinting, a birth certificate proved a person's identity. Finding no father's name appended, that only half an identity is known and recognised, can be traumatic, and uncertainty can drive an adopted child to seek out its natural parents. In Freda's case there appears to have been no attempt to find out who her father was, which again suggests to me that she already knew.

Barbara found it difficult to accept the evidence of the workhouse archival records because 'my mother loved Ripon so much, and she always spoke happily and lovingly of her childhood.' But the evidence is cast iron, written by hand at the time in the official record books of Ripon Workhouse, and Freda's workhouse experiences do not discount the possibility of happiness at other times. If, as I think likely, Edith was 'looked after' as the Marquess's mistress up to 1910, when she was first listed as a pauper in the workhouse with her children, there would have been

material happiness during Freda's first and most impressionable years – years when, as she told Barbara,
she made frequent trips to Studley Royal. There would
also have been love all around, for if Edith had three
children by Frederick she would have loved him, and
almost certainly he would have loved her. In the first
flush of Edith's relationship with Frederick we have a
credible image at which all Freda's subsequent education of Barbara was aimed. That image, regenerated
by Freda's natural desire to recapture who she really
was, is surely what drew her back with Barbara to
Ripon, and time and again to the Studley Royal Estate
after Studley Hall had been destroyed, as well as to
other stylish, historic and aristocratic domains which
helped to identify what kind of man she believed her
own father to have been. Of course she told Barbara
they were happy times. They were everything she had
desired and lost, and now they were everything she
desired for Barbara who she perceived rightly had
inherited from Edith the fighting qualities necessary
to reach far beyond the situation of her birth. The
telling point about Freda's 'educational programme'
for her daughter – force-feeding her 'books and art
and furniture and style' – is its uniqueness. No other
mothers of Barbara's friends did anything similar for
their daughters, and the desire to put Barbara where
Freda felt she herself ought to have been explains why
she did it.

Freda's longing to be who she really was drew her
back to Ripon from Armley and from the loving arms
of the Taylor family at the least opportunity. Indeed,

as in *Act of Will*, it set her in opposition to her mother-in-law, Esther Taylor, who was concerned that Freda was giving Barbara ideas above her station. But it also engineered this extraordinary 'educational programme', preparing Barbara to resolve the problems of identity and loss Freda suffered, and be what Edith might have been. The nature of Freda's love was to give *and* take; for Barbara became the unwitting instrument of resolution in her mother's loss.

Pulling herself out of the dismay that my revelations had initially caused, Barbara began quite naturally to be concerned about what people might think. 'I don't want the press to say that I have grandiose ideas about my background when I have always said that I come from a working-class background in Leeds,' she said, and urged me to verify the link with the Marquess of Ripon. It is not possible, at this distance of time, to verify the identity of Freda's father, given that Freda's mother never married him, his name does not appear on Freda's birth certificate, and there is no DNA evidence available. Equally, it is not possible to discount the likelihood of Freda's father being the Marquess of Ripon either. In fact, it doesn't matter whether Frederick Oliver Robinson actually was her father. It doesn't matter if the evidence is circumstantial. What matters is that we can perceive the fiction arising out of the problems of identity Freda experienced as an illegitimate child, which she believed included loss of status, and how these problems determined the environment in which Barbara was brought up and so fed through to the novels. The happy ending is that Barbara's novels did resolve these problems.

It is nevertheless interesting to see how closely we can push the link with the Marquess, and logically we should start with the birth certificates themselves. To recap, Edith chose not to name the father of her first three children on their birth certificates. Refusal to do so was unusual even in cases where the true name of the father was unknown, because it openly declared the child's illegitimacy, and in those days illegitimacy was a terrible stigma, which a mother would do anything to avoid. I quote an official Ripon illegitimacy return, where in every single case a father is named, whether or not the nomination is authentic. I show that this is consistent with the case of Catherine Cookson, born illegitimate around the same time as Freda, whose birth certificate carries the name of a man believed to have been her father, even though Catherine's father had known her mother, Kate, for a very short time (by Kate's account they made love only twice) and had long left her in the lurch by the time Catherine was born. Finally, it is in research terms unusual to find no father mentioned on a birth certificate, for a name not to have been conjured up from somewhere, especially on three consecutive certificates, as was the case for Freda and her siblings Fred and Mary. So much so that it begs explanation.

The unusual nature of Edith's omission of the father's name suggests a definite decision on her part not to invent one, as if the truth about Freda's paternity was barred to her, that she had agreed to withhold the truth but that she was not prepared to compromise the truth with a lie. Second, it is implicit that Edith didn't name the father because she wished to protect his reputation, and therefore that the man had a reputation worth protecting, that he was a prominent man, a man of position whose public reputation would suffer were his 'indiscretions' made known. The three children are bound to one father by the fact of his not being named on all three certificates (as well as by the telling choice of their names, to which we will come). It suggests that each birth was not a one-time fling, that Edith was enjoying an ongoing relationship with one man, whom she didn't name because she loved him enough not to want to blacken his reputation.

It is logically possible that the father was an ordinary married working man, as Barbara pointed out to me, but this is, I think, unlikely. First, would an ordinary working man have been able to persuade Edith he was worth waiting for through three births and the passage of seven years, from 1904 to 1910? And would such a man have refused to detach himself from his spouse? (The Marquess, a highly visible Catholic, had much to lose.) Again, how would an ordinary working married man have afforded to keep Edith?

Photographs of Edith in fine clothing, and the image handed down of her as 'the beautiful Edith Walker', plus the fact, passed down to Barbara, that Edith didn't work because she didn't need to, are consistent with the father of her children being Edith's benefactor and protector (again like Audra's father in the novel). Being pregnant so often would have made it impossible for Edith to hold down a job of the sort that she had been doing prior to 1904 – no one would have hired her as a domestic – yet she does not appear as a fully fledged workhouse inmate until after the birth of Mary in 1910 when the affair is abruptly curtailed. She could not have avoided the workhouse earlier unless she was supported – either married (which we know she was not) or being kept by the children's father. Again, Freda's very obsession with the lifestyle of the aristocracy, a main plank of Barbara's education, steers us away from the idea that her father was from the working classes.

This is all reasonable argument. All in all, it is likely that her suitor was a man of substance, someone able to support a mistress. So, we come to the question as to which man of substance in the locality is a likely contender.

Edith's first two illegitimate children, Freda and Fred, were given names derivative of their father's name as a kind of lifeline to their true identity. It was a typical thing for a single mother to do. In A *Woman of Substance*, Barbara chose to name Emma Harte's illegitimate child Edwina, after her aristocratic lover Edwin Fairley, not because she knew or suspected that Freda and Fred were illegitimate and had been named after a father called Frederick, but because the practice was recommended to her as typical.

There was only one contender among local families in village-sized Edwardian Ripon. And not only was

Frederick a family name of the Robinsons of Studley Royal for hundreds of years, but their family seat was a magnet for Edith and Freda in Freda's childhood, and later Barbara in hers, and is a key focus of the novels. Finally, of course, Edith's naming her third child Mary ties down the father's identity more successfully than if she had chosen to name her Frederika, because Mary had been the name of Frederick Oliver Robinson's dear sister, who had died in infancy.

Of course, it is possible that the very visibility of the Robinsons led to Edith naming her first three children after his family as a sort of joke, but it seems unlikely that such a joke could be made to run for seven years. By naming her children Freda, Fred and Mary, Edith was, I am certain as certain I can be, pointing the finger of paternity at Frederick Oliver, and she made sure he had nowhere to hide by desisting from inventing a fictitious name for their birth certificates.

There was, as I have shown, access and opportunity for such a liaison. Despite the huge social gulf, there were certain points of contact between rich and poor in the Ripon community, among the most likely being places of entertainment, theatres, music halls and inns. Edith was living in the thick of these in Water Skellgate. The nearby music hall and theatre, the Victoria Hall, was the ideal venue for an ambitious girl – or indeed anyone – to mix with 'the other half'. Closer still was the Palace Theatre, a casino and a permanent funfair. Then, opposite the music hall, was the Masonic Temple, where the Marquess's very own

Lodge held meetings throughout the year, and round the corner was the popular inn, the Unicorn, owned by the Marquess and a venue he would have attended regularly as the Masons used to gather there after meetings. The Masons were involved in providing support for the poor. Frederick Oliver was patron of the Ripon Home for Girls (ironically his own wife seems to have drawn him into this). All of which brought him in person into the poorer parts of Ripon that I have described.

Edith gave birth to Freda not at home but in an apartment in Water Skellgate, where the Studley Royal Estate owned numerous properties. Although the ownership of Freda's birthplace, 9A Water Skellgate, is not known, it was given over to the Irish League, an organisation of support for the many Irish workers in Ripon and very likely one sponsored by the Estate. Then there is Frederick's own need. His wife, Gladys Lonsdale, had all but deserted him, taking a long lease on a house in Sussex and becoming part of a racy arts set in London. Someone like 'the beautiful Edith Walker', with a love of glamour and a natural vitality, would have made an attractive antidote to such a loss.

Then there are the dates, which bring the business to ground in actual events in Edith's and Frederick's lives, the ups and downs of Edith's fortune coinciding with crucial dates in the lives of the Robinsons of Studley Royal. It is clear that when Edith's long stint in Ripon Workhouse began in 1910 she was no longer operating under the protection of her lover. Something had happened to curtail their relationship. Is it pure coincidence that the first Marquess died the previous summer? Was this occasion for son and heir Frederick Oliver to tussle with his conscience and put his new responsibilities as Marquess before his love for the woman who had borne him three children? Or had the philanthropy of the first Marquess sustained Edith, charity which, with his death, simply dried up? What seems certain is that the Robinsons closed the door on any contact with Edith Walker for the time being, and handed the matter over to the State.

While still incarcerated in the workhouse, Edith married John Thomas Simpson in what looks very like an arrangement to settle the matter for good, at least to all appearances. Edith travelled from the workhouse to Ripon Cathedral to marry him, and travelled back again. Why did she not move in with Simpson straightaway if this was a love match? Why, when her next child was born in 1912, did the registrar enter different addresses for father and mother – Edith in Bedern Bank (another property owned by the Estate), Simpson in Bondgate? Simpson was a labourer, six years younger than Edith. Was he perhaps in the employ of the Estate, a solution that would distance the problem of Edith by keeping her in a more profitable fashion and at arm's length? There have been Simpsons in Ripon for hundreds of years. The name takes us back to the John Simpson who, as I said, was head gardener during John Aislabie's landscaping of the Studley Royal Estate, and in Edith's time the family gardening business was still kept up by a John Simpson who lived with his wife Elizabeth at Cemetery Lodge in Kirby Road, until 1919 when George and Lavinia Simpson took over.

Then there was Edith's sojourn in Morpeth, miles away to the northeast in Northumberland, which would have distanced Frederick's little 'problem' still further – geographically speaking – and which once again provides a connection with the Studley Royal Estate, the Morpeth 'solution' later becoming a major part of the Studley Royal charitable portfolio, a whole project where workers could relocate, live in their own house and work a piece of Studley Royal land in far-off Northumberland. The connection is further boosted by the discovery that here, at Winton House, was also the headquarters of the Freemasons, in which the Robinsons of Studley Royal were leading lights and through which Frederick may well have funnelled the 'solution' in the first place.

Barbara was staggered when she read about Edith's sojourn in Morpeth. 'I saw "Morpeth" and I remembered immediately Mummy saying that when she was little – I don't know how old she was – she used to go to Morpeth.' Freda's half-sister Frances was born there in 1914. This period could well have been another particularly enjoyed by Freda, for if Edith's marriage had begun as stratagem, it appears that she and Simpson were now (perhaps as a result of the Morpeth experiment) close. Certainly when they returned to Ripon they continued to live together, taking up lodgings at Yorkshire Hussar Yard, where Edith's sixth and last child, also called Edith, was born in 1917.

It is likely that Freda did not live with them in the Yard, and one should remember when considering how happy Freda told Barbara she had been in Ripon, that despite the roller-coaster ride Edith led her, she was part not just of Edith but of the extended family of Walkers who lived in the city, particularly those living at 8 and 9 Bedern Bank. Besides, up to 1910, along with the patriarch John Walker there was Edith's brother Thomas, his wife Frances, son Jamie, and three daughters, Lillie, Elizabeth and Minnie in residence. Elsewhere in Ripon, until his death in the First War, lived another brother Joseph and his wife, Ruth Matilda, who had been witness at Edith and Simpson's wedding. Then there was Gabriel Barker, either Freda's Aunt Elizabeth's or Aunt Minnie's child, who also lived in Bedern Bank for some time, and very probably there were others that have eluded my researches. Ripon, with its winding streets and strong family continuity, would have seemed a magical playground even allowing for the workhouse years.

Being the eldest, Freda would never suffer the ultimate degradation of deportation, when, in 1924, it all fell apart. In that year, three of the children were put in the hands of the NSPCC, who delivered them to Dr Barnardo's Homes, thence to Canada and Australia. Why in 1924? Surely because Frederick Oliver Robinson, Second Marquess of Ripon and the last of the line, died the previous year and Edith's protection finally came to an end. No one else could afford to look after them.

Subsequently, John Simpson would decline and meet an early death in Ripon Workhouse, but the spirit of Edith found its medium in Freda, who went forth to ensure that the emotional circle of her mother's life was as yet far from complete, and that her dream would at last be realised.

A lifetime later, Freda herself died, but only after the publication of *A Woman of Substance*, as if to announce that her job was done. She saw the book become a success; she saw the two ends of the circle meet. The midwife's feelings are never thought of in the joy of a mother's first birth, but Freda's part in this is nurse *and* mother. The scope of her life took her from the Edwardian era into which she and the woman of substance were born, right through to the modern world in which people like Maxim West operate. Her feelings following her daughter's success are unimaginable, and one must believe that she had a few things to say quietly to her mother, Edith Walker, whose ambitions lie at the fount of all this.

'My parents died in 1981 just as I was at the end of *Voice of the Heart*,' Barbara told me. 'They were both alive to see *A Woman of Substance*. I remember after my father died in the October I said to Mummy that I wanted to bring her to New York, but she insisted on staying where she was. I suppose an old person doesn't want to be moved. She said, "Just do me a favour, go back and finish that book, I want to read it." But she died before it came out, just five weeks after he did. She was seventy-seven, and I think that she had decided she didn't want to live any more.

'The housekeeper rang me one day and said, "Your mother's really not well," and the doctors came and were going to put her in hospital. I said, "Can she come to the telephone?" And Brenda said, "Let me go and see if Rose and I can help her to come to the telephone." There was another lady there, a neighbour called Rose. I heard the phone go down – of course this is six o'clock in the morning in New York, six thirty because it was about eleven thirty in Yorkshire. They were ages and I'm then saying, "Hello?" and there isn't anybody there – and eventually Brenda came back, about five minutes later. She said, "I don't really know how to tell you this, Barbara, but your mam just died."

'I couldn't believe that she'd just died. I didn't want to believe she was dead at all. Then I thought she must have died earlier and that they had talked it out between themselves because they hadn't known how to tell me. I felt so helpless. Later I found out what they told me was true. Mummy had been sitting in the chair and she had smiled at Rose. Apparently Rose said, "It's me, Mrs Taylor," and my mother didn't answer her, but finally she looked at her and she smiled, and it was a very radiant smile and she had extremely blue eyes. Rose said, "If you could have seen your mother's eyes, they were shining." She told me this when I got to Leeds. Apparently Rose sat and held her hand and talked to her for a few minutes and Mummy looked at her and said, "God help me, please have God help me." Rose said, "He will if you're asking him." She smiled again and Rose said the eyes seemed bluer than ever, and she said, "She smiled at me a third time and her face was so radiant, I don't know what it was that she saw." And Brenda was there – this lady who'd looked after Mummy – and Brenda said, "Well, what she saw was Winston" – my father – ". . . she was happy when she died."'

Emily stared at Paula. Tremulously she said, 'I've always been afraid of death. But I'll never be afraid of it again. I'll never forget Grandy's face, the way it looked as she was dying. It was filled with such radiance, such luminosity, and her eyes were brimming with happiness. Whatever it was our grandmother saw, it was something beautiful, Paula.'

Hold the Dream

ACKNOWLEDGEMENTS

Principally I would like to thank Barbara Taylor Bradford and Robert Bradford for their friendship and generous contribution to this book; also Amanda Ridout for suggesting the idea in the first place and Patricia Parkin for performing the requisite balancing act to see it through.

Among those who kindly agreed to be interviewed I would like to thank especially Billie Figg, whose journalistic skills were rigorously applied to our discussions, and who, unprompted, offered me some of her own early interviews with Barbara, as well as many personal memories. My thanks are also due to her husband, Jack, whose gentle humour added a very welcome dimension to the book. I would also like to thank Doreen Armitage, Judy Blanchland, Mark Barty-King, Arthur Brittenden, Bobby Caplin, Margery Clarke, June Kettlelow, Roderick Mann, Shirley Martin, Frederic Mullally, Beryl Thompson, Vera Vaggs and Bob Wyatt. I am also indebted to the late Richard Whiteley.

Once it became clear that the book would require as much detailed archival research as interview I fell into the hands of a number of professionals in institutions and libraries in the North of England, to whom I am very grateful. In particular I would like to acknowledge Doris Johnson, whose scholarship in archival science and incisive appraisal of material was not only useful to the book, but taught me a lot along the way.

I would also like to thank the following: *Architectural Digest*; Lonnie Ostrow of Bradford Enterprises; Chapel Allerton Hospital; Mr B. C. Smith of the de Grey and Ripon Masonic Lodge; Mr P. Allen of the Morpeth Masonic Lodges; Granada Television; Guardian Newspapers; Leeds Library; Mike Yaunge and Ros Norris of the Ripon Local Studies Research Centre; Morpeth Library; Northallerton Library; Northallerton County Archives; Northumberland Record Office; Observer Newspapers; Adrian Munsey and Samanta Elliott of Odyssey Video; Probate Subregistry: York; Public Record Office: Kew; Registrar: Leeds, York, Harrogate; Christine Holgate of Ripon Library; *Ripon Gazette*; Ripon Workhouse; Scarborough Library; West Yorkshire Archives (Sheepscar and Wakefield); Yorkshire Archaeological Society; Louise Male of the *Yorkshire Evening Post*; David Hartshorn at *Yorkshire Post* Archives; and Doreen Stanbury and Pat Smith for their typing.

There are, in addition, some crucial literary sources, works that I have acknowledged when quoting from them in the text: in particular, by Keith Waterhouse – *City Lights* and *Streets Ahead* (Hodder Headline, 1994 and 1995); Alan Bennett – *Telling Tales* (BBC Worldwide, 2000); Paul Murray Kendall – *Warwick the Kingmaker* (Allen & Unwin, 1957);

Jack London – *The People of the Abyss* (Journeyman Press, 1977); Anthony Chadwick and Beryl Thompson – *Life in the Workhouse* series (Ripon Museum Trust, 2003); Jim Gott – *Bits & Blots of T'Owd Spot* (Crakehill Press, 1987); Judith Summers – *Soho* (Bloomsbury, 1989); and Daniel Farson – *Soho in the Fifties* (Pimlico, 1993). Other works which have informed my text include *Lancaster and York: The Wars of the Roses* by Alison Weir (Pimlico, 1998), *Oliver Twist* by Charles Dickens (Penguin Classics, 1966 etc.), *Wuthering Heights* by Emily Brontë (Penguin Classics, 1965 etc.), *Backing Into the Limelight: The Biography of Alan Bennett* by Alexander Games (Headline, 2002), *Empty Cradles* by Margaret Humphreys (Doubleday, 1994) and *Neither Waif Nor Stray: The Search for a Stolen Identity* by Perry Snow (Universal, 2000).

I would like to acknowledge all the picture sources. Maps are by Ordnance Survey and photographs are by or from Ripon Library, the Robert and Barbara Taylor Bradford Photographic Archives, Leeds Library, Yorkshire Tourist Board, Skyscan Balloon Photography, English Heritage, Cris Alexander, Lord Lichfield, the *Yorkshire Post*, Columbia Pictures and Odyssey Video.

While every effort has been made to trace copyright sources, the author would be grateful to hear from any unacknowledged ones.

NOVELS BY
BARBARA TAYLOR BRADFORD

INDEX

A Woman of Substance

Barbara Taylor Bradford

In 1905 a young kitchen maid leaves Fairley Hall. Emma Harte is sixteen, single and pregnant.

By 1968 she is one of the richest women in the world, ruler of a business empire stretching from Yorkshire to the glittering cities of America and the rugged vastness of America.

But what is the price she has paid?

A magnificent dynastic saga, *A Woman of Substance* is as impossible to put down as it is to forget. This multi-million copy bestseller is truly a novel of our times.

'An extravagant, absorbing novel of love, courage and ambition, war, death and passion'   *New York Times*

The storyteller of substance'   *The Times*

'Few novelists are as consummate as Barbara Taylor Bradford at keeping the reader turning the page. She is one of the world's best at spinning yarns'   *Guardian*

ISBN 0 586 20831 3

Hold the Dream

Barbara Taylor Bradford

Emma Harte is eighty years old and ready to hand over the reins of the vast business empire she has created.

To her favourite grandchild, Paula McGill Fairly, Emma bequeaths her mighty retailing empire with these heartfelt words: 'I charge you to hold my dream.'

A towering international success, this is the powerfully moving tale of one woman's determination to 'hold the dream' which was entrusted to her, and in so doing find the happiness and passion which is her legacy.

'Steamy sex, romance, financial chicanery . . . I enjoyed every word.'   *Daily Express*

'Queen of the genre.'   *Sunday Times*

'Few novelists are as consummate as Barbara Taylor Bradford at keeping the reader turning the page. She is one of the world's best at spinning yarns.'   *Guardian*

ISBN 0 586 05849 4

To Be the Best

Barbara Taylor Bradford

Set in Yorkshire, Australia, Hong Kong and America, this remarkable contemporary novel continues the story of an unorthodox and endlessly fascinating family.

As the spirit of Emma Harte lives on in her granddaughter Paula O'Neill, an engrossing drama is played out in the glamorous arena of the wealthy and privileged, underscored by a cut-throat world of jealousy and treachery.

Paula must act with daring and courage to prevent her formidable grandmother's glittering empire from unscrupulous enemies – so that Emma's precious dream will live on for the next generation.

'The storyteller of substance.' *The Times*

'Queen of the genre.' *Sunday Times*

'Few novelists are as consummate as Barbara Taylor Bradford at keeping the reader turning the page. She is one of the world's best at spinning yarns.' *Guardian*

ISBN 0 586 07034 6

Emma's Secret

Barbara Taylor Bradford

The legendary Emma Harte, heroine of *A Woman of Substance*, returns . . .

At the centre of this sweeping family saga stands Paula O'Neill, beloved granddaughter of Emma and the guardian of her vast business empire. Paula believes all that Emma left to the family is secure. However, beneath the surface sibling rivalry and discontent flare.

Into this volatile mix walks Evan Hughes, a young American fashion designer. She is looking for Emma Harte. But Emma has been dead for thirty years. And Evan bears an uncanny resemblance to Paula O'Neill.

Troubled by Evan's presence, Paula turns to Emma's recently discovered wartime diaries to find the truth . . .

The decades fall away. It is London in the Blitz. Emma Harte comes vividly back to life, accompanied by Blackie O'Neill and David Kallinski. Emma is holding her family together as bombs drop, sirens wail and her sons go off to war. As she struggles with her grief, her indomitability, willpower and strength come to the fore.

As the pages unfurl, Paula discovers the secret Emma Harte took to the grave to protect others. Its repercussions irrevocably change lives.

Emma's Secret is vintage Barbara Taylor Bradford. Emotion, drama, suspense, intrigue and passion fill the pages in a spellbinding novel which only she could write.

ISBN 0 00 226135 9

Unexpected Blessings

Barbara Taylor Bradford

A great dynasty began with one exceptional woman ...

A stranger just a year ago, Evan Hughes is now at the centre of the Harte family – in love with Gideon Harte and part of the powerful empire. But joining the dynasty that Emma Harte – the original Woman of Substance – created so many years ago re-opens old wounds. As determined as she is, can Evan make her mark on this extraordinary clan?

As Evan reads the letters Emma wrote to her grandmother in the 1950s, and Emma comes vividly back to life, she realizes that the Harte women have always had to match adversity with bravery and what she must do.

Emma's other great-granddaughters are strong, passionate women too. There's Tessa Longden, battling for her daughter's – and her own – future; Linnet O'Neill, a brilliant but envied businesswoman; and India Standish, who surprises everyone with a shock decision.

With a much anticipated family wedding approaching, it seems their collective strength will be needed more than ever. Because a deadly enemy has vowed to destroy everything that these remarkable women hold dear...

'A sweeping saga full of passion and intrigue...a gripping read.'
Hello

ISBN 0 00 651442 1

Just Rewards

Barbara Taylor Bradford

Linnet O'Neill, great-granddaughter of Emma Harte, finds herself following in the footsteps of the original woman of substance as she battles to save the family business. She and Emma's other great-granddaughters face heartache and tragedy and are tested to the limit as the final chapter in the extraordinary story of the Harte family draws to a dramatic close…

Linnet O'Neill returns from her honeymoon full of fresh ideas for bringing the Harte empire into the new century. Will she become the new Emma Harte, as so many have predicted?

Evan Hughes, American great-granddaughter of Emma, is pregnant and planning her small family wedding but after her marriage, tragedy strikes.

After an acrimonious divorce, Tessa Fairley is ready to start a new life, and is madly in love with the Frenchman Jean-Claude Deléon. But having always believed herself to be her mother's rightful heir, and jealous of Linnet, Tessa is reluctant to forego her chances of the top spot.

But it is Evan's sister Angharad who, latching on to Jonathan Ainsley, puts them all in danger.

The four young women must draw on the strength of character and determination inherited from their formidable great-grandmother to win through.

'The storyteller of substance.'   *The Times*

ISBN 0 00 719758 6